TRANQUILA

Published 2024
Printed in the United States of America
Print ISBN: 978-1-64742-674-3
E-ISBN: 978-1-64742-675-0
Library of Congress Control Number: 2023921527

For information, address:
She Writes Press
1569 Solano Ave #546
Berkeley, CA 94707

Interior Design by Tabitha Lahr

She Writes Press is a division of SparkPoint Studio, LLC.

TRANQUILA

A DOCTOR-MOM
ATTEMPTS THE SLOW LIFE

in Spain

AMY BREEN

SHE WRITES PRESS

Chapter 1

AUGUST 2013

arcelona in August was very quiet. We were American ghosts in a Spanish ghost town, wandering around in the hot, thick air, trying to struggle out of the personal fogs we'd been drifting in since flying across nine time zones.

This was not going according to plan. At least not the plan I had dreamt up a few months earlier, after Tim and I had somewhat spontaneously decided to move our family to Barcelona for the year. That plan entailed a year of experiences and adventures in which Tim, the kids, and I all laughed a lot and spoke Spanish fluently to each other. I didn't even know what we were saying to each other in this daydream, since I didn't speak Spanish. But whatever we were saying, we were saying it fast and well, and we were very happy and smiling while we said it, and sometimes in these dreams Tim and I had glasses of cava in hand and were basking in the Spanish sun as the kids ate tapas. We looked like we were having a very good time.

But the only adventures we'd had since landing a week earlier had generally been *mis*adventures as we'd tried to procure necessities for our flat and find our way around our new neighborhood. Lately we'd been venturing out into the oppressive mugginess to find school supplies for the kids' impending start of the school year. There hadn't been much smiling, rarely any laughing. We were hungry and dazed and living on Oreos. And who knew that they didn't speak Spanish in Barcelona? We kind of knew, but in the rushed decision to move there we'd chosen to ignore the fact that Catalan, which to our ears sounded like a mixture of French, Italian, and Spanish, was the primary language of Barcelona. And the area of town where we lived was far from the touristy area, so not only did the fiercely Catalan people not speak *castellano*, Spanish, they didn't speak English either.

Tim had taken Spanish in high school and college, but his Spanish was rusty after twenty years of nonuse and he said his Spanish helped him not one iota in understanding Catalan. Still, his rusty Spanish and no Catalan beat my no Spanish and no Catalan, so he was the designated communicator for our family, whether he liked it or not.

After no success at two stores looking for a certain type of school notebook, we were all about to enter a café for lunch when Tim got a phone call. As I stood on the sidewalk waiting for him to finish, sighing in resignation at the dark grey patches of sweat blooming on my light grey T-shirt, I could see he was struggling to understand what the person on the other end was saying to him. (While speaking a different language is hard, it's even harder when you don't get to read a person's lips or body language, the nonverbal cues, as you talk. We had become intimately familiar with this fact in recent days.)

Despite the kids hanging on me and squirming in the heat, I thought back to a blog I had come across right before we flew to Spain, written by a professor of linguistics. In it he said he always laughed when people said they were moving to Spain to learn Spanish, and then chose to live in Barcelona. Back then, his words had filled me with a slight bit of concern. Now, standing in humid Barcelona with three bored, hot, and hungry kids, I only wanted to punch that guy.

After a bit of back-and-forthing, Tim hung up and turned to me. "That was Antonio." Antonio was our *portero*, our doorman, in our new apartment building. "A guy from the cable company is waiting for us in the lobby. Or I think that's what he said."

"Now? They weren't supposed to come 'til Wednesday I thought!"

We were getting our first taste of our future Spanish life. "Tomorrow" might mean next week. "Next Wednesday" might mean today.

Our five-, seven-, and nine-year-old kids were bickering and wilting simultaneously. They loved Oreos but the cookies caused predictable sugar crashes. Which we now found ourselves in.

"Can you stay and order sandwiches for them?" Tim asked.

My world expanded and contracted in a second. I felt I'd just stepped out of my body. Had he just asked *me* . . . to *order sandwiches*? By *myself*? I didn't understand what he was saying. Was he speaking in Spanish? Did he know *I* couldn't speak Spanish?

And so, with Tim dashing back to the flat, I entered the café with three cranky kids hanging off me like wilting leaves off a vine, approached the gentleman behind the counter, and did my best pantomiming, with an apologetic smile though I was not smiling on the inside, that we would like three ham-and-cheese baguettes.

We sat down and waited for the sandwiches. I had gone from tired to having a major headache in the five minutes since Tim had left us. The kids' complaining hadn't stopped. I saw the server heading over with the sandwiches and slumped back in my chair, relieved and exhausted: My ordeal was about to end.

But after taking one bite, Patrick, my seven-year-old, said, "Gross! This has tomato on it!" He picked up the top half of the baguette and showed me the underside, which had a pinkish-red-dish hue with seeds. Tomato had been crushed into the bread.

"Mine too!" cried Mae.

"Mine too!" Kieran said in disgust.

And the fury was unleashed. Out of my mouth came warnings and threats like, "You better get used to different things!" and "It's just tomato!" and "It's the only thing you have to eat!" and "Do you have any idea?"

The kids looked down at their plates. Kieran, my nine-year-old, picked up his sandwich and began to eat. The other two didn't.

I reached across to Mae's sandwich, grabbed the ham and cheese off the sandwich, and said, "Eat this."

Mae had the guts to say, "There's still tomato on it," pointing to the seeds clinging to the meat.

After I choked down my anger, I ate their two baguettes, straight up, sans ham and cheese; Kieran ate half of his sandwich; and we left.

We walked the four blocks back to our flat in silence. I felt awful—unclear if it was from the baguette ball in my stomach or from my tantrum. My behavior was so different from that happy and carefree mom I had naively envisioned in our future life in Spain—the one who'd laughed merrily with her kids as they did cartwheels around her, never knocking and spilling her cava, daisies floating in the air—back when we had made the decision to move here. Even though the decision had been rushed and abrupt, it had felt absolutely right. We had wanted a change; Tim and I felt stagnant in our work lives as well as our personal growth, and we had long felt a desire to show our kids a life outside of the success-driven and entitled bubble of Silicon Valley—outside of our homogenous community.

But those motivations were hard to summon now as I struggled in my daily life. At that moment I needed to look at street signs, and steer the kids around the dog poop on the sidewalk, and hold our breath as we walked past a smoker on the corner, and what in the world were we going to do for dinner that night? Restaurants didn't open until 9:00 p.m.; the kids would be asleep by then. Could we find a place to order pizza? *That's a joke*, I thought. I couldn't order a pizza on the phone even if I wanted to.

We arrived at our building. As we entered through the large wooden doors, I decided to leave my frustration there. I chose to think about how next week school would start, and so would my Spanish classes. And then all my problems would disappear. Like magic.

Like a ham-and-cheese sandwich served without tomato.

Chapter 2

ANYTIME 2012

I slowly turned the patient's forearm outward. He moaned groggily.

"You're doing great," I told Mr. Pisaro. "We should be done soon."

He nodded slowly with his eyes closed. He was a fifty-two-year-old who had fallen off his bike and dislocated his shoulder. I had ordered Dilaudid for him to make him comfortable, but "comfortable" is a relative term when your shoulder is out.

I kept his right elbow at his side and slowly, gently rotated his forearm away from his trunk. Gabe, the nurse, stood by watching, in case I needed anything.

I began to feel resistance—Mr. Pisaro's shoulder not wanting to externally rotate anymore—and then the gratifying but subtle "clunk" as the humeral head went back into the glenoid fossa. Mr. Pisaro let out a sigh of relief, accompanied by a languid, narcotic-hazed smile. This wasn't his first time dislocating his shoulder, and he knew that moment when the shoulder went back in as well as I did.

"Dr. Breen?" Lydia asked from the doorway. "The patient in 3 has some questions for you."

Of course she did. Even after you've discharged a patient and have moved on, it doesn't mean *they* have. But I still had to let 10C know about his lab results, and I had just picked up a laceration in 7 I hadn't seen yet.

"Tell her I'll be there in five minutes, thanks Lydia," I said over my shoulder as I palpated Mr. Pisaro's shoulder, making sure the normal contour was restored. "Gabe, can you get Mr. Pisaro in a sling? I'll get his discharge papers and prescription ready. And let me know when he's more awake and I'll come back and talk to him. Thanks." I walked out to the hall down to the counter and started filling out a prescription for Mr. Pisaro before ducking into 3.

"I told Matt to meet you in there to translate," Lydia said as she walked up to me at the counter. "How are the kids?"

It was always jolting to switch from my "work world" to thinking about my "family world." It didn't seem like too long ago I had been rushing out my front door to work, even though it was going on six hours. I had kicked a piece of chalk on our walkway as I was looking down and checking my maroon scrubs for any stains from the afternoon dinner I had just scarfed down in three minutes. I'd looked up to see my four-year-old daughter, Mae, drawing chalk figures in the driveway with the babysitter. Patrick and Kieran were riding their bikes in the cul-de-sac behind them, yelling something to each other. This was a familiar routine: rushing off to work on a beautiful California afternoon, chasing each kid down and interrupting their blissful play to give them a goodbye bear hug and kiss, maybe getting the briefest "Bye Mommy," without even eye contact in return.

Doing the evening shift in the Emergency Department was my choice; since having kids, I tried to maximize my time with them by being around all day and then working the 5:00 p.m. shift so I only had to leave when their day was winding down. All three kids were under the age of nine, so theoretically they were asleep for the majority of my shift. But I missed their dinner, I missed their story times, I missed their bedtimes.

As I turned on the engine and buckled up to come to this shift, I had thought: *But it's good they don't care I'm leaving. It's good they are totally engaged with the sitter.* Which then predictably morphed into: *But why do I have a babysitter when I should be the one playing with my kids? I'm paying the sitter so I can go to work to make money so I can pay the sitter so I can go to work?* Pulling away from the house and exiting the cul-de-sac, I'd looked in my rearview mirror and seen the kids happily darting around—and felt dejected. And then I'd gotten mad at myself for feeling sorry for myself. *This is the life and career you've chosen*, I'd told myself. *Put on your adult pants and suck it up.*

Lydia reached in front of me for a lab slip and pulled me back to my "work world."

"They're pretty good, thanks. Well, that's not exactly true," I amended, thinking back to wiping Mae's sweet face after her puking incident that morning. "One was vomiting today, but I've been too busy to call home to check in." I finished the prescription for Mr. Pisaro and looked at Lydia. "Hopefully Tim's got it under control."

"Ugh, vomiting. That's the worst. Which kid?" she asked.

"My four-year-old."

"God, aren't you so glad you're here and not at home dealing with *that*?" she tossed over her shoulder as she headed off toward the lab.

"No—actually, I'd much rather be at home," I said to no one, out loud, because this was the Emergency Department, and speaking out loud to oneself was not out of place here amongst the angry drunks and patients being admitted for psychotic breaks. I talked to myself all the time at work. Especially now that I was feeling sorry for myself again.

Apparently my adult pants had fallen off somewhere.

"So keep giving him Motrin, it'll help make him comfortable," I said to the mom in room 3 who was holding her toddler to her chest.

Her eyes quickly darted to Matt, an ED tech and our unofficial translator. He wasn't fluent, or maybe even good, but he was the best we had.

"*Dalo Motrin,*" Matt told her. "*La medicina va a hacer el bebé más cómodo.*"

Her eyes were still on Matt. I could see no relief in them as she bounced her toddler in her arms. And I hadn't said the word "baby," which I had clearly heard Matt say.

Since we weren't provided with a translator and had to rely on someone with decent but not expert Spanish to unofficially translate for us, this lack of knowing whether what you had said had actually been passed on to the patient happened too frequently for my comfort. But finding a legitimate translator somewhere in the hospital at eleven at night was as likely as Matt translating word-for-word what I had said.

"*Pero, ¿qué pasa con la erupción?*" the mom asked, her eyes still on Matt.

I never knew how to construe this; it happened quite often, where the translator became the patient's point of focus. Was it comforting to focus on the translator, since they had a language in common? Was she embarrassed? Did she not trust what I was telling her? Regardless, I didn't like the gap that existed between me and my patient, any of my patients, when language became a barrier.

"She wants to know about the rash," Matt said to me.

I looked at the mom, whose eyes darted to mine and then came to rest back on Matt's. I had already explained, through Matt, that a virus was causing her child's rash and crankiness and there was no medicine to treat it per se. For the hundredth time, I worried what information had actually been passed on to the patient and what hadn't.

"Dr. Breen?" Gabe popped his head in the door. "5A is awake and wanting to go. You want to talk to him, right?"

"Yeah, definitely," I said, thinking of the discharge papers I still needed to fill out for Mr. Pisaro.

"And do you want me to irrigate the guy in 7?" he asked, referring to my new laceration—the guy I had yet to see.

"Let me numb him up first, thanks, Gabe. Could you put some lido at the bedside for me?"

Gabe nodded and let the door close behind him.

Turning back to Matt and the mom, I said, "Tell her it's a virus causing the rash, that it will go away in a few days, and that there's no medicine to treat it but she needs to keep her son hydrated." I was already thinking of what type of suture material I would need for the laceration. "And please go over the precautions in the discharge papers with her, and point out peds' number so she can follow up with them."

The mom looked at Matt expectantly, her body stiff, as she moved her toddler to her other hip. I knew she wasn't fully understanding or accepting of the situation, but I accepted this with resignation. If I had another ten minutes to sit with her and answer all her questions, I would. I would love to. But I worked in the ED, where time was a luxury, and I never got that gift. I had done a good work-up on this child and knew my diagnosis and treatment plan were solid. But I didn't like leaving that mom feeling uncertain like that. I knew she was trying hard to advocate for her child, despite a language barrier. I felt compassion, from one mama bear to another—and frustration that my job had to be this way. But it was. I had to move on to the lac. And Mr. Pisaro. And my patient in 10C.

I walked out of the room, toward the lac, and looked at my watch. I hadn't been able to call home yet to check in on Mae. And Tim. And now it was too late to call.

After I had talked to Mr. Pisaro and sewn up the laceration in 7, I was heading to 10C to discuss that patient's test results with him when a thought muscled into my consciousness: *I don't want to be doing this when I'm fifty.*

I was forty-one. Tonight was no different from any other night. But I was tired of this. Of the pressure, the continual high-stakes clinical decision-making, never having enough time, missing out on taking care of my family. It wasn't fun. It hadn't been fun for a while.

As I walked into "room" 10C, more a slot for a gurney separated from 10B and 10D by flimsy floral curtains, I saw my patient now had his daughter and wife at his bedside. They were standing, because there was no room for chairs.

After introducing myself and shaking hands with the wife and daughter, who appeared to be in her early twenties, I said, "So some of his blood tests that look at his pancreas are higher than they should be. The next step is getting a CT scan to make sure his pancreas looks okay."

"Will he be okay?" the daughter asked me anxiously, her eyes wide. Her question had a whiff of drama; her vantage point was that her dad was not in pain, had walked himself in there, and had been chuckling with his wife when I came in.

"Well, we don't have the information we need to know exactly what's going on, but your dad's looking good. He'll need to drink some contrast, which helps the radiologist—"

"How much longer will this take?" the daughter interrupted me.

"Well, it'll take a few more hours," I answered with growing wariness. "The contrast has to make its way to his abdomen, and then after we get the CT we need to get the results from the radiologist. But that's good, because it means we can keep our eyes on him that whole time to make sure he's getting better, not—"

The daughter put her hand in my face, arm outstretched—the universal "stop" or "shut up" sign, depending on how you wanted to read it. In this case, I think she definitely intended for me to read it as "shut up."

"If you're not going to help him right now, right here, we're leaving," she said, squared up to me.

My own nerves flared. I don't like confrontation, either emotional or physical, and this was both. Simultaneous to feeling my own heat and not knowing how to handle it, I was surmising that I wasn't dealing with a totally rational person, given how outsized her reaction was in relation to the context.

While I tried to calm my own nerves, I also tried to defuse the situation, using extra care in explaining why her dad needed to stay and what harm leaving now could cause him, all the while wondering if I needed to ask security to escort her to the waiting room to prevent any further escalation. It was a hard thing to do: talk calmly and with care to a person who had just put a hand in your face.

After the daughter had calmed down and they had agreed to the work-up, I walked out of 10 toward the office to do my charting with anger, embarrassment, and shock coursing through me. Unnerved, I felt like my adult pants had fallen off, once again.

I am not *doing this 'til I'm fifty. No fucking way.*

Chapter 3

AS GOOD AS IT GETS

*A*nother shift over, I walked out to the parking lot in the dark early-morning hours, climbed in the cold car, and drove the twelve minutes home in silence. At least this shift nobody had shoved a hand in my face. Just some vomit on my work clogs. I could handle gross better than confrontation.

El Camino Real, the road home, was quiet now. The stores were all closed. Barely any cars were on the road—maybe two to three other lonely travelers, with the occasional cop pulled over on the shoulder, waiting to catch a swerving or speeding driver. Usually, the drive home was when I decompressed from the shift. *Was I wrong to push for admission on the guy with the belly pain? Why is it always contentious when I needed a consult from Dr. Stephanopolos? Mostly the surgeons are pleasant, but not him. Why do we call him Dr. Stephanopolos, anyway, when the rest of us all call each other by our first names? Such an ass.*

My mind turned to tomorrow morning. When I got in bed tonight, or rather this morning, I'd need to set the alarm for four and a half hours later. I wanted to make it to Kieran's concert at school. Tim could go, but I wanted to; I didn't want to miss it. I also had to get a few things from Target, and I'd promised a friend I'd take a walk with her.

I looked down at the gas tank. Damn, I needed gas too. So, concert, errands, gas, walk. That should still leave me a few hours before work to get some things done around the house—laundry, folding, did I have enough food for dinner? Damn, add grocery store to the list. And damn! My work availability for next month was due tomorrow!

Each month I had to fill out a calendar for work with my availability for shifts for the following month, and then the scheduler for our department put together the puzzle of all our availabilities and requests and sent us our shift assignments for the month to come. That blank calendar of possibility always changed my mood from perhaps sunny to at best gloomy, and at worst "stay away from Mommy." When the calendar was blank, it was a month of joy and possibility, of 100 percent time with my kids. But every day of availability I had to mark down—each Monday at 5:00 p.m., every Saturday at 10:00 a.m.—was 30 percent less time with my family, 40 percent less time. Every shift I offered, I resented the fact that I had to.

But most times when I filled out the calendar I knew, of course, that I had to work. Financial reasons aside, the arguments would play through my head: *Are you really not going to work after all the time you've dedicated to getting here—four years of college, four years of medical school, and three years of residency? If you reduce your number of shifts, you'll feel rusty at work. And being rusty makes you slower (not good for your colleagues), makes you feel incompetent (not good for your psyche), and makes you second-guess everything (not good for anybody). If you don't work, what are you?* "Hi, I'm Amy, I'm a doctor. Well, I was a doctor. I mean I still am, but I'm not practicing anymore. Which was a choice I made . . ." This is the point where the person I was talking to would excuse themselves to go fill up their already full drink.

So every month I did this mental dance between wanting more motherhood and knowing I needed to work. What was the lowest number of shifts I could sign up for in order to not feel rusty but still feel as if I were getting the time I wanted with my kids?

Zero.

Okay, well, that was unrealistic and dumb. But that was what I really wanted.

Yeah, but again, dumb.

Okay, three shifts.

Yeah, that would be nice, but I would definitely feel rusty.

I knew I should probably do eight shifts a month—two a week—minimum. But that would qualify as full-time, which is what I had walked away from after Mae was born, including all those nice benefits. So why would I do that?

What about seven?

Seven would be okay, but what about six? Six. Yeah, that would come out to a shift and a half per week. I guess that might be enough to not feel rusty.

Okay, five it is.

When I had just finished residency and was working alone, a newly minted attending, on a shift at a community hospital, I confided to an older colleague who was going off shift that I felt I still had so much to learn. He said, "You'll never know as much as you do right now."

I think he may have had to reach over and pick my chin up off the floor after that comment. *How could that be?* my petrified brain was screaming.

With the benefit of time, I had decided he was only partially right. Sure, I definitely had much more information in my brain back then, just coming out of residency, than I would ever have again. But what that attending had not conveyed, and what I now knew made a huge difference, was the importance of experience.

That was what ate at me every time I looked at a blank work calendar. I felt behind because of the three maternity leaves I had taken, and after reducing my hours to part-time to accommodate being a mom. Every shift I didn't sign up for was experience passing me by. And I was digging myself deeper into a hole every month I signed up for only six—no, five—shifts. Part of me thought I hadn't gotten far enough in my career before going part-time; knowledge hadn't cemented like it should have. But you can't hold off having kids indefinitely. And I hated even allowing that question—*Did I damage my career, and psyche, by stepping away too soon?*—to enter my head. Women should be able to start a family without feeling they've sacrificed their careers.

Surprisingly, I was the first woman in my group to get pregnant, let alone need to take a break to pump her breasts. And this was in 2004, for god's sake, not 1970! What I needed was a slew of women who had come before me and with me who had also taken maternity leave and come back part-time and now felt slower and needed to look up correct dosages and what fractures needed referrals; what I needed was to see that being unsure was normal. But I hadn't had that and didn't have that. And so this internal debate raged on in my head, every month that I had to fill out the damn calendar, and it left me feeling dejected and restless. Because I hadn't found the answer.

And my current situation was not it.

Almost home from my shift, that thought took me back to a conversation I had had with Paul, one of my best friends from high school. It was 2009 and I was back East for our twentieth high school reunion. Paul and I were driving on the Schuylkill Expressway in Philadelphia, on our way to the reunion. In that forty-five-minute car ride, we tried to catch up on our lives the best we could. (Thanks to med school, residency, and subsequently work, and on top of that living in California, I had fallen out of communication with him and everyone else from my past who was important to me outside of my immediate family. I'd even missed nearly everyone's wedding.)

Like me, Paul had a young family, and as we barreled down the Schuylkill he told me about a recent conversation he'd had with one of his friends back home in Seattle. One hand on the wheel, the other arm resting against his door, so at ease, Paul said, "We were watching our kids run around the playground and my friend turned to me and said, 'This is as good as it gets, man.'"

I held my reaction, waiting to hear what Paul had replied. *Are you serious?* I assumed he had told his friend. *This isn't as good as it gets. We're so young! We have so much more to do! No way this is as good as it gets!*

Instead, I heard Paul saying to me, "I was like, 'Man, you are so right! This *is* as good as it gets.'"

At that, he looked over at me with his characteristic easy smile, like he knew I agreed.

Since I had no poker face, I turned my head and said to my window—with a little laugh, so as not to tip off Paul—"Yeah."

Now, driving down El Camino after my evening shift in the Emergency Department, I found myself wondering, again, *Is this as good as it gets?* And I felt exactly as I had felt driving along the Schuylkill with Paul a few years earlier. Nope. "This is as good as it gets" felt depressing. It felt lazy and complacent. As if you weren't hoping for anything better. As if you were just accepting the status quo.

Of course the best was yet to come. *Of course* it was.

And with that I pulled into my driveway, walked into the dark, silent house, found my way to the bedroom without banging my shin on furniture and waking up a kid, changed out of my scrubs into a T-shirt, and climbed into bed next to a sleeping Tim.

Chapter 4

MAY 2013

"*Y*ou are not going to believe what the Moellers are renting their house for." Tim had just returned from a mountain-bike ride with some friends, one of them being Brian Moeller. Brian and his family were taking a year-long sabbatical in Barcelona starting that summer and were renting out their house while they were gone.

I bent over to get peas out of the freezer and guessed a number, venturing what I thought was high. As I rummaged around the drawer, Tim told me the actual figure.

"They are getting *how* much?" I stood up straight in disbelief.

"I know. Ridiculous, right?" He paused a few beats, leaning against the kitchen island. "I wonder how much we would get for our house."

"Probably more," I said as I looked for a dish to microwave the peas in. "Our house is on a cul-de-sac, their street is a cut-through. Our house is a little bigger. Yeah, we'd get more." I looked up and saw my husband's wheels turning.

Living abroad was something we had always wanted to do. We'd had a fleeting opportunity to live in Switzerland six or so years prior, for Tim's job, but that chance hadn't materialized into reality, which had disappointed us more than we'd realized it would. That tease of change had stuck with us—had awakened something that had been lying dormant, but hadn't announced itself.

Since that missed opportunity, life had gotten busier. Back then, when Switzerland had been dangled before us, we'd had a one-year-old; now we had a nine-, seven-, and five-year-old. We both had jobs, and we owned a house we had remodeled just four years earlier. Why would we consider pulling up roots just because our friends were managing it? And it was already May! The kids would need to be in a new school in *wherever* in August. As in, in a handful of months. As in, you can't up and move to another country in a span of *three months*, with *three young kids*. Where would they go to school? What country would that school even *be* in?

"They listed on craigslist," Tim said. "It was rented within a few days." He let that sink in for a moment, then added, "That kind of rent could almost finance a year abroad."

"I huh." I handed him the bag of frozen peas. "Stick these in the microwave."

Tim and I had been married long enough that we recognized certain hallmarks of our marriage, one of which was that every few years, we felt the need for change. Luckily, we somehow both felt it, and both liked to act on it. Which was serendipitous—a homebody plus a spouse with wanderlust does not a perfect marriage make. We'd started dating as freshmen in college and gotten married at the end of my time in medical school, and somewhere along the way we'd developed a profound need to take a hard turn left whenever our life was decidedly pointed straight ahead.

So, every few years, we turned. The bigger the change, the more attracted we were to it. The last time we had acted upon the hunger for change was when I'd needed to rank where I wanted to do my residency in emergency medicine. I was in medical school in Philadelphia then—where I'd grown up, where my parents still lived, where Tim had a good job, where we were only a few hours from his family in DC—but after interviewing at Stanford, I knew

I wanted to rank that program number one for residency, and Tim liked the idea. Stanford, in California. California, where we knew no one and where Tim didn't have a job or connections. Because, why not. Because we liked change.

I matched at Stanford and we moved to California, and then the need for change started to get pushed far below the surface of our lives—beneath the epidermis and subcutaneous fat. Residency and then work in the Emergency Department for me, work and then business school and then back to work for Tim pushed that need beneath the muscles, beneath the fascia. By the time we had had three kids, our mutual desire for change was safely buried under the normalcy of life. Diapers, preschool, evening work shifts, overnight work shifts, breastfeeding, nannies, grocery shopping, cutting crusts off sandwiches, trying to be social despite our profound sleep deprivation with other sleep-deprived young parents, the occasional trip back East to see family, rinse and repeat for many years.

But all that time, without our knowledge, our need for change was fighting against the weight of normalcy. Unbeknownst to us, it was slowly making its way upward—around the organs, up through the cobweb of fascia and the bundles of muscle fibers, all the way right back up to the epidermis.

Hello, change.

Chapter 5

HOW ONE MOVES ABROAD

*H*ow a family normally goes about moving abroad.

One to two years before moving abroad: Depending on size of bank account, go visit several cities (or countries) you might like to live in; return home; narrow choices over several weeks to months; decide. Tell friends and family you are moving abroad.

One to one-and-a-half years out: Apply to schools for your children in chosen city; depending on bank account, visit chosen city again, this time evaluating neighborhoods and schools; look into lawyers in destination country to help with visa process; look into lawyers stateside to help with visa process stateside.

One year out: Talk to a relocation specialist in destination country to help find flat/house.

Six months to one year out: Go to chosen city again to see flats or houses relocation specialist has chosen for you; look at cars, furniture; visit schools to which your children have been accepted.

Six months out: Hire someone stateside to help with preparations such as moving furniture into storage, storage of cars, etc.; find caretaker for your house; go to the many appointments your lawyer sends you to for fingerprinting, consulate meetings, document translation, etc.

Two months out: Throw your bon voyage party; start packing.

How the Breens went about moving abroad:

Three months before moving abroad: Wistfully remember wanting a family experience abroad when discussing the fact that your friends are renting out their house and moving to Barcelona.

Two months and two weeks out: List house on craigslist, "just to see."

Two months and one week out: Panic because house got rented; after putting kids to bed, narrow "experience abroad" to "Spanish-speaking country" to "Spain versus Argentina" to "Spain," then consider "which city is best for living in as well as seeing the rest of Europe" and land on "Barcelona"; ignore that you have never been there; find schools in Barcelona on the internet; apply to said schools.

Two months out: Discuss merits of telling kids we are moving to Spain for a year versus asking kids how they would feel about moving to Spain for a year; decide on "telling"; tell kids; deal with aftermath for the next year.

One month and three weeks out: Start calling the admissions person at the International School in Barcelona weekly, and finally hear that there is room at the school for two of your three kids; think, *Maybe home school for the third?*; hear weekly from Jordi, the guy in Barcelona who's helping you find a flat, that July, the month you're in, is the worst month next to August to find a flat because everyone is winding down for their summer holiday; pray; buy plane tickets; forget to tell your parents and siblings and then remember to tell your parents and siblings you are moving to Europe for a year; scramble to assemble the documents needed to get a visa to Spain for one year; make daily runs to the post office or UPS store for fingerprints, passport photos, and passport applications, making sure you print five copies of all documents as per the visa application; fill out endless forms; find certified translator for all documents, as required for the visa; make five copies of those translated copies; make appointment at Spanish consulate in San Francisco for visas.

One month out: Go to consulate appointment; discover that visas won't be ready until mid-September and must be picked up in person by all persons applying; have it dawn on you that your plane tickets to Spain are for August 21, which means all five of you will have to return to the States a mere month after moving to Spain to get your visas in person, if that is in fact necessary. It is, says the consulate guy.

Two weeks out: Find a friend to house your car for the year; sell your other car; start packing; tell Jordi, yes, you will take that one flat, out of the two options presented.

One week and six days out: Outfit an entire apartment, from furniture down to potholders, in two nights on IKEA.es; realize there are many things you have not done, like figure out if you need to have a car in Spain, tell your neighbors and friends you're moving, and learn Spanish; ask yourself what the hell you have done.

Move to Spain.

Chapter 6

TOUCHDOWN

We knew we had arrived at our flat when Jordi pulled his minivan up on the sidewalk. We were on a one-way street, and cars could barely squeeze by his left rear fender, which—they let us know by honking at us as they slowly passed—was sticking out into the road. Jordi seemed unfazed.

Jordi was a local whom our friends, the Moellers, had hired to help them find a flat and then recommended to us. He'd met us at the Barcelona airport after we landed and helped load up our five giant duffel bags—everything we had brought for five people to live for an entire year—into his minivan.

And now we were double-parked on Carrer Francesc Pérez Cabrero—our new street, a street name whose R's my tongue would never be able to wrap itself around the entire time we lived there. (Which had nothing to do with the fact that I was an American with zero Spanish ability.) As we piled out of the minivan, we saw a long block of elegant stone-and-brick buildings about ten stories high with one building connected to another connected to another—shops on the ground floor of each, residences above. On our left, across the narrow one-way street, lay Turó Parc, a shady expanse of dense foliage that was the namesake of the part of town we now lived in. As we peered beyond the black wrought-iron fence, we could see sand paths winding past a pond.

Looking back up the block at the long line of tall buildings and cars honking at Jordi's minivan, the "cityness" of our new living situation acutely penetrated this suburban girl's brain as acutely as the blaring car horns.

Our brains were being tricked by the bright afternoon sunlight; our bodies knew it was roughly 2:00 a.m. but the Spanish sun said otherwise. We had transitioned from West Coast time to East Coast time when we visited with Tim's family in DC before our jump across the Atlantic, then tolerated a long layover in Heathrow in a daze before landing in Barcelona's gleaming, modern airport.

In a fog, we followed Jordi through the twelve-foot-high wooden doors of our building and down two marble steps into a dark, cool foyer with walls covered in dark wood, marble floors, and the occasional potted plant in the corners. An older gentleman came out from behind the desk at the far end of the foyer with a smile. He was in dark polyester pants and a button-down, short-sleeve blue shirt. With his grey hair and dark-rimmed glasses, he was one pocket protector away from being a 1950s office worker. He gave Jordi a handshake as he gripped his shoulder, a friendly greeting, and smiled at us as Jordi made introductions in Spanish, none of which I could understand except "Breen."

This was Antonio, our *portero*. He smiled and spoke very rapid Spanish that somehow didn't sound like Spanish to me. I looked at Tim and saw a panicked look on his face as he concentrated on Antonio's face, trying to decipher what he was saying. (Jordi would tell us on his next visit that even he had a hard time understanding Antonio. "Antonio is from the south," Jordi would explain. "They only say the first half of every word." Which was why I didn't understand Antonio; nothing to do with me not being able to speak Spanish.)

Jordi continued to translate for us—Antonio was apparently giving us a warm welcome—then explained a few things about the building. Antonio then led us a few steps to the right, back up two different marble steps to a foyer with a staircase. As we gazed upward at the winding staircase, Jordi said, "This is original. It's gorgeous, no?"

It was. The staircase was something out of an M.C. Escher drawing: polished wooden stairs with white spindles rising up to meet a gleaming wooden railing that wound up and up and up into the far reaches of the building, a never-ending spiral of a seashell.

Antonio was opening a door I hadn't noticed in the wall behind us. "This is the elevator," Jordi translated. "Antonio is saying it is very important, when you get off, it is important to remember to close the inside door *and* the outside door. If you do not, the elevator will not work."

Antonio signaled me onto the elevator, which he had already entered. I stepped in. It bobbed slightly. I felt as if I had entered an antique telephone booth—the same polished wood panels of the lobby lining the bottom half, glass on all four sides of the upper half, shiny brass knobs and buttons. Antonio closed the inside door and said something to me in Spanish as he opened and then closed that inside door. Jordi smiled at me and said, "That is the door he is saying is very important to close."

Antonio stepped out and ushered in the three kids. He reached in, pushed the number six button, closed the interior door for us, and then the exterior door, leaving me and the kids alone inside. A moment of stillness in a frenetic day, broken by the bob of the elevator as it began to slowly rise. Through the glass windows, we watched the inside of the elevator shaft slowly pass downwards as the elevator took us up to our flat.

I looked at the kids, who were alert but glassy-eyed, running on fumes. I was too; I was too aware of the difficulties I was encountering, like not being able to understand anyone. Instead of my first impressions being dulled and foggy from jet lag, they were sharp and jagged like glass shards.

I took a deep breath. One of many that day, that week, that month. Life suddenly felt onerous, and I hadn't been prepared for that.

The elevator stopped and bobbed at the sixth floor. Seven-year-old Patrick opened the interior then exterior doors, and the kids filed out. "Kids, do not forget to close this interior door, too, or else the elevator won't work," I said as I closed both doors. It would be a mantra for many months. In front of us were stairs leading down to the left, up to the right. On our left and right were identical double French doors with the panes shaded out. Jordi, who had just made it up to the stairs, said, "Your flat!" as, panting, he took out a key.

He opened the French doors on our left, and as he did a brightness met our eyes. We stepped inside the foyer and saw a flat with whitish faux-wood floors, white-white walls, and brushed nickel doorknobs on all the doors we could see, which were many. A very modern flat.

As I stood in the foyer and stared at the myriad doors to my right and in front of me, I turned to find Tim coming down the long hall to the left. In my fog, all I could muster was confusion as to how Tim was already in the flat, to which Tim replied, "Service elevator," and nodded back behind him.

Taking the lead, he went into a room off the left of the hallway. The kids and I followed, passing rooms on the left and right—the laundry room, a tiny room with the service elevator, a bedroom, another bedroom, and the galley kitchen off to the right, among others, before the hallway ended in a bright, long room, the dining and living room. Light poured in from the four large windows that spanned the length of the room with views out over Turó Parc, Jordi's minivan still jutting into the street down below.

The flat was better than I could have imagined. As Jordi had told us, starting a search so late, in June, had left us with very slim pickings, given that Barcelona emptied out in July and was a ghost town by August. So to land this nice of a flat, in such a prime location, was a godsend.

As I looked around, I recognized the couch, the dining room table, the chair, all of which I had picked out on IKEA about two weeks earlier. Jordi had said, "If you buy your furniture on IKEA, I can have it delivered and assembled for when you arrive." I had spent two late nights in my sister's kitchen in Spokane two weeks earlier, picking out everything we would need to outfit our home, from bunk beds to laundry baskets, towels to frying pans—all sight-unseen, on a very crappy website. And here it all was now, assembled and in place. Or in *a* place, anyway. Jordi had put stuff where he thought it should go, but he hadn't had much to decide; it was only barebones furniture—no rugs, no art, no plants, no decor. Looking around the living room, another glass-shard impression: Our new life felt temporary. And that unsettled me.

Thanks to jet lag, my mood bounced from unnerved to elated. The flat was so bright! *Look at those gorgeous big windows lining the front of the flat and the newly painted white-white walls!* Cue the crash from elation to apprehension—*Oh my god, these are white-white walls! And three kids will be living here! Why couldn't the walls be painted a color like "Soccer Ball Smudge" or "Sole of Sneaker"?*

Sensing a need to smooth out my jet lag–induced emotional volatility, I walked over to the beautiful windows to soak in our view. Down below, across the street, was the pond we had seen, with lily pads floating on the surface. Lots of treetops, some sandy paths, and then, across the park, building after stately building, just like our block.

Just then, Jordi asked if there was anything else he could help us with before he left. Thank goodness he caught my erratic emotions at a stable moment, or else I probably would have begged him to stay for another week. Or until I had learned Spanish. Instead, I let him say his goodbye, and as the door closed behind him, the finality of the moment sank in. We were here. On our own. In Barcelona. In our new life. Our white-white, bright new life. With no food, no car, no family, and an inability to communicate with the other inhabitants of our new land.

On cue, the kids started complaining of hunger.

Well, let the adventure begin.

Chapter 7

HOW DO YOU OPEN THIS THING

*W*e had partners in crime in Barcelona. The Moellers, the family from Menlo Park who had set off our wild speculation about what we could rent our house for, had arrived a few days before us and were renting a flat a few blocks away.

We had chosen Barcelona for several reasons, one of which was that the Moellers were already many steps ahead of us and could advise us on visas, school application, and flats—priceless, given how little time we had. But I had also made sure before we left the US that they did not feel we were hopping on their adventure.

Thankfully, the Moellers had reassured us that they were happy to have us as partners in crime too, and after our arrival, we shared information eagerly. This place has cheap but good produce. Hey, the kids get a pass that allows them to ride the metro for free! This is where we can buy fresh milk as opposed to the shelf-stable boxed milk. Okay, don't buy fresh milk because it goes bad in two days.

A week after we had settled into our respective flats and a few days before school would start for the kids, we all felt the need to explore. We also wanted to give the kids a little fun away from the hot, muggy emptiness of the city. God knows they needed an escape, especially from me.

We decided to try a beach north of the city. Since neither of our families had cars, we needed to become familiar with Barcelona's impressive transit system. With Brian Moeller, who was fluent in Spanish, leading the way, our plan was to walk the nine blocks to the bus stop, take a bus to the train station, and then travel by train up to a beach town called Mataró. Lisa Moeller and her three girls were all proficient but rusty in Spanish. My three kids and I were helpless hangers-on. But with the combined knowledge of Spanish our rag-tag group possessed, we set out—laden with towels, hats, and a beach ball—optimistic that we could handle this small adventure.

After walking the nine blocks to the correct bus stop—in flip-flops, as only Americans would do—and waiting for what felt like forever to the kids, our bus finally came barreling towards us. And then whizzed past us. I was pretty sure the driver gave us the bird. We had just learned our first of many, many cultural lessons that would serve us well living our daily lives in Barcelona: Just being at a bus stop when your bus approaches does not entitle you to getting on that bus. If you would like on that bus, you must raise your hand in the air as it approaches. That is the only way a bus driver can possibly know that he needs to stop at a bus stop that is a scheduled stop on his route.

And so we applied our newfound lesson, got on the next bus that came (after waiting for a second eternity), made it to the train station, and somehow purchased tickets for the right train. All told, everything—reading the map, figuring out the system for how to purchase a ticket (is this ticket one-way or can we return on it too?), even navigating how to get through the turnstiles to the tracks (are you supposed to put your ticket in? will you get it back?)—added up to a much more mentally taxing and time-consuming affair than taking a trip by train in the United States.

After waiting another eternity, which we passed by sprawling ourselves out on the floor of the train station and passing the beach ball back and forth, not caring how American we looked, we finally got on the right train, and then were on our way to the beach.

Lesson two of that day: You are a dumbass foreigner if you think the doors of your train will just open at your desired stop. Just because the train has slowed and come to a stop at the platform does not mean the doors will magically open for you, like any other train you've ever been on. We diligently paid attention to the stops on our way north out of the city. As we approached our destination, we hustled the kids to grab their stuff and get in the aisle, preparing to file out of the busy train car. "The next stop is ours!" we said, urging them toward the doors. "Get ready!"

"Here it is, Mataró!" Tim exclaimed as the train came to a halt, the MATARÓ sign gleaming bright in the sun on the small brick building at the station. The ten of us stood in a line, eagerly looking at the train doors. And then, nothing happened. And then nothing happened again. We were all just starting to nervously look at each other and chatter, "Why isn't the door opening?" when a young man standing in the crowd around the door, sensing our distress and utter stupidity, pressed the magic button on the door.

As soon as the doors opened for us, Kieran, at the front of our line, hustled off the car with nine-year-old Tess Moeller—then a *beep, beep, beep* sounded and the doors began to close. Liz Moeller, the oldest of the group at age twelve, rushed off the car. I locked eyes with Kieran out on the platform, his wide with disbelief and his mouth agape, as the doors closed in front of me. I lunged forward and over Mae, thrusting the only part of my body that could make it through the door without pushing Mae out the door with it.

The doors closed, tight and secure, on my arm.

As the realization sank in that my nine-year-old son was about to be left on a platform in a country he didn't know and where he couldn't speak the language, I began to claw at the door, desperately trying to pry it open, a mama bear ripping a car door off a Volkswagen so her cubs could get to the food inside. The same young man who had pushed the magic button grabbed one of the doors with two hands and leaned back with his body weight. The doors let go of their death grip on my right bicep and parted, and the remaining seven of us hurtled off the train onto the platform, shouting "*gracias*" over our shoulders to the kind young man as we streamed out into the baking heat of the high Spanish sun.

The nearness of what had almost just befallen us was fighting in my brain with the need to let my son know all was well. If I freaked out about this, I would set the tone for what Spain was going to be like for him—he could be abandoned at a moment's notice, left alone on a platform in an unknown town, because his parents made dumb foreigner mistakes like not knowing how to open train doors.

So, as I bear-hugged Kieran, I forced a laugh and said, "Well that was close!" Then the anxious side of me kicked in, and I followed up with, "If you're *ever* left alone at a train station, *stay there*. Do not get on another train! We will come back for you!" My alter-ego everything-is-fine mom then took over again: I kissed him on the head, patted him on the butt, and sent him forward to the wide beach full of topless women who were sure to gross out his nine-year-old self.

Mae stopped in front of me and turned around, anger in her five-year-old eyes. "You got me smushed in the doors!"

"What?"

"You pushed me forward and I got stuck in the doors!"

"Wait, you did? What part of you?"

She drew a line with her finger from the top of her head, down the middle of her face, down the middle of her chest and belly . . . I got the picture.

Apparently in my rush to save one child, I'd almost sacrificed another.

33

I gave her a bigger hug than I'd given Kieran—not only an attempt to squeeze away her confusion and fear at almost having been made the sacrificial cub but also to suffocate the utterly awful and incompetent feeling permeating my body.

After she let go and the ache began to settle into my right bicep, I wondered how this experience would actually settle out with Kieran and Mae. How would Mae process being squashed in a door because of her mom, who was trying to save her other child? And Kieran? No doubt he had been frightened, but he was nine, and I had played it pretty cool, not making a mountain out of a mountain.

Even so, for as long as we lived in Spain my eldest son would walk up six flights of steps multiple times a day rather than risk being trapped in an elevator. I wondered how else that day's trauma would manifest in the months and years to come. Maybe I should have bagged the safety talk and instead just hugged him longer, tighter—like the train door on my arm. And Mae's face.

Chapter 8

THE MORNING COMMUTE
(OR PLANES, TRAINS, AND AUTOMOBILES)

"Stop jumping!" I hiss-whispered at the boys as they flew down the stairs from our flat, me and Mae in close pursuit, on our way to school at 7:55 a.m. *Bam bam bam BOOM, bam bam bam BOOM*—the boys took the old wooden steps by two and then jumped onto each wide landing, racing each other to the bottom. I stole a peek down the old winding banister, six spirals down to the bottom, catching flashes of the boys' heads and backpacks and other body parts as they flew down—*bam bam bam BOOM*.

Tim and I alternated who did kid drop-off, who did kid pickup. Today was drop-off day for me.

Getting out of the flat each morning, Kieran complained that Patrick was making him late, and Patrick got upset and mad that Kieran was complaining about him. The only resolution was a race down the stairs.

I jogged down the steps holding Mae's hand, her backpack keychains clattering against the railing, in pursuit of the boys. *Bam bam bam BOOM* echoed up to us.

35

"Do you want to get us kicked out of here!?"

Now that we were in the foyer and not necessarily in jeopardy of waking up any of the Spanish (whose national wakeup time seemed to be nine-ish), I raised my voice to a hiss instead of a hiss-whisper. "We live in an apartment now! Which means we have neighbors above and below us, probably still asleep; and this place is old, which means our neighbors above and below us hear *everything* you do! And when you trample down the stairs each morning like a herd of elephants, every other neighbor hears you too! You *cannot be this loud*!"

I'd never known how stressful living in a flat could be. If the kids kicked a soccer ball into the wall at home, a home we owned, I chastised them for inappropriate behavior—"If you want to kick a ball, go outside and do that!" If they kicked the ball at our white wall in our all-white flat in Barcelona, a flat we did *not* own, my stress level ratcheted up. "Do not kick the ball in the apartment! If you leave a mark, you're going to have to paint it over yourself! Do you have a can of white paint? And do you want the neighbor complaining to the *portero* about the noise we make, who will then complain to the owner of this place, who will then kick us out?"

In Barcelona, there was no "outside" I could send my kids out to, because "outside" was six floors down and across a busy city street. I couldn't send a five-, seven- or nine-year-old out to play in that "outside" without me going with them. And most times I just didn't have the energy or patience to go with them on that twenty-minute to one-hour outing just because I wanted them out of the flat. I was appreciating moms who raised their kids in cities much more these days.

Adding to my stress level on school mornings like this was my *awareness* of my stress level. After this daily rebuke of my kids, my amygdala and prefrontal cortex launched into a daily argument.

Amygdala: "The kids should know better than to act like that! And they can't keep acting like that; neighbors will complain! We don't know them, they don't know us, but they do know that flat 6-1a is generating too much noise!"

Prefrontal cortex: "But we've only lived here a few weeks. The kids have never lived in an apartment. They'll take a while to learn the rules. And think about *their* stress—they're in a new country, they don't know the language, there's no food they like, there are no snacks in the kitchen, they are at a brand-new school, they know no one, they are the 'other' kids, the 'new kids,' they miss their friends. And on top of all that, this new country seems to have turned their mom into a super bitch, and they have no idea if the old mom is ever coming back."

As the kids and I passed through the building's giant wooden doors—glancing at the golden hands holding apples that served as their door knockers—I left my anger trailing behind me in the foyer.

We took a left onto the wide, wet sidewalk and into morning air thick with city smells and the start of humidity, beginning our twelve- to fifteen-minute trudge up the hill to the metro stop.

Barcelona is sea to mountain. At the sea is the Barcelona most people know—Barri Gòtic and el Born, the Olympic Village, the beaches. As you travel away from the Mediterranean up the mountain, you get to neighborhoods like Turó Parc, areas where many Catalans live. Toward the top of the mountain is where the private schools are located, and then over the mountain to the other side is where the suburbs, like San Cugat, are. That's where many school families live, having traded city living for a yard and swimming pool.

Back home in Menlo Park, the kids had an easy commute to school: a half-mile bike ride on flat road. We could send them off with a quick peck and a wave. But in Barcelona, sea to mountain, no kid would be biking to school. Every day started with a combination of walking, taking a metro, and taking a bus two and a half kilometers up the mountain.

In the gray early-morning light Patrick settled in next to me, taking one of my hands. Mae took the other. Every day that we lived in Barcelona, those two held my hands to and from school. In the US they hadn't done that, but here, with their world feeling so unsure, a handhold seemed to be what they needed. This made us impassable to anyone walking on the sidewalk, a wall of uncertain humanity. Our walking human chain had to stagger backwards at an angle to allow people to pass on their part of the sidewalk.

Today, as usual, Kieran was a step ahead, an edge of anxiety in his voice as he complained that he was going to be late for school because his brother and sister were so slow/lazy/uncaring, and Patrick, as usual, shot back, "Kieran!" in a hurt voice. We passed the Jofre store, the *farmacia*, the store that oddly sold only hosiery, the corner store with fruits and vegetables, Maxipa, the bakery. By this time, I was pulling Mae. We nodded and said *"bon dia"* to the *portero* who was always out in front of his building at this same time, in his royal blue smock, spraying the sidewalk, and he returned the greeting, smiling. We passed the "Circle Church," the round Catholic church in the middle of the roundabout just past the stores.

As we got closer to La Bonanova metro stop, the buildings became more residential and sat a few meters back from the sidewalk, some greenery between their entrances and the sidewalk. My head was always down as I brought the kids along with me up the hill, scanning for dog poop. The sidewalks were made of a slick cement stamped into tiny ten-centimeter squares that made the sidewalk look much nicer but also, when dog poop was smeared across them (and it often was), turned our journey into a more complicated ordeal.

By the time we reached the top of our block, I was pulling Patrick along, with Kieran still upset in front. Mae, at my side, was getting frustrated at Kieran complaining over her talking: "Kieran, I was talking! UUUuuh!"

I wasn't really listening to her, as I was thinking about poor Kieran, who was dealing with anxiety over a new school, over being late to a new school. And I was showing him no patience. By the time we reached the top, we were walking in silence, because I had to give Mae a piggyback the rest of the way and I was too out of breath to talk. On days when I had the mental and physical reserve, I spent this time asking Patrick questions about his teacher or which bakery he thought made the better baguette, Maxipa or L'Obrador—anything to distract him from the ire of his brother. Today was not one of those days.

As we got to the mouth of the entrance to La Bonanova metro station, Kieran asked what time it was, knowing we had to catch the 8:10 a.m. metro. Every morning he asked that same question just as I was pulling Mae and Patrick up the last bit of hill to the mouth of the station.

"I don't know," I answered as we jogged down the steps into the station—not wanting to let go of my younger ones' hands to look at my watch, knowing that frustrated Kieran. In that moment, a thought pushed its way into my head: *This is what you wanted. You wanted to not work so you could have time with the kids.* I was enjoying my freedom from work, but the fact that I was irritable with the kids and frustrated by something as simple as a daily commute shamed and embarrassed me.

I pushed that thought to the back recesses of my mind. I had a metro to catch.

Through the metro station doors we went, the now-familiar whoosh of hot, stale air greeting us. Kieran checked the board for our metro, listed on "*vía une*," track one. "Come on, guys, track one!" he called out as he pushed his T12 metro pass into the slot. The clear plastic partitions parted; he darted through and collected his pass on the other side, then hovered to make sure I got through, his separation anxiety always present since that day in Mataró. I went last to make sure everyone got through before me, so we wouldn't end up with me stuck on one side and unable to reach them on the other. Another Mataró in the making.

We jogged down the steps into the muggy, stagnant air of the metro platform. We collapsed onto the tiled bench, stared at the grungy yellow floor-to-ceiling tiles across the tracks, and waited. No one talked, tired from the walk and the early-morning start, and I was trying to suppress my earlier thought about appreciation, or lack thereof.

"I see it! It's coming!" Kieran exclaimed as he peered into the dark tunnel.

His anxiety wafted past my anxiety: "Kieran! Step back from the edge!"

The same recorded overhead male voice I would hear every day for our time in Spain told us the metro was approaching. Only later, when I was actually getting better at Spanish, would I realize the voice was speaking in Catalan.

The metro pulled up, and we saw the typical wall of people inside each car. I knew by now that you had to push your way in. The door sometimes closed on a kid's backpack, then reopened.

Every seat was taken by the time the train reached our stop. There was room in the aisles, but all the young commuters seemed to prefer to pack together in the middle area in front of the doors, nonchalantly looking at their phones and chatting. So Mae would be face-to-butt with someone, Patrick face-to-hip, Kieran face-to-backpack for the two stops, six minutes, we were on the metro.

Most of the train piled off at the Sarrià station, where we also got off, and made their way to the escalator without any jockeying to get ahead—no rush. We un-Americanly fell in line and made our way up the escalator, put our T passes through the system again, walked out the long yellow-tiled tunnel, passing posters advertising upcoming shows in the city or an event at a local university—I couldn't read any of them because they were in Catalan—Patrick trailing his hand down the wall over the posters, me reprimanding him for touching the grimy walls.

We emerged into cooler, more alive city air full of sounds of cars honking, motos zipping through the traffic, and buses' air brakes hissing. Kieran checked behind us to see if he could see the

V7 bus, the bus that would make its way up the hill through the traffic and take us the rest of the way to school.

When the V7 arrived, we were confronted with the same issue as with the metro. We entered at the front of the bus, put our T passes through the system again, and then hit a wall of humanity. The bus driver peered into his rearview mirror and saw the space in the aisle at the back of the bus, but he never said anything. No one moved. And he would not pull out if people were standing next to him or on the steps into the bus. It was a silent stand-off. Today there was enough room for the four of us to get past that magic line next to the driver, and we held on as the V7 stopped and started up the hill in morning traffic.

We circled around the Ronda del Dalt at the top of the hill before finally coming to our stop, where the whole bus emptied. We crossed the busy onramp leading through the tunnel to San Cugat and then made our final push up the pedestrian ramp to a higher road where the school was, joining other families filing in— Patrick holding one hand, Mae holding the other, Kieran ahead. A line of parents in cars trying to drop off kids inched along the narrow residential streets, the apartment buildings now replaced with individual city houses. Apparently, taking public transportation to school was a very American thing; all the non-American expat kids and Spanish kids walked or were driven.

We took a left onto a narrow street and, as usual, saw the vice principal of the upper school greeting every student with a handshake. We crossed over to the right, past the gigantic trash dumpsters, to the elementary school, said hello to the principal, and walked through the gates to the "patio," or playground, swarming with kids.

We had enrolled the kids at Lincoln International School— or, rather, we had enrolled two of our three that LIS had room for, with less than two months to go before we moved to Spain, and under a lucky star LIS made room for the third as we were flying somewhere over the Atlantic. The classes at LIS were taught mainly in English, with an American-type curriculum. Half of the teachers were American, but the student population was international: 30 percent of the kids were Spanish, and less than 25 percent were American.

LIS was smaller than any school our kids had attended before, with only two classes per grade. If the school was smaller than what our kids were used to, the patio was smaller than a California backyard. Other than a cement basketball court, the patio—a square covered in gummy, track-like material, with one jungle gym—was the only place the kids had to play at recess. LIS was a city school squeezed into city space.

The kids threw down their backpacks and each found someone they knew. Kieran started playing *fútbol*, Patrick got involved in some kind of chase, and Mae was soon hanging upside down on the monkey bars. Amid the squeals and yelling of the kids, I had to make small talk with parents I was getting to know—the coup de grâce of my long morning ordeal. After many years of small talk before school at the kids' elementary school in California, I think I had used up all my chitchat chits; I found small talk exhausting.

The bell rang and the cacophony followed the kids as they rushed for the building. I tried to get my eyes on each of my kids as the crowd bottlenecked at the steps into the school, bumping shoulders with Spanish dads in tailored pants, crisp button-down shirts, and trimmed beards, Spanish moms in hip jeans with thick, beautiful scarves around their necks, and other Americans in athleisure wear.

I found Mae and made my way with her into the first floor of the building, where we hit another wall of this time pint-size humanity. You couldn't bend over to reach the cubbies without your butt taking out a little kindergartner. I kissed Mae, and she went into her class and found her place on the carpet. I then ran up to the second floor, which held the two classes of second graders on the left and two classes of third graders on the right, the hall lined with cubbies and windows into the classrooms, a replica of the floor below and above. I was lucky today and found Patrick as he jammed his backpack into his cubby with his foot. I cringed, thinking what was happening to his lunch in that backpack.

He leaned away as I tried to kiss him—the same kid who'd sweetly held my hand the entire way to school—and went in and sat on the carpet of his second-grade classroom. I then jogged up the stairs to the third floor, home to the fourth- and fifth-grade classes.

Kieran had been complaining about his teacher. "She doesn't like me," he said. I spotted him at his desk—my happy-go-lucky kid who'd loved school in California, now sitting stiffly, at attention, eyebrows arched. I could almost feel the electricity shooting out of his frayed nerve endings. My heart felt heavy.

I went back down to the second floor and passed Patrick's room, stragglers still going into the class. Patrick sat on the floor surrounded by his classmates, his eyes on the teacher, another boy eagerly whispering something in his ear. I went down to the first floor, which was now devoid of people, and sneaked a peek through the big window of Mae's kindergarten class as I hurried by—fully aware that I seemed like a helicopter parent but still trying to act like I was definitely *not* a helicopter parent. I saw Mae sitting crisscross in the circle of wiggling kindergartners. She looked up as I passed and gave a quick half-smile as she raised her hand out of her lap an inch, the start of a wave, only to quickly drop it back down as her eyes darted back to her teacher.

I exited the building with a heaviness and started the commute home. I usually walked all the way, a much shorter affair without the kids. I passed women taking a *café* together, *porteros* sweeping the entrances to their buildings, newsstands, and people walking to work down leafy side streets with motos zipping past.

The sun was shining, and I found my sighs turning more into deep exhales as I walked. The kids were tough in the morning, lots of complaining and pulling along. But they were dealing with a lot. We had moved to Spain so we all could experience life outside the bubble we knew, and Tim and I had known the experience would likely be uncomfortable, for all of us—at least at the beginning. But that knowledge didn't make seeing your kids dealing with the challenge and the discomfort any easier.

I needed to have more patience with them. Mae's needing to be piggybacked was partially because her kindergartner legs weren't as capable as ours, but maybe also partly because she needed comfort, a way to release her burden. Perhaps Patrick's oversensitivity to his brother's ire in the mornings was his nervous system's way of saying, "I'm a bit overloaded." And Kieran's anxiety about being late to school, same thing. I needed to step back from the situation and see it for what it was—their struggle as they adjusted to their new life. And I needed to support them in their persistence in these struggles. That is, if I was capable of separating myself from my annoyance with our morning routine.

As the sun shone on my face, the truth revealed itself brightly. My complaining about the commute, my anger with the kids' loudness as we left the flat each morning, my irritation at the commuters who wouldn't make room on the metro, even my avoidance in the metro station of admitting I wasn't able to appreciate my situation—being with the kids and not working—these were manifestations of my own difficulty adjusting to our new life. I was too busy yelling at the kids to see that not only were they struggling, *I* was struggling.

Maybe that was why they held my hands in the morning and I held theirs: We were each other's anchors in our new life. A hand-hold meant everything was okay—that even though our world felt unsure, we had each other. I needed to hold their hands as much as they needed to hold mine.

Chapter 9

GAL-VAHÑ

*T*he majority of people who lived in Turó Parc were some of the wealthiest, oldest Catalan families of Barcelona. Amongst them were people like us, a smattering of American expats. Had we known it was the area of choice for Americans to live in Barcelona, we might not have chosen the flat we did.

Who was I kidding? This was our only choice.

The expat crowd was a group of ever-changing members, as is the nature of being an expat. Some had been there for five or more years; some were brand-new like us. In the early days, the expat group reached out to the group of new arrivals and invited us to dinner parties and cocktail hours, most of which we didn't attend. We were too busy settling in, finding our way around. My need to be situated trumped my need to be social.

The expats we did meet were kind and fun for the most part. I noticed that they seemed to do things together—the men had a self-titled group called the Loafers; the women just did things together without the puerile need to name themselves. In the second week of our living in Barcelona, Tim accepted a lunch invitation from the Loafers, not knowing what the group was all about yet. Lunch started around 1:00 p.m. Tim didn't get home until 1:00 a.m. Lunch morphed into cocktails morphed into dinner morphed into more drinking. What that group was all about was *partying*. Luckily, Tim arrived at the conclusion all by himself that he had no interest in reliving his college years, which was what it seemed some of those guys were trying to do.

I understood that some people find comfort in sameness; perhaps gravitating toward other expats helped these people feel comfortable, made them happy. But for my part, along with my need to get situated, I felt a strong need to find a life that felt "new and different," even "challenging." And hanging out with Americans or other English speakers felt "comfortable," "easy," and "same." I had not moved my family to another continent just to hang out with people like the ones I had left on the first continent. And so we politely declined most invitations, until they stopped coming.

Luckily, my need for "new and different"—and, thanks to the language barrier, "challenging"—was fulfilled without me even trying. The smallness of LIS did not give the kids a lot of choice when it came to making friends. Kieran could pick Vasily, the big Russian kid who picked fights with everyone, or a group of sporty Spanish boys. And as most parents know, your social world becomes an extension of your kids' social worlds. A friendship with the moms of Kieran's Spanish friends began to blossom on the patio before the morning bell rang and while we waited for the afternoon bell. My growing friendship with them felt like a door opening to the sunny side of why we had uprooted our lives and moved to Spain.

Two of those three Spanish moms were, like me, new to LIS. Alba and family had just moved back to Spain from Cuba because of her husband's work at the ports. Carmen and family had just moved back from Italy because of her husband's work. Carmen and her husband, David, were both Catalan, but had moved to Italy when Kieran's friend Guillem was three. So, in Guillem's household, the family spoke Catalan to one another but also spoke

Italian and English. When they moved back to Spain, Guillem didn't know *castellano*. Kieran loved that Guillem had to learn Spanish with him, though knowing Catalan and Italian meant Guillem picked it up light years faster than Kieran, who had zero language ability outside of English.

The third woman in my newly forming crew was Claudia—mom of Jaime, and the only one of us not new. Though born and raised in Barcelona, she had a seemingly perfect command of English, as she had spent more than eleven years in London as she worked her way up in the private equity world.

They all spoke English for my sake. Alba wasn't comfortable with English but tried her best. Claudia could switch between the languages fluidly; Carmen could as well but wasn't as fluent in English as Claudia. We spent many a morning and afternoon getting to know each other through the topics of what was happening in the classroom, what the teacher had done, and what birthday party was happening. Some of my best Spanish lessons were when I approached the three of them while they were already mid-discussion and tried to understand their conversation. My Spanish would improve rapidly during my time in Spain, but my comprehension always far exceeded my ability to speak. And so I could sit and listen to their conversations but could rarely participate. If I did, it was like a four-year-old speaking to a group of women.

Claudia, who would become my best friend in Barcelona, would remind me many times over the months to come that my Spanish would never improve without me trying to speak the language—but when I did, she chastised me for how badly I spoke. That must have been why she was in private equity and not a kindergarten teacher.

One day, walking into pickup at school, I ran into my Spanish teacher. (My Spanish classes that year were hosted at the kids' school.) In Spanish, she asked what I had done that day; I started listing some activities that I had the vocabulary for, leaving out more complicated descriptions.

This happened every time I spoke Spanish, and I found it so frustrating. That morning I could have fallen down the steps and scraped myself up, or witnessed an awful car accident as I came home, but the only thing I could convey to someone about what happened in my day was that I'd bought carrots at the market. And I couldn't even put it in the past tense. I would have to tell that person, "I buy carrots."

"...*y voy al mercat*"—I go to the market—I said to my teacher, even though I had already gone that morning.

"*Mercado*," she said in a clipped tone.

Since I was still stuck on how much like a four-year-old I sounded, it took me a beat to pick up on what she was saying. She wasn't criticizing my verb tense, she was taking issue with my noun. Apparently, what I had said, *mercat*, was Catalan. *Mercado* was *castellano*. My Spanish teacher was from Valencia—definitely not Catalan. She was not only making a grammatical point, she was making a nationalistic one as well.

It wasn't the first or the last time I would say a Catalan word not knowing it wasn't *castellano*.

A few minutes later, I saw Claudia on the patio. In those early days, I still foolishly attempted to speak a bit in *castellano* to her. I slowly pieced together a few lines about my trip to the market in Turó Parc, Mercat de Galvany.

"Gal-VAHŃ," Claudia said, crisply.

"Gal-VAHN?" I tried, still not pronouncing it the way Claudia just had.

"In Catalan, when a word ends in 'ny,' you do not pronounce it like 'ee.' It is not 'Gal-vahn-EE.' It is 'Gal-VAHŃ,'" she said, without the patience of a kindergarten teacher.

Fast-forward a few months and into a better friendship, and I would have been able to say to Claudia at that moment, "Gal-VAHN, Gal-vahn-EE. *Mercat, mercado.* How am I supposed to know a word is Catalan and not *castellano*? They both sound foreign to me! I can't be held accountable for mispronouncing a Catalan word when I don't even know it's Catalan! Who has to learn two languages simultaneously, anyway?"

For now, I couldn't and didn't say that. But I would need to soon. Or else I was going to have to switch friend groups to the expats, who raved about the wonderful produce they had bought that day at Gal-vahn-EE.

Chapter 10

CHICKEN ON THE BOTTOM

I may have looked like a dork, pulling my shopping trolley to the market, but who was I trying to impress? I didn't even know anyone in this city, anyway. And who was I kidding? I *was* kind of a dork. And honestly, this shopping trolley was the best invention ever, next to being able to pick out your own produce at the market and the market delivering it to your flat—something I hadn't discovered yet. So, today—every two or three days, in fact—I could be found pulling my black shopping cart, handed down to me by an expat who had moved back home, to the market.

I lugged what looked like a golf bag for groceries into the elevator with me from our flat, down six flights, down two steps into our lobby, up two steps to street level, out into the bustling city and across the street into Turó Parc, across the sand paths of the park past the palm trees and large green shrubs, past the elderly women and *las chicas* also pulling their shopping carts through the park (with a mutual nod, like a secret handshake of the coolly initiated—if you knew, you knew), to the other side of the park, across the street, past Bar Turó, past the place I got my eyebrows plucked for three euros (Spanish women didn't believe in eyebrow waxing, I was told, because it made your eyebrows sag), past some small boutiques, around the sidewalk dog poop, and down a few more blocks to Mercat de Galvany (Gal-VAHÑ). Even though I was finding that I enjoyed the obscurity of big-city life, there was something comforting in having a routine like this.

Mercat de Galvany was a large, very old, stone-and-brick church in the shape of a cross, surrounded by a high stone wall, that had been repurposed into a market. The former church took up an entire block. Just inside the stone wall, vendors were arrayed around the perimeter of the lot surrounding the market, selling various wares—piñatas for parties, uniforms for cleaners, clothes for women, pots and pans and irons and hairdryers. The entrance into the church was a set of automatic sliding-glass doors that seemed oddly out of place in a centuries-old building; they sighed as they opened into the cacophony inside, long rows of vendors sprawling out in front and off to the sides, the wet cement floor under it all.

I had an established route I followed and always purchased from my regular vendors. Today, as usual, I first walked down the row straight in front of me—past stalls of produce, cases of cuts of beef, barrels of dried goods, a stall only selling mini green bananas, and more produce stalls, a shock of color in the dark church—to a place in the middle of the church that I could smell before I arrived; there, at the center of the cross, were the fishmongers. The fish were laid out beautifully on ice, symmetric and colorful in their death. Not being a seafood fan, I held my breath and averted my eyes from the widened eyeballs of the dead fish, mouths agape at my passing, instead looking up toward the stained glass windows high up and off to the sides of the market church.

Eyes still on the windows, I took a left and hurried out of that area toward my chicken lady. Not that I was in a rush to get to the horrors that awaited me at the chicken stall, but dead fowl was better than dead fish. Just.

I went to my chicken lady first because the paper wrapping containing my purchases from her almost always had raw chicken scraps clinging to it, and I didn't want chicken going on top of my fruit and veggies. Chicken on the bottom, meat second, produce third, eggs on top.

I had become friendly with the proprietors of the chicken stall, Verónica and her husband Joan (John in Catalan, pronounced *zshwan*; not to be confused with Juan, pronounced *hwan*, which was John in *castellano*). They were my age, friendly and welcoming, and, most importantly, patient with my Spanish.

We had somehow fallen into a routine where I walked away from our interaction with some new phrase. And the phrase was always inappropriate, at best. Verónica would laugh as she told me my new expression and Joan would shake his head.

When you learn a curse word in a foreign language, it doesn't sound like a curse word. It's just another word in a language where all words sound foreign. *Joder, hostia, coño*—which is the curse word? They all are. But not knowing Spanish, all three sounded like any other Spanish word to me. One would think I would try to perfect phrases like, "Excuse me, how do you open this train door so that I don't leave my child stranded on the platform?" Instead, I spent the most time trying to parse out exactly what level of curse word Verónica was teaching me. If I said *joder*, was it kind of bad, or *really* bad? Could I say it in front of the kids? If I did, would a passerby call the Spanish equivalent of Child Protection Services?

As Verónica chatted with me, I never knew where to rest my eyes. If I looked down, I saw skinned bunnies sitting in her case, all eyeballs and red meat, front and back legs stretched in rigor mortis, forever frozen in their last big leap. If I looked up, I saw Verónica slicing out the breasts I'd just ordered from the plucked chicken she was manhandling. Nothing had done more for my decline in meat-eating than living in Spain. I was seafood-avoidant living in a city renowned for its unique fish and crustacean cuisine, and quickly finding a distaste for meat. Not a great combination.

I tried to find the silver lining in my chicken shop of horrors in that I knew exactly where my meat was coming from; no chicken breasts in foam and plastic packaging, sitting in a refrigerated section of the store for who knew how long, like back home. If I asked, Verónica could tell me that chicken's name and exactly when it died. Not really the name part. The Spanish would never name their chickens.

Today, after finishing with my order and receiving my inappropriate Spanish lesson of the day—feeling like I should cross myself, given that our conversation had transpired in a church—I did the part of the exchange that I really dreaded, even more than looking at dead bunnies with bulging eyeballs and chicken hearts on display: paying.

Verónica wrapped up my order in paper, still wearing the gloves with which she butchered the chicken, chicken juice and the occasional raw scrap of meat transferring from her gloves to the paper.

"*Veintiuno treinta.*"—Twenty-one thirty.

I handed her my debit card.

Verónica took it in her chicken-juice gloves.

Gag.

Rang it up. Handed it back to me.

Gag.

I took the card and put it back in my wallet. *Gag.*

Every time. Never got used to it. I loved Verónica, but... *joder!*

The experience was slightly better at the butcher. The body of a cow couldn't fit in the display case. And this sight was more familiar to me; it wasn't so far off from American meat cases. But there were more cuts of meat, and all had names I didn't recognize—partially because I hadn't covered cow parts yet in Spanish class and partially because that wouldn't have helped, the names were all in Catalan.

After a few visits, Sergio, the charming young butcher from whom both Claudia and her mom purchased their meat and to whom Claudia had introduced me, had said to me, "*Tú dime siempre lo que vas a preparar para la cena y yo te diré el tipo de carne que necesitas. Así es más fácil.*"—Always tell me what you're making for dinner, and I will tell you what type of cut you should get. It's easier that way.

Absolutely brilliant. Why couldn't American butchers be this helpful? And when I got home, I always found a sprig of rosemary on top of the cut of beef I had bought.

I would later find out that I didn't even need to show up to get my beef. I could email Sergio what I needed each week and one of his workers would deliver my order. For free. And there was no website to navigate. I could literally email him and say what I'd like. *Dear Sergio, this week I'm making . . .* I have no idea how owners like him could float the economics of this business model, but the Spanish had hit a homerun in the customer service department when it came to food. Not in other parts of customer service, like anything to do with the government, or cell service, or transportation. But getting food from the market to my house? Top-notch.

But that was for the future. Today, Sergio had to still to puzzle through my spoken Spanish.

After testing the limits of sweet Sergio's patience, I strolled to my produce people, around the corner and past the gentleman selling olives and the woman selling nuts. Within the first week or two of the kids starting school, word had traveled among us Americans: "You know you can't touch the food at the produce stands? Absolutely taboo. You tell them what you want, and they pick it out." I can only imagine how that would've played out for me had I not been warned.

Not being able to pick out my own apples seemed strange, but these vendors, again, were experts; they picked out good ones, or else they wouldn't get your repeat business. But there were some customs that needed clarifying. When I asked for "*tres pimientos rojos,*" three red peppers, my produce lady grabbed three shriveled pimientos. "*Disculpe, no esos. Más firmas, por favor.*"

Unfortunately, I just had said, "Excuse me, not those, more signatures please," when I meant to say, "more firm, please." If this had transpired in France, she would've rolled her eyes, maybe even walked away and helped someone else—anyone other than this stupid American wasting her time. In Spain, they didn't even signal that I was talking like an idiot. She said, "*¿Por qué más duros? ¿No los vas a cocinar?*"—Why more firm? You're not going to cook them?

"*No, voy a comer como eso.*"—No, I'm going to eat like that.

"*Ah, vale. Crudo.*"—Oh, okay. Raw.

"*Sí, crudo.*" A new vocab word! Though I had no idea if *crudo* was *castellano* or Catalan. As always. At least now the produce lady knew that the American who spoke like an idiot wanted firm, not shriveled, red peppers. And not signatures.

With each trip to the market I learned new words, and my people learned my likes and dislikes. I walked away from my produce people with a "*Nos vemos pronto!*"—See you soon! From there I walked past the bar with the late-morning *café* drinkers sitting on stools and up to my egg guy.

Seeing me, he said, "*Buenos días, guapa! ¿Una docena?*"—Good morning, beautiful! A dozen?

"*Sí, gracias,*" I responded gratefully. "*¿Cómo estás?*"

And he answered, speaking slowly and clearly for my benefit, as he picked over the forty or fifty white, tan, brown, and speckled eggs in front of him—looking for what, exactly, I didn't know—to choose my dozen. His stall was tiny, five feet wide by a few feet deep, but he inhabited it with a seeming love.

I was acutely aware of how different this life was from the hustle of Silicon Valley—always the next greatest thing around the corner. This man—about my age, with glasses, an apron, and a great head of brown hair—appeared unworried and happy. He emanated pride and purpose in what he did. He did not seem to have his eyes trained on a better something around the corner. His eyes seemed contentedly focused on his task and helping his customer. He would be there the next time I went to the market, and happily greet me.

I walked out of Gal-VAHŃ, the glass sliding doors sighing closed upon my exit, leaving behind the place where I knew people and was known, and merged onto the sidewalk with my cart, becoming another nameless pedestrian. I made my way home, careful not to jolt my cart as I lifted all thirty pounds down the two steps into my cool, quiet lobby and then again up two steps to the elevator landing.

Antonio, our *portero*, said hello. Then he tried to tell me something in his southern half-word way, and I didn't understand him. As if I would definitely have been able to understand him if he had spoken in full words. I did not sense that Antonio was telling me that my flat was on fire, however, so I just smiled and nodded and backed away, waving and thanking him, then slipped into the elevator.

I took a deep breath as the elevator dipped and then started slowly going upwards. Instead of being annoyed by the interaction with Antonio, which would have been my usual reaction, I was surprisingly amused. I was in a good mood coming home from my market outing. Thinking on it, I realized that here, that was more the norm than not. Back in California, every errand was a race against the clock, to be done with the least amount of interaction possible—get in, get out—usually because I had to get to work and my eyes were always up ahead on the next task. But in Spain I was forced to slow down. I had no choice—I had to think through what I needed to say and process what was said back to me, not to mention because I had to walk everywhere. And surprisingly, I was enjoying this slower approach to life. I savored the experiences during those two hours of shopping.

It seemed I was taking the time to smell the rosemary. While I wouldn't necessarily gain energy from something like socializing at a party, I always did from my interactions with Verónica, Sergio, my egg guy, my produce people. *Maybe I'm an extroverted introvert*, I thought, *if there is such a thing.* I was enjoying carving out a small known existence within a life of big-city anonymity.

The elevator bobbed, signaling that I was at my floor, pulling my mind away from its contented contemplation of that day to focus on what needed to be done next—unload the groceries and sanitize my credit card and shopping cart from the chicken juices. *Joder!*

Chapter 11

SCHOOL FOR ANGRY CHILDREN

nother successful commute to school—check that box. Successful meaning made the metro, no piggybacking necessary, no backpack left on the metro platform, and the V7 pulled up right as we walked up to the bus stop, which meant less walking and less pulling kids uphill. On top of that, I was fairly certain everyone had remembered their lunch boxes. Was it possible I was beginning to master my daily life in our new city? I didn't want to be smug, but I was feeling like I was getting the hang of life in Barcelona—even, I dared say, crushing it.

That day we had Mae's and Patrick's teacher conferences. Tim and I went in pretty confident we would hear that Mae was doing great all around and Patrick was performing strong academically. We wondered how he was doing socially, though. He kept his affairs close to the vest, and we just didn't know if he was venturing out and making friends.

At Mae's conference, we learned two things. One was that she was a chatterbox. Her teacher literally called her Miss Chatterbox. That was surprising information to us, as she didn't dominate conversations at home. But with two brothers who probably didn't want to hear her and didn't often let her talk, maybe when given the freedom to speak and a listening ear, Mae took full advantage. The second was that the teacher felt Mae wasn't reading at the level they would expect a native speaker to be. The teacher assured us she thought it would be fine, but said she wanted to make us aware.

I don't appreciate when someone is concerned enough to give a warning, but then plays off the warning and leaves it in your lap to do something with it. Or not. Your choice! In medicine I could never get away with saying, "Sir, your ECG shows more abnormal heartbeats than expected, but it should be fine." Even if I knew it would be fine, I would need to explain how I knew that. Not, *Here's some information you don't know what to do with, go ahead and think the worst; drive home worrying your heart is going to explode. Take care!*

At Patrick's conference we learned that he was doing great academically, doing very well all around. His teacher asked us if we had any questions.

"We worry a bit about how Patrick's fitting in," I admitted. "Does he have many friends? Who does he play with?" Patrick told us nothing at home, he was a closed book. How was school? *Fine.* Anything interesting happen at school? *No.* So I'd been assuming the worst about his transition to this new school and had dragged Tim into my anxieties so I'd have company.

The teacher stared at Tim and me blankly for a beat before saying, "Patrick is the most popular kid in second grade."

Come again?

"Everyone wants to play with Patrick!" she went on.

Well, that little imp. Tells us nothing, leads us to assume the worst, when he's actually mister man about town.

Kieran's conference would be the next day. Kieran, unlike Patrick, had been communicating with us extensively about his school experience. He gave us daily briefs about the Russian boy, Vasily, and what trouble he had gotten into on the patio. I surmised from what Kieran described that Vasily physically took out on other kids whatever emotions he was dealing with at home or at school. He was, in short, a bully.

While Kieran's communication was constant, however, it wasn't direct. His prefrontal cortex wasn't developed enough—that would wait until his twenties, or maybe his forties based on my experience with his father—to be able to say, "I'm feeling really anxious about school." Instead, he complained about his teacher. "Miss Duda doesn't like me. She only lets me ask five questions a day." Miss Duda was young and American, and this was her first year abroad too. Kieran's anxiety manifested in asking a lot of questions, and his teacher's anxiety left her unable to cope with Kieran's anxiety.

On the way out of school that day after Mae's and Patrick's conferences, while kids were still madly running around the patio letting off steam from their day and pairs of chatting parents dotted the patio, I asked Kieran how his day had gone.

He gave me another rundown of the reasons Miss Duda didn't like him, as well as what antics Vasily had gotten into trouble for that day. Then, squaring up his body to mine, he said, "Mom, can I ask you a question?"

"Sure, what?"

"Why did you put me in a school for angry kids?"

I stared so hard into his eyes, trying to understand what the hell he meant—where that question had come from. It was so stunning, I waited for the punchline.

"Do I have anger issues?" he asked, his eyes a little wet.

"Kieran, no!" I said, kneeling down to be eye-to-eye with him. "Why would you think you have anger issues? And this isn't a school for angry kids! This is a normal school! Normal kids! Sweetie, you're fine! Why would you think that?" I asked, wrapping him in a hug, crushing him to my chest.

I wasn't sure which felt worse: Kieran thinking we thought he had emotional issues or the fact that I hadn't picked up on any of this. I was so busy trying to get through my days—getting to school without issue and on time, figuring out what food to get from the market so I could make a meal every night—that I couldn't see the bigger issues my kids were wrestling with. Like Kieran's concerns that he might be emotionally unstable or Mae's reading problems. Maybe I was getting better at checking the boxes of daily life, but I hadn't stopped working and moved my family halfway across the world to get good at checking boxes; this was my opportunity to be present, be the mom I wanted to be for my kids. Today's conversation with Kieran was a harsh reminder that I was falling short.

The shock of realizing I was so out of touch with his worries felt like a punch in the gut. Or maybe that pain was this morning's smugness being slapped clean off my face.

Chapter 12

EL C-WORD

*I*t's not so common to like a parent of your kid's friend as much as your kid likes his friend. But I really took to Claudia, mom of Kieran's good friend Jaime. She worked full-time, so we couldn't take long Spanish lunches to get to know each other like so many people did. But after dropping her four kids off at school she would walk the two and a half kilometers down the hill to work, and often I would walk with her just so we could keep talking. She was whip-smart and direct, and I very much enjoyed our discussions.

Her husband, Tomás Alemany, to whom I often talked at school drop-off, was diplomatic almost to a fault, in contrast to Claudia's directness. Like seemingly all Spanish parents dropping off their kids at LIS, Claudia and Tomás dressed impeccably for work. Claudia and I were quite a pair walking down the hill, she in her tailored pants and sweater with her shirt collar peeking out stylishly, elegant but understated jewelry to finish off the look, and me in my Lululemon pants and sneakers, the American uniform.

Claudia's outstanding English, courtesy of her many years in London, meant a much easier road to friendship for us. I found it impossible to get to know someone well if I had to speak in Spanish. My brain couldn't translate fast enough for conversation, and

I would be thwarted from saying something about eighteen times a conversation because I had no idea how to make that quip in Spanish. And 95 percent of the time I didn't have the vocabulary for the witticism anyway.

But this wasn't the case with Claudia and Tomás, who'd also spent years working in London. Conversations naturally started and ended in English and were generally English in the middle parts as well, especially since Claudia's general impatience with my Spanish made engaging in that language with her feel like a formidable task. My Spanish at this point was restricted to the present tense, and to the subjects of food or modes of transportation. So with my desire to deepen our friendship with Claudia and Tomás, I pushed the English.

Tim and I had already gotten together with them a few times, mainly for take-out Indian food at our flat, since we didn't have a babysitter. Claudia and Tomás were worldly, interesting, and interested people who also loved to laugh, which made conversations easy, engaging, and fun. Conversations gravitated towards commiseration over what awful parents we had been that week, and the shared feeling that we were ruining our kids.

Even though Claudia and I were becoming very good friends, the four of us agreed that Tomás and I were twins separated at birth. He and I seemed to interact with the world in a similar manner, needing to be emotionally attuned to the people we were speaking with. Tim or Claudia would sometimes jokingly ask Tomás how I would handle something, or vice versa.

Tomás was a wonderful person, full of love for his kids. He also got frustrated quickly with them, but every time he got to his boiling point and reprimanded them, his guilt kicked in and he then immediately smothered them in love and kisses. We saw this cycle of anger, guilt, and love play out at least once every time we were together.

Several times, *la familia* Alemany hosted us at their swim club, Bonasport, for lunch and swimming. Bonasport was close to their house, which was just down the street from LIS—almost atop the mountain, looking down over the city. We had to take a taxi to get there because the club was not near a metro or bus stop, but we were happy to get out of the city proper and spend time with our friends in such a lovely setting.

Lunch was served on the terrace, awash in sun, overlooking the pool, which then overlooked the rest of Barcelona. The kids would swim before and after lunch and play on the playground and down on the basketball courts, all while the adults enjoyed our extended lunch and then *cafés* over several hours. That is how you did lunch on a weekend in Spain—a family affair, no rush. The conversation usually encompassed talk of kids and parenting, and very rarely work. Work wasn't something one usually talked about in social settings in Europe, we had learned. For my own part, my inability to speak about work, because I wasn't working, didn't bother me at all. I hadn't missed working at all yet, in fact; learning Spanish was a full-time, challenging, unpaid job for me.

One time after a lunch at Bonasport, when we were done with our *cafés* and were looking for the kids, I told Claudia and Tomás as we walked toward the *bàsquet* courts how Verónica, my chicken lady at Mercat de Gal-VAHÑ, had been a surprisingly good source of useful phrases.

"Like what?" they wanted to know.

"Well, like '*envasar al vacío*,' when I want my meat vacuum-packed." Who knew you could even do that? "Or when I'm feeling frustrated, I can say, '*Estoy hasta el coño.*'"

Claudia and Tomás stopped mid-stride. Claudia grabbed my arm.

"Don't ever say that," she warned me.

I had stopped walking too. "Why?"

"That is not anything you would *ever* say," Claudia said in a low voice. "I would *never* say that. It's very low-class."

I stole a quick glance at Tim and his face was as perplexed as mine, though not as red. I peevishly managed to ask, "Why? What does it mean?"

"Well, it's a way of expressing frustration, but it means"—and here she dropped her voice to a whisper—"you've had it up to your *cunt*."

Oh my god, I wanted to die. I had just said a word, in Spanish, out loud, not even lowering my voice, that I had never even said in English, to people who we liked immensely but admittedly didn't know us fully. I couldn't begin to describe the depth of my embarrassment. I couldn't look Claudia in the eye, and I definitely could not look at the expression on my twin's face.

"Okay! So never say the C-word," said Tim, who was finding this all a bit amusing.

"'*Coño*' is okay to say," Claudia corrected him. "You just can't say '*Estoy hasta el . . .*'"

Huh? "But it means the C-word. What difference does it make if you say it alone or in that expression?" I asked, completely confused.

"Like if I hit my hand on the counter, I might yell, '*¡Coño!*' because it hurts. But I'd *never* say it in the expression you said." She wouldn't even say the expression *I* had said.

I shook my head. "I don't get it. It's the same word. It means the same thing in the sentence as it does alone. In English we'd never say that word, alone or in a sentence. Why is it okay to say it alone in Spanish?"

"It just is," Claudia said. "It's like saying 'Damn!' when you say it alone."

How did that make any sense? How was *cunt* alone benign, but *I've had it up to my cunt* super low-class? How in the world was I supposed to learn this language when little bombs like this were planted everywhere? I could only hope my mistakes were more of the *mercat/mercado* variety and not the C-word variety. I was beginning to be *hasta el* C-word with Spanish.

Chapter 13

ON THE ROPES

The bureaucratic gods were smiling down on us. Through a communication error on the part of the San Francisco Spanish consulate, only Tim was having to fly back to San Francisco to retrieve our visas instead of all five of us. The Chancellor of the San Francisco Consulate had even sent Tim an email saying how highly unusual and irregular it was for them to allow just one of us to go. Why they did, we didn't know. But we had an email from the Chancellor himself, verifying that it was true. Only Tim was required. We would take that rare victory.

Even though those visas were going to allow us to live legally in Spain, in my mind the sole purpose, the most glorious reason, that Tim was going back to California was to max out his two-luggage limit with food. Food we missed, food we could not get. Those duffel bags would come back stuffed to the gills with bags of chocolate chips, boxes of mac and cheese, bags of chocolate chips, jars of peanut butter, and bags of chocolate chips.

And there would be the five visas in Tim's pocket.

In the days leading up to his flight, we wondered out loud who actually had it worse—Tim flying Barcelona to San Francisco (not direct) and back (not direct) with a mere thirty-six hours on the ground in California, or me, who would be alone with the kids, some of whom were sick, for five days in a country where I could barely communicate with anyone. Tim felt genuinely awful for the challenge that lay ahead of me, and I felt like a boxer mentally preparing to head into the ring.

The weekend before Tim left, we had taken a four-day trip with the Moellers. The first two days were spent on the Costa Brava, a gorgeous coastal area north of Barcelona on the Mediterranean, and the following two days in a country house in Setcases, near the Pyrénées.

On day one, Mae had come down with a fever. And then nausea. And then lethargy. As any parent who is a doctor will tell you, knowing too much is a curse; every day I ran the differential in my head of what could be wrong with Mae and looked for the worrisome symptoms that meant we would need to pack up and get medical care.

By the time we were home and Tim left for his trip, Mae was better but only operating at 60 percent, and I was exhausted from both constant vigilance and caregiving and was headed into five days as a solo mom. The times in my life where I had to be with the kids, alone, for an extended period gave me an appreciation and respect for what single mothers dealt with on a daily basis, forever. Not just one week here and there. I was worried how I would fare in this role and, worse, how I would feel if I discovered I was punching above my weight.

Tim left at 4:45 a.m. on Monday, and while Mae had always been more of a trooper than Tim or me, she wasn't ready for school that day. The bureaucratic gods may have been smiling down on us, but other gods were laughing at me; Kieran woke up feeling hot and complained of a headache on Monday as well. So, two for sure were staying home.

How to get Patrick to school? Mae had slept two-thirds of the day on Sunday. Was I going to pull her out of bed at 6:30 a.m. and make her walk the fifteen minutes to the metro, ride the metro, and ride a bus crammed with forty other people in order to get Patrick to school, then repeat on the way home? Then repeat again in the afternoon when it was time to pick him up?

It was an easy call: The kids were all staying home from school.

It's possible that with those five long days still ahead on my mind, and while staring at the very large duffel of dirty laundry from our trip, I let the kids play on their iPods and eat the sugary cereal, right out of the box, that I had bought for moments during the upcoming week when I found myself against the ropes and needed a treat for the kids so I could catch my breath.

Guess I was already there on day one.

Doing laundry in Spain was not for the weak—the washer was maybe one-quarter the capacity of what I had at home, and the flat had no dryer. So load after load got hauled back to the kids' room, where I leaned out their window and hung the wet clothes on the line strung outside, between buildings, six stories above the alley. Even if I was super efficient and did load after load in the washer, my rate-limiting step was Mother Nature and how fast the clothes on the line could dry. Only when they finally did could I hang up more wet clothes. And then more. It took two to three days to cycle through laundry from a trip. But where else was I going? I had two sick kids at home.

Oh, that's right, food—I had no food for lunch or dinner in the flat. And with no one to watch the kids, I had to take the kids to the market with me, despite Mae feeling so punky. We ventured out on scooters to Gal-VAHŃ a few blocks away. Scooters were a godsend to me and Tim; they enabled us as a family to get around the city faster and with less complaining. But he and I still suffered the very high risk of getting bashed in the ankle while a kid carried their scooter through a door or into an elevator. Happened at least once a day.

My girl Mae, usually game for anything, could barely scooter, she was so beat. When we finally made it home, Mae crawled right into bed and slept for the next two hours. I let the boys play Minecraft while I made chicken soup with stars (minus the chicken, because I hadn't gone for my inappropriate Spanish lesson since before our trip) and then lentil soup, trying to stock up for at least one more meal.

I then attempted my single-mom homeschooling. I made the boys read for a while. I then made Patrick work on a story he was writing for class. That lasted five minutes. So I made him write an email to someone, anyone (since "keystrokes" was a legitimate form of writing in school curriculums, and therefore a legitimate homeschooling activity). Then on to art. That lasted ten minutes. Okay, on to music. Patrick and Mae danced every morning at school as part of the morning routine, so we danced to "What Makes You Beautiful," the song Patrick's class was working on.

Later, after Mae was up, we went outside to the park for some "PE"—in our case, wandering around in fresh air. When we returned, one of the kids yelled from the front room, "Thanks for homeschooling us today, Mom!" Their appreciation made me feel more apprehensive than happy.

After a day of lessons, I collapsed in a heap of exhaustion next to the heap of wet laundry piling up by the window. I couldn't even muster the energy to respond to Tim's multiple emails checking in on us, making sure I wasn't down for the count.

The day Tim left, he had sent an email saying, "Btw, the boys have their *fútbol* physicals on Thurs, sometime b/t 5:15 and 9p."

The next morning I read it a second time, hoping I had misinterpreted the message. What he'd written meant that we'd have to get to their *fútbol* club by 5:30 p.m. for Patrick's practice and then stay there until 8:00 p.m. for Kieran's practice, squeezing in two physicals, and all the while keeping sick Mae at the club. And navigating this in what language? *Joder!*

By Thursday, Mae was still sick but on the mend, and Kieran was fine. Once we had scootered the twenty minutes to the club's fields, I got instructions about where to go and what to do from three different people *in Catalan*, paid for their physicals (an ordeal when you don't know how to say numbers in *castellano* or Catalan), talked Patrick through the ECG that was part of the physical (which admittedly did resemble the torture machine in *The Princess Bride*, which they had just watched), handed in only partially filled-out forms, because I couldn't read what they were asking for (*nombre* doesn't mean number, and who's going to read these forms anyway, really?), and got both Kieran and Patrick to their full practices. Mae was on repeat of, "I'm so tired!" from 7:15 onwards while an American parent talked my ear off. I just needed the bell to signal the end of this round.

On Saturday, Kieran had a game. I hired Liz, the Moellers' sixth grader, to stay with Patrick and Mae. I could not put them through another several-hour ordeal. Right after Kieran went into the locker room for his one-hour pregame talk in Catalan, I sat on the cement steps of the city school next to the turf fields, staring ahead at the five- and six-story buildings beyond, motos zipping past, cars honking. As the buildings turned fuzzy in my vision, I tuned out, deaf to the city's heartbeat thumping around me.

I was exhausted. I had been pacing myself to make it the five days and wasn't enjoying my time. Here I was, getting to do exactly what I had wanted to do when I had been working—be with the kids, and during a once-in-a-lifetime opportunity of living in another country, no less—and yet I was barely showing up, either for the kids or to my own life.

A dad from Kieran's team pulled me out of my mental rope-a-dope by asking me something, but I only understood one word, "WhatsApp" (which sounded more like *wushup* when a Catalan said it). I pieced together that he was trying to add my info to the team roster, and so I tried to explain to him that you had to use the +1 when you put in my number since it was my US number, and none of this was going well. And so a crowd of team parents gathered, listening to his Spanish not understanding my English. Luckily one of the dads spoke English, and we gradually sorted things out.

The English-speaking dad turned to me at the end and said, "We go get *café* while they are in the locker room. Would you like to join with us?"

I didn't drink *café*, and I certainly wasn't in the mood to be social, but I didn't want to go back into the ring with my thoughts either, so I said yes.

As awkward as it was sitting among this group of new "forced friends" that I couldn't converse well with, I felt reenergized by the experience. Meeting a group of new people, conversing in a language I was just learning, picking up on nuances of culture, similarities and differences—this wasn't what my life was back home. It was different. It was part of the adventure.

When we headed back to the field, I quickly picked up on the fact that the moms sat to one side of the players' bench and the dads stood to the other. I wasn't thrilled with this development, but keeping myself open to the possibility that something intriguing could come of this, I took my place with the moms.

Kieran scored a goal in the second half, which meant that some focus turned toward me—normally not something I enjoyed, but the interactions with the moms allowed me to learn that one of them, Flor, spoke great English. We chatted for the rest of the match, and after, she and her husband, Oriol, offered Kieran and me a ride home, since it turned out they lived around the corner from us. They had three boys around our kids' ages and were a kind, warm, outgoing family.

We loaded up in their Volvo SUV—which, after having spent some months in this continent of tiny cars, felt luxuriously big— and headed home.

When Flor texted later that day asking if we'd like to join her and the whole family at a city fair, my mental progress vanished. Even though I had just proven to myself that by making the smallest effort—simply by being open to putting myself out there—new and interesting experiences could happen, I couldn't envision going all the rounds that afternoon and evening: taking three kids to a city fair, then making dinner, and then doing the bedtime routine.

I thanked her and said hopefully another time soon—not closing it off entirely, just pushing it a bit further ahead, hopefully to a time when my ability to see the value of these interactions would outweigh my need to survive.

When Patrick's game time rolled around the next day, I was still in survival mode. So, after Patrick went with his team for warm-up, I found a corner, the farthest place I could sit away from people and still watch the game, and parked myself there. But being in the corner didn't protect me from my thoughts, and soon I was again self-inflicting body blows about my performance over the previous five days. I'd been given the opportunity to show up, as a mom and as a participant in my adventure, in my life here. And I'd responded by giving just enough to get by, by pacing myself. Was life so hard that, at the end of a day, survival was success? *Is this how I want to live my life here?*

I stared out across the turf field. After a few moments and a final deep breath, I got up off the ropes and left the corner. I wanted to show up. With that determination, I crossed the field, over to where the parents were seated. And I joined the moms on the moms' side.

Chapter 14

DON'T QUESTION IT

*S*ome days we felt as though we weren't that in control of our lives in Spain; we were merely following along, sometimes flying blind. How else could life go when you were unclear of the rules, both spoken and unspoken? (Especially since even when they were spoken, you couldn't understand what they were saying?)

One rule we were aware of and knew we needed to do something about was applying for the *Número de Identidad de Extranjero (NIE)* and a *Tarjeta de Residencia* (Residency Card). Both were required if you were going to live in Spain for more than a month, and both were absolutely necessary to function in Spain. Paying utility bills, buying a cell phone, and getting an annual transit pass all required the *Tarjeta de Residencia*, which was like a driver's license—a card with your picture and personal details, as well as your fingerprints—and your individual *NIE*. The *NIE* was the key, a unique number to you, that allowed us foreigners to do things like open a bank account, work, or buy a car.

We knew enough about the process to know that going through it would make our visa process back home seem uncomplicated and easy. When we had received the fortuitous news that only Tim would have to go back to California to retrieve our visas instead of all five of us, we'd known not to question it. Convinced that the lucky star Tim seemed to live his life under was at least partially responsible for our good fortune with our visas, we hoped that lucky star would be above us as we went through the *NIE* process. Or at least above Tim, who would be shouldering most of the burden and doing 100 percent of the talking. My basic French would be not helpful at all in obtaining our *NIEs*, and while I was confident with a few medical phrases in Spanish, asking a government official to open his mouth and take a deep breath would serve no clear purpose. So Tim remained our chosen representative. Never mind that before Barcelona, he hadn't spoken Spanish in the twenty years since we'd graduated from college—go get 'em, Tim! (I didn't realize how stressful it was to be the designated interpreter until we traveled to France and I became our family's chosen representative. But he had more Spanish under his belt than I did French, so . . . go get 'em, Tim!)

Obtaining our *Tarjetas de Residencia* and *NIEs* would be, at best, an adventure. One comes away from any dealings with the Spanish government thinking that it actually tries to find a reason to screw you. That it is part of a bureaucrat's job. Transacting business with the Spanish government is akin to dealing with the DMV in the US, except that the process is much vaster. Anything involving paperwork in Spain entails a high likelihood that you will not have what is required and will have to go back another time; you feel the government is smirking, knowing you will fail, and enjoying it. Back of the line! And the Spanish government doesn't warn you where the pitfalls might be. The bureaucrats just tell you when you screw up and then demand that you start all over again. Just because a process exists doesn't mean the steps are written down anywhere. Or are clear. Or fair.

I thanked Tim's lucky star that I was not working or able to speak Spanish, and therefore by default was in charge of the kids while Tim went through the craziness. First, he had to go to our local *comisaría de policía*, police station, to get something called a *padrón* certificate, which we needed for the next step in the process. For the *padrón*, he needed to show our rental contract and passports. Someone had warned him in advance that he needed to make an appointment at the *comisaría de policía* for all of this, but failed to also tip him off to the fact that even with that appointment, he would still need to take a number when he arrived. He then had to make an appointment at a bank to get another form, handed to him at the police station, filled out (no number needed at the bank appointment). And all these steps were just groundwork for the actual *NIE* application.

Once all those documents were in hand, Tim had to call and make an appointment for our family at the more regional *comisaría de policía*. Luckily, another family was a few steps ahead of us in the process and warned us: Make an appointment for each person in your family. Five people, five appointments. They had made one appointment for their family of five and gotten turned away. Back of the line!

The morning of our appointment for our *NIE*s we kept the kids home from school and Tim anxiously checked and double-checked that he had all the documents required. Passports, photocopies of passports, *padrón* certificate, fifteen passport photos (three for each member), *NIE* application form filled out and three photocopies of that, bank document with official stamp and photocopy, receipt of payment of the administration fee with stamp by the bank—Spanish and English copies, and photocopies. It was blissful to focus on getting the kids fed and ready while Tim worried about that mess; once again, I didn't question my good fortune.

We had the kids bring their scooters, and we all headed for the bus stop on a sunny October morning, the kids in shorts and T-shirts. A thirty-minute bus ride later we arrived at the *comisaría de policía* that held the key to our *NIE*s. A police officer directed us down a wide concrete ramp that led to a large interior cement courtyard. The government buildings encircling the courtyard were tiled in a royal blue, with the occasional and purposeful different-colored row of tiles that popped visually, or sometimes vertical rows of cement breaking up the tile. The courtyard floor was made of many small squares of cement rather than a huge slab.

New buildings in Spain didn't look like so many in the US, where the contract went to the lowest bidder. In Spain, they seemed to prioritize aesthetics above the price tag. I am more practical than I am an aesthete, but as I experienced more and more days where I would walk past an interesting building or an alluring mural, I found myself appreciating the intentionality and effort the Spanish put into aesthetics, making beauty out of what could be just another building to walk past.

As we approached a long line of people coming out a door, we told the kids to scooter around in the courtyard, but they kept close to us, seemingly sensing our unease.

"Tim, we have five appointments starting at 11:06," I said. "Why would we need to get in line?"

"It's just how it is here," he responded, seasoned from the many appointments he'd gone to and the incessant hoop-jumping he had done leading up to this appointment.

And so we waited in line, the kids sticking with us. When we arrived at the front of the line, we told the gentleman when our appointments were and he gave us five tickets, like at a deli counter. Tim asked if we should all go when the first number was called or if we had to go individually, and the bureaucrat essentially answered in rapid Spanish that he didn't know.

A large digital clock on the wall in the waiting room said it was 10:59 a.m., a few minutes before our scheduled appointment, and next to the clock was a digital sign with the number 83. Our deli tickets had numbers 117 through 121. We had come prepared for this Spanish bureaucracy and had packed snacks, school workbooks, and iPods.

We told the kids the wait might be a while and to scooter about. The courtyard was ideal for scootering; no one was out there, and it was flat and concrete. This time, they ventured out.

The fun lasted for about ten minutes before a woman in uniform yelled down from the ramp, "*¡Aquí no podéis usar patinetes!*"—You can't ride scooters here!

As we told the kids to just go over to the wall and sit and listen to music or do some schoolwork, Kieran pointed out that the woman who'd yelled at them was smoking. No big deal, as every other person in Barcelona seemed to smoke. But she had been standing under a *No Fumar* ("No Smoking") sign when she yelled at them.

The clock on the wall read 12:05 p.m., an hour after our scheduled appointment, when number 117 finally appeared. We decided we would all go in together. I was on edge; I wanted this to go well, or at least to *go*. I wanted us to come out of this experience with our *NIE*s. We left the scooters in the courtyard; we would risk them getting stolen over being denied our *NIE*s because our kids had ankle-bashed some bureaucrat.

The room was large and fluorescent-lit, with six large tables set up three opposite three, a worker behind each one. Number 117 was posted on an electronic board at a far table, so we filed over to that one.

A nice-enough-looking middle-aged woman, dressed in a black blouse, hair dyed a sandy blond and partly pulled back, was seated behind our table. No smile as we approached.

Here we go.

Tim sat in one chair, Mae sat next to him in the other, and the boys and I stood behind them. I shushed the kids when any utterance came out of their mouths. In rapid succession, the woman asked for passports, bank documents, and *padrón*, all in Spanish. Tim rifled through the papers. And then I saw it—a shadow of anxiety passed over his face and then came to rest there. We were one photocopy short.

He turned to me. "You're going to have to make a copy of our visa."

I may have gulped. I definitely didn't say anything. I couldn't even walk into a Kinkos back home without getting nervous—the process of making a photocopy was confusing enough there, with everything in English. How was I going to do this in Spain? In Spanish?

At some point I awoke from my visualization of how I would mime, "How can I make a photocopy?" to see Tim sifting through more papers, handing documents to the woman. He looked at me, the unease on his face not quite mirroring the DEFCON 1 level of anxiety on mine, then said to the lady, "*¿Necesita un copia todavía?*"—Do you still need a copy?

She replied no.

Relief washed over me like the spinal of morphine at Kieran's delivery. Why would she require it two minutes ago and not now? It was one of the mysteries of Spanish bureaucracy we would experience more than once and learn quickly not to question.

Mae was climbing on Tim in the chair, and much to the attestation of what a good dad he is, he wasn't losing his cool with her the way someone else in the family would have under these tense circumstances. I gave the kids their iPods and calmness quickly descended. Pretty soon the lady was making little jokes and smiling as she asked Tim to sign here and here. I laughed along, like a hostage trying to appease the deranged captor so as not to unhinge him.

As it turned out, she was a very nice lady—no appeasing necessary. Maybe she had a wall put up because so many expats turned up with the wrong damn forms, or no photocopies, or without their bank stamp. But we were turning out not to be one of those families, and so her job was getting easier. Tim put his finger on the scanner to provide four sets of fingerprints, and then it was my turn. Sign and fingerprints. She was very nice to me too. I was all sincere smiles back. As Kieran did his signing and fingerprinting, she commented on how beautiful the kids were.

When Kieran was done, she called for "*el mediano*"—the middle one—Patrick, whom she smiled at the whole time, and finally, "*¡la princesa, muy guapa!*"—the princess, how pretty! Mae made the kindergarten equivalent of a signature, a crooked lowercase "mae."

And then we were done. We couldn't say "*muchas gracias*" enough. Tim asked her how we would know when our *Tarjetas* were ready for pickup.

"*Vuelve en un mes. Estarán listos. No necesitas pedir hora.*"

Come back in a month and they'll be ready? You don't need an appointment?

Spanish bureaucracy. How could we just show up and collect our *Tarjetas de Residencia* when to get to this point we'd had to jump through a hundred hoops to even get an appointment, which had turned out to be an appointment to get an appointment?

I banished those questions from my mind; we had done it. We had been prepared with all the correct documents, thanks to Tim's tremendous efforts and preparation, and even sailed through with a missing photocopy; the kids had been calm; no ankle-bashing had occurred; and we were now official residents with *NIEs*.

Walking and scootering out of the police station, feeling uplifted by our success and a glimmer of optimism that maybe we were getting the hang of life in Spain, I turned to the kids and said, "Kiddos, let's find some gelato before we go home!"

Mae turned and looked up at me, dubious—about the smile or gelato offer, I wasn't sure. "But we haven't even had lunch . . ."

Patrick was also looking at me like I'd maybe hit my head when he wasn't looking.

Oh, children. Did you learn nothing in there? When life is going your way, don't question it.

Chapter 15

RAMMING INTO WINDOWS

*T*he end-of-the-day bell rang, and outside Mae's classroom the hall was packed with kinders and first graders, the beautifully dressed Spanish, the nicely but not as stylishly dressed other expats, and the easy-to-spot Americans in their workout clothes all jostling through the sea of little ones, trying to grab backpacks from cubbies while avoiding stepping on any kids underfoot.

The kids had already darted out on the patio and I was trying to make my way down the short, jam-packed hall when a Spanish mother I recognized but did not know made eye contact, raised her chin, and smiled—the universal *"¡un momento!"*

This recognizing but not knowing happened often. We had three kids at this school, and many other families had multiple kids there also. I saw some faces more often than others as we battled through the same two or three hallways every day.

This mom came up to me, bumping past kids and adults, and asked me in Spanish if I was Patrick's mom. *Sí.* She asked if Patrick wanted to come to Nico's birthday party on Sunday. Patrick had mentioned Nico, a nice boy in his class.

Back in the US this might have caused a logistical problem—trying to squeeze a last-minute birthday invitation into our schedule. Here in Spain that was never the problem, because we were always either out of town or in town with no plans whatsoever other than a *fútbol* match. The logistical problem, always, was getting there.

"*Muchas gracias. ¿Dónde está la fiesta?*"—Thank you. Where is the party?

Don't say San Cugat. Don't say San Cugat. San Cugat was the suburbs, on the other side of the mountain from downtown, from us, from the school. Many Spanish families from school lived there, enticed by the bigger properties. But for a family without a car, getting to San Cugat was an almost two-hour round-trip ordeal by metro. And that metro only got you to the central square of San Cugat. You still had to get to the house. There was no Uber. There may or may not be a taxi, especially if the party was on a Sunday. It would be *muy difícil* getting my kid to a party in San Cugat.

"San Cugat," she said brightly.

Damn it.

I told her in Spanish that Patrick would love to but we didn't have a car to get there. I'm sure what I said actually came out to, "Patrick is happy but without car."

She flagged down another Spanish mom I was sure had kids in some of the same classes as my kids but whom I also didn't know, and they had a short conversation in *castellano muy rápido*. This second woman said in broken English, "I can take Patrick. I go to party."

Without my processing what this all meant, we began to exchange WhatsApp information.

That finished, I started to walk to the patio, totally unsettled, wondering what had just transpired. My son was going to the party of a family I didn't know, and would be driven there by a woman I also didn't know. And it was a swim party. He was only in second grade. He was not a strong swimmer yet. What had just happened?

Among the shrieking kids and parents paired off talking, I found Claudia on the patio.

"Claudia, do you know that woman over there?" I asked, pointing to the woman who was going to give Patrick a ride.

She cocked her head. "No."

"How about that woman?" I pointed to the mom hosting the party.

"Yes, I know who she is but I don't know her. Why?"

I explained the party situation.

"Well, if it's who I think it is," she said, "they had a party for one of their other children earlier this year and their Rottweiler bit a boy on his face."

What was going *on*? Was I on camera?

I walked up to Nico's dad across the patio and introduced myself. I then explained that it was so nice of them to invite Patrick to their son's party, but Patrick was scared of dogs (lie)—did they have any?

They had three dogs, he told me. One stayed "put away"; the other two were good with kids, but if those two got to be a problem they'd be put away too.

I couldn't bring myself to ask if one of those dogs had removed a boy's face a few months earlier.

That night as I tried to go to sleep, I pictured two events. The first was Patrick playing hide-and-go-seek at the party and opening a closed door to find a Rottweiler two feet away with a low growl and saliva dripping from its jaw. The second was Patrick playing with the other boys in the pool, lunging for a ball as another boy lunged too, getting knocked underwater, trying to take a breath of what was now water instead of air, and sinking down to the bottom of the pool, all of this transpiring as a group of parents stood around with *gintonics* in their hands, chatting, no eyes on the pool.

I barely trusted my own husband to watch our kids, let alone another parent. Now add in the fact that they were Spanish parents, who weren't nearly as neurotic as American parents?

I didn't sleep.

I found it strange that birthday party invitations in Spain never had an end time. Then I attended a few and realized that they end whenever they end. Families planned their days around the party. A birthday was the entire family's day, because the Spanish are all about family and kids are to be enjoyed. So why not relax and soak in the sunshine, the good food, and good company, have a *tranquilo* day?

Because I'm an American, and we drop off the kid and hightail it out of there to go get the next kid somewhere or to enjoy an hour without that kid. We are busy. We have places to go.

But not in Spain, I was learning. And the rules of engagement for playdates in Spain were similar to the rules for birthday parties: similar food, similar assumption that parents might stay and enjoy the food and company, and similar length of time (i.e., forever).

The following weekend, Patrick had a playdate with a friend whose mom, Sonia, was American but had lived in Barcelona for so long, married to a Catalan man, that she actually spoke English with a bit of an accent. She had a car and had offered to pick up Patrick for the playdate—thank God, because they lived in San Cugat.

At 9:45 a.m., Patrick and I met her outside of our building. As I was getting Patrick into the car, another car or two beginning to pile up behind, I asked, "What time should I come pick him up?"

"Well," Sonia said, "what time do you eat dinner?"

Later that day—well before dinner time, not believing any family would want to host a kid all day long—I set off for the metro. I was going to need at least forty-five minutes to get to this family's stop in San Cugat.

I arrived at their house around 4:00 p.m. after walking the ten minutes from the metro stop. A six-hour playdate so far—Sonia and her husband must be exhausted. I couldn't handle hosting a *three*-hour playdate.

Sonia's husband, Javier, answered the door. His English was excellent, and he greeted me warmly.

"Come in! Come in!" he said with a broad smile before kissing me on both cheeks.

I immediately tried to lay the groundwork for my exit. "Oh, I can't stay. I'm sure you want your weekend back, Patrick's been here for six hours!"

"Nonsense, come in!" Javier ushered me through their cluttered living room and out onto their sunlit *terraza*, which overlooked their apartment-complex pool. Grass and greenery everywhere, blinding my city eyes.

Sonia came around the corner onto the terrace and greeted me with kisses.

"We didn't even know the boys were here, they've been so busy!" she said as they took seats on the *terraza*, me following their lead. "The pool, NERF guns, running around . . ."

"Please," Javier said, "let me get you a drink. What would you like? Wine? Beer? *¿Gintonic?*"

"Oh no, thank you, I'm fine, really, I should just get Patrick and leave you to your weekend!"

"Would you please stop?" he said. "You're making me nervous with your . . ." He flapped his arms, mimicking my *Oh no, no, I can't stay*!

I'm not an excitable person, but to these Spanish people, with my fast speech and my gesticulations, I must have seemed like a bird who's accidentally flown inside the house and keeps ramming into windows trying to get out. I chastised myself for being anxious. Why *was* I needing to run? Seriously, what did I have to get to? Nothing. Why couldn't I sit and enjoy these people's company?

And so I did. I attempted to be *tranquila*, and for the next forty minutes I proceeded to have a very nice visit, chatting easily with two people who were not pressed for time, who were not counting the minutes until their child's playdate finally ended. Which I still was having a hard time wrapping my head around. We were "so busy" back home in California, but so were Spanish parents. They had work and school pickups and drop-offs and food shopping and activities to cart kids to. How was it that they weren't harried and haggard and needing some downtime? How was it that they could just sit and enjoy an hour-long conversation after hosting another child for six hours?

If only the person I am now could tell the person I was then that these moments, exactly these, were going to be the most important moments of my time in Spain. Not the trips to Rome and Budapest but these moments on the *terraza*, opening myself up to new people and new ways of life, over a *gintonic*. A slow unwinding of whatever was wound.

I took the opportunity to ask Sonia and Javier's opinion about that upcoming birthday party.

"So, is Ramón going to Nico's party next weekend?"

"Yes, why?" Sonia replied.

"It's very American of me, I'm sure, but I don't know the parents, and it's a swim party. It just makes me nervous—I don't know what kind of supervision there will be, and you know, they're boys . . ." I knew I was over-worrying out loud, but their warmth and kindness opened the door for me to air my anxiety.

"Oh, they'll be fine," Javier said, waving his hand in dismissal.

I nodded, his confidence putting me at ease.

"Well, honey, it's true, the Spanish really are so bad about watching kids around a pool," Sonia said.

Aaaand that's a wrap. Patrick wasn't going.

On the metro back, with Patrick content after playing many hours with a new friend, the outskirts of Barcelona whipping past, I thought about my anxiety and how it had been whiplashed that day like a kid in a pool with a bunch of rough-housing boys. I knew I needed to be true to myself; Patrick wouldn't go to a party where I thought he might not be safe. That decision was fine and felt right. But what didn't feel right that today's visit had highlighted, what didn't sit right with me, was my need to flee—my perpetual need to go instead of *enjoy*.

I could stand to slow down. I could stand to sit down. I could hope that with each party, with each conversation with a new person, with each glass of wine or *gintonic*, I would open up, I would unwind. I would attempt to be *tranquila*, and I would learn to control my flapping arms.

Chapter 16

OH, PARIS

*B*ack in California, when we were in our frenzy of trying to figure out where we were going to move to, Barcelona had quickly become a top contender for several reasons, including its accessibility to the rest of Europe for travel. Now that we were there, we found ourselves taking full advantage of that accessibility.

In our first few months in Spain, we started locally, going on day trips to Montserrat, Sitges, and nearby beaches, then expanding a bit farther up the coast of Spain to Cadaqués and L'Escala, and then down to Valencia.

Next, we ventured on to destinations we had to fly to. Rome was our first. We wanted a big win for our first trip, and treats of daily pizza and gelato intermingled with visits to all the historic sites, plus a day at gladiator school, got us the W.

It was Christmas Eve, and we had just returned from a trip to Munich and Garmisch. I had always wanted to experience Europe's fabled Christmas markets, and since I'm the trip planner, I'd made sure we did. The trip to Germany had been fantastic, replete with an ice gorge hike and sledding (all despite woefully inadequate clothing), drinking steins of beer at beer halls, sausage eating, sleigh rides, and of course gleefully meandering through the Christmas markets. Now we were in Barcelona for Christmas proper, two days after which we'd be off on a trip to Paris and Bruges. The kids had three and a half weeks off over Christmas, and we were not going to sit at home when all of Europe beckoned.

Because I had delayed planning for our Paris trip until after we were back from our trip to Germany so as not to burn myself out, I now had only two days to plan our week in Paris. So of course I sat in our flat, looking out at streetlamps adorned with Christmas decorations, and sipped my glass of wine, not planning.

Barcelona's neighborhoods converted into Christmas wonderlands at this time of year, with lights and decorations crisscrossing above the streets. Paris, oh huge Paris, was looming— but all I could do was sip wine and stare out the window. And sip wine.

Somehow, the sparkling Christmas lights and possibly the wine eventually infused me with some initiative and inspiration. And with a jolt of realization of how lucky we were to be living this life, I walked over to the computer and dove in.

Carcassonne, Valencia, Costa Brava, Rome, Munich, and Garmisch—I thanked these destinations for teaching me valuable lessons in trip planning. Find options for food for every place you plan to visit, ahead of time. Find a park every day for the kids to be kids in. Have a plan for where you would like to go but be flexible. If the kids don't like dinner, let them have dessert anyway, because there is no kitchen cabinet of food in your hotel room to go to when hunger strikes at 9:00 p.m. Pay extra for the fast pass, skip the line, and save yourselves hours of waiting time—otherwise you could face a tearful bedtime with at least one kid, or possibly an adult, who is way past the point of exhaustion.

Most importantly, we now knew our family was a family of doers, not viewers. A guided tour through the Vatican had culminated with Mae almost causing me to miss the Sistine Chapel because she was D-O-N-E. Yes, it was a guided tour—but *know your audience, Amy*. I should've anticipated that a three-hour tour of four miles' worth of art in the Vatican could result in something like a kindergartner on my hip repeatedly whining into my ear, "I want to gooooo!"

Many hours of planning and a few glasses of wine later, our family found ourselves walking over the polished black marble floors of the Barcelona airport for the fifth time in a month, off to Paris.

After takeoff, I couldn't help but think that our getting served chocolate croissants and drinks gratis was a good omen of what lay ahead for us, we who were used to cheap seats and the typical amenities that came with them: nothing. But while the free croissants and drinks on our flight were wonderful, the idea that they were a good omen would prove to be delusional.

Before leaving, I had made sure to check in with the owner, Julien, of the Airbnb we would be staying in. He would be in Qatar while we stayed in his flat in the 7th arrondissement, his trip no doubt subsidized by our renting his flat over the holidays. What I should have done as a self-proclaimed rockstar trip planner, but did not, was confirm that not only would Julien be gone but so would all of his personal effects. Like from the bathroom (*do you really not need your toothbrush in Qatar, Julien?*). And the opened containers of food in the refrigerator. And the linens on the bed that looked used, old, or both.

That's okay. Onward and upward.

We had a new city to explore!

The next morning, we awoke to a drizzly gray December day. We navigated the metro and arrived at la Place de la Concorde. There were so, so many things to see in Paris. I had flashbacks to my eighth-grade trip to France with my French class. We had extensively studied the famous landmarks before going—the Pompidou, Notre-Dame, the Louvre, the Eiffel Tower. And when we arrived in Paris and traveled to those famous places, if no tour had been planned, we would linger outside, all of us saying, "There it is, Les Invalides!" and then that slight letdown—*Yup, there it is.* Pause. *What's next?*

And so, after emerging from the metro to the Place de la Concorde and steering clear of the Christmas market set up there—more like Rome's plastic crap market than Garmisch's authentic one—I was able to point to a large avenue that radiated from the plaza all the way down to a building off in the distance and say, with confidence, "Kids! See this big street there? It's called the Champs-Élysées. Very famous. But it's like Passeig de Gràcia back home in Barcelona—famous, but with a bunch of shops you can find anywhere in the US. But way down the other end of it, do you see that building with the arch?"

Silence.

"Do you see it?" I made sure each kid's eyes were staring at the arch. "That's the Arc de Triomphe. Very, very famous."

Silence.

"It's a memorial of sorts for the French who fought in wars."

Silence.

"Stand over here and let me take a picture of you in front of it. That way when you're older and studying it, you can say 'I saw the Arc de Triomphe!' and I'll have proof for you. You're welcome."

Our next destination to be seen and not entered was the Louvre. One controversial call in my rockstar planning was choosing the Musée d'Orsay over the Louvre as the museum we would visit.

The museum? As in *one* museum?

Yup.

What? said just about everybody. *Not the Louvre?*

Controversial, check and check. But I knew the Louvre would be overwhelming with three young kids; the Musée d'Orsay was far more manageable.

As we crossed through the Jardins de Tuileries on our way to the Louvre, the kids spotted a section that might as well have been designed for our family—small individual, ground-level trampolines. Within seconds they were flipping and yelling and having the best time.

Did we have a trampoline back in Menlo Park? Yes. Did we move to Europe to jump on Parisian trampolines? No. But this was a small gift that would recharge their happiness batteries and give us an extension to our sightseeing by at least an hour. Worth the stop. Especially because we had *the* museum on our docket that day.

At the far end of the Jardins de Tuileries stood the incomparable Louvre. In order to lure Mae away from the trampolines, we played "I Spy." I kicked it off by spying a glass pyramid (that didn't exist when I'd visited Paris as a girl).

The kids bit at first, but after looking at the exterior of the Louvre for about as long as it takes to say "trampoline," they turned their attention to the myriad crap that was being hawked in front of it. The same light-up toys that vendors had sent flying through the air with a buzzing sound in Rome and in Munich were also buzzing through the air here in Paris (and we would see them again in Florence and Budapest and Morocco). The kids were not happy that they would be getting neither a light-up flying toy nor an Eiffel Tower keychain (*well, you have to go up the Eiffel Tower to get one of those, and that's tomorrow!*).

At our urging, they begrudgingly crossed with me and Tim over the Seine, a fine drizzle wetting our faces, to the Musée d'Orsay.

This time the kids had *plenty* of time to appreciate the exterior of a museum, because I'd broken a key Breen travel rule and failed to buy a fast pass to get in the short line to enter the Musée d'Orsay. And so, as we snaked slowly and more slowly toward the entrance, we gazed up at the train station-cum-museum built in the late 1800s, another iconic building of Paris. But the hunger signal from the kids' stomachs overpowered any curiosity they may have

had about the building, so gazing was soon replaced with beau-
coup complaining.

Once inside, following the Breen *food first!* travel rule, we
stood in another outlandish line to purchase muffins that tasted
like ones I've eaten in many a hospital cafeteria. How was that
possible, in Paris? *Onward and upward!* I thought—a bit less
enthusiastically this time.

We immediately put into action the plan I had laid out a few
days back in Barcelona. I had researched famous paintings housed
in the museum on the Orsay's website, then told the kids to each
pick their favorite one and draw it. It had helped kill some of the
day-after-Christmas letdown, and I'd hoped it would allow them
to have purchase in the experience at the museum. Now, with
muffin-laden bellies, we set out to find the masterpieces the kids
had made reproductions of just a few days earlier.

As we passed by rooms full of Monets and Manets and van
Goghs, my cringing turned to delight as I watched the kids'
faces light up when they found their paintings. They compared
and contrasted their favorites; they appreciated each other's
paintings. We are not a cultured family, but we were having our
cultural moment.

As we entered other galleries, Tim told the kids to just scan
the room and see what painting captured their eye, and then go
look at it more closely. We were missing hundreds of paintings,
but seeing the kids so engaged with the art and enjoying their
time *at a museum* exceeded our expectations so thoroughly that
we couldn't be disappointed.

When we found the Orsay's giant clock, which ran floor to
ceiling, Tim and I could sense the kids' wonder of being on the
"inside" of a clock, looking out past the backwards numbers, to
all of Paris stretching out on the other side.

Simultaneous to us reaching the maximum of our kids'
attention span was an overhead announcement, repeated several
times, about an "unclaimed package." Tim and I noticed as we

walked toward another exhibit that security had cleared one whole floor below us. Unclaimed package plus a floor being cleared by security? Okay, kids! Enough culture for today! But not before quickly ducking into the gift shop to purchase postcards of the famous paintings they had drawn. Balancing a Breen travel principle—try to make it fun for the kids—with assessing if a bomb was a credible concern, we didn't linger in the gift shop, however, and after hastily paying for the postcards, out we went into the gray Paris day.

Waking up on day two felt a little overwhelming—did we really have four full days in Paris ahead of us? I also had to face the fact that I was now the one in charge of communicating, with my studied-it-in-high-school-but-haven't-spoken-it-in-the-intervening-twenty-four-years French—no small task. The weather had cleared, and Tim and I tried to do the same with our attitudes. We set off for Le Marais—a cool, authentic neighborhood of Paris.

It turned out to be a total a bust for our family, even with hitting a park on the way. Our visit to Le Marais culminated in a very rude Frenchman barely containing his disdain as we ordered four crêpes from him. "*Oui?*" he sniffed as he turned his head away from me.

I hadn't spoken yet, so it wasn't my French. And my kids weren't messing around or dressed in neon, so it didn't seem like he could be exhibiting his disdain for American tourists. If the crêpes hadn't been so delicious and my kids hadn't been so hungry (*food first!*), I think I would have dumped our food in the trash right in front of Monsieur Disdain. Establish eye contact, raise eyebrows, pause, tilt plate, maintain eye contact, slide crêpe into trash, walk away, pride intact.

Instead, once we'd finished eating, I just sniffed, "Let's go kids," turned my head away from him, held it high, and walked off.

Next on our list as we made our way through my itinerary was Notre-Dame—a building I found exquisite. The plan was to not fight the lines and crowd to go inside the cathedral but rather do the less popular attraction of climbing the cathedral towers to see the gargoyles and the views of Paris. A trade-off—a smaller line in exchange for experiencing the cathedral, albeit from the stairwell.

When we were a block or so away, we came upon a line. Tim and I looked at each other, and I could tell he was having the same sinking feeling I was. Hoping we were wrong, we followed along the line to its point of origin—*please don't let this be the line for the Tower climb, please don't let this be the line for the Tower climb*—where we found a sign that read "Tower climb."

Merde!

Giving up our hope of experiencing any part of Notre-Dame close up, we moved around to the back side so we could at least get a better view of the famed flying buttresses. Tim and I sank down onto a free bench as the kids chased each other in the sand-lot behind the cathedral.

We were beginning to think that Paris sucked—that everyone in the universe was wrong about this city. We'd need at least one win to convince us otherwise.

In search of that win, we opted for something on my Paris to-do list: ice cream at Berthillon, a famed ice cream shop that I had been told made ice cream scoops into the shape of a flower. Tim and I gathered the kids and made the short trek to Île Saint-Louis, and I gave our order *en français* to the woman at the counter—who, based on how she treated the couple in front of us, seemed to strongly dislike tourists. The woman handed us three cones with three regular scoops of ice cream. No flowers. The kids turned to me to complain, but, seeing my face, quickly decided their best course of action was to start licking instead.

As we walked over to the Left Bank, I tried to do some emotional reconfiguring while Tim oversaw the kids' purchases of some tiny prints of artwork at the art stalls nearby. We stopped into the famed Shakespeare and Company bookstore and wandered through the rooms. My emotional upgrade was complete when I saw Patrick reading to Mae, nestled in a small cubby in a corner. My heart melted, much like the flower petal ice cream my kids should have gotten to enjoy.

The last visit on our list for the day was Jardin du Luxembourg, the second-largest park in Paris and home to the Luxembourg Palace. I ducked into a shop on the way to buy some sandwiches—*food first!*—and ordered *en français*. Unexpectedly, my attempt was met with amiability, and as the woman taking my order smiled at me and we exchanged pleasantries, the layer of ice that had been forming around my heart since day one in France thawed slightly. I walked out of the café with tasty baguette sandwiches, a smile on my face, and an elevated mood.

The kids wolfed down their sandwiches as their eyes beheld the wonder of the Jardin du Luxembourg. The park offered fountains and pony rides and playgrounds and tennis courts, though oddly all of it, even the playground, required payment. After feeling the freedom of running around an open space with no worry of a car mowing them down (unlike everywhere else we'd seemed to inhabit that year), what ended up fascinating them the most were the tables of chess matches—rows of mainly older men seated across from each other at tables off to one side of the park. One gentleman in particular—a bespectacled, balding, late-middle-aged man with a dark winter coat and tan scarf—held the kids' attention. He was playing speed matches, and each time his opponent made a move he would quickly retaliate while yelling, "*Nein! Nein!*" and then slam the clock. After each match he would stand, turn to my kids, and give them high fives before sitting back down for his next challenger.

That night as we went to bed on Julien's probably unclean sheets, decidedly trying not to think about that fact, I felt like our trip had turned a corner. Or maybe it was just that my attitude had.

Upon waking up the next day—day three—I wondered if it was possible that what was on our agenda that day, climbing the Eiffel Tower, could have a direct correlation with our Paris experience. Was it possible that as we went upward in the Tower, so too would go the trajectory of our trip?

The day was very cold, so we layered as much as we could, donned our puffy jackets, and headed out. I had tried to purchase tickets to the top of the Eiffel Tower before leaving for the trip, but even that wasn't early enough: The tickets to take the elevator to the top sold out weeks and weeks in advance. So we were going to have to wait in line to purchase tickets to walk up the Tower to the upper elevator—a shorter line than the one to buy day-of tickets for the ground-floor elevator, but a line nevertheless.

Some days Mae was a trooper, and some days she just wanted to be piggybacked everywhere. Today, she was going to have to girl up. We were taking the stairs.

After a forty-five-minute wait in the "shorter" ticket line, we stepped forward, buffeted by a biting wind, to the next available ticket window with numb toes and dwindling patience. The man closed the shade down. Lunch break!

By now this type of occurrence didn't faze us; we lived in Spain, where this happened all the time. The kids had also been champs while waiting in line. So I smiled to myself—*tranquila*— stepped up to the next window, and purchased our tickets.

The next thing we knew we were boldly taking the steps up the Eiffel Tower. We counted every step out loud—partly to entertain the kids, partly to keep our minds off the increasing cold. After 350 steps, we made it to the first platform.

The weather was getting windier and colder, but the kids were tackling the challenge. We made it to the second platform the highest we could go by foot, 674 steps up. The kids, including Mae, had walked every step of the way without a word of complaint. We funneled into the line to take the elevator from there to the top—the reward for the most brave and fit—frigid wind blowing, no one talking, all of us determined and on a mission. Or maybe our faces were just frozen so stiff that speaking was no longer an option.

We got off the elevator 905 feet up in the air. We stepped out to take in the view, and as we rounded a corner of the platform we were almost pushed backward by the blasting, icy wind. We snapped a picture, attempted to register the view, and then got back on the elevator to descend.

That we had worked so hard to get up to the top and only spent a fraction of that time at the destination didn't seem to bother a single one of us. We got off at the second platform and hightailed it down the 674 steps to the bottom, the air feeling almost tropical in comparison to where we had just been. Excitement flooded us like the blood rushing back into our fingers and toes.

After eating celebratory crêpes—celebrating our climbing accomplishment or mercifully rising body temperatures, it wasn't clear—we walked to an ice cream shop, continuing our quest for flower-shaped scoops of ice cream. As it turned out, my information had been wrong: Berthillon was not renowned for flower-shaped ice cream, just for having amazing ice cream. The famed flowers were the product of another purveyor, so I was still on a mission.

We found the shop, but it was closed. Our flower-shaped prize would have to wait for another day. Still, we had had a good morning, and that success carried us. I wanted that upward trajectory to continue, and I would not let Paris—or my attitude, if I was keeping myself honest—get in the way.

We ate dinner at our Airbnb that night, which the kids appreciated—pasta with red sauce, a baguette, salad, and a bottle of red wine for Tim and me. Somehow that basic meal, which would normally have made me feel like I was cheating as a mother, made us all joyful and content. Sitting in that small flat, our family squeezed around a little table with a flowered cotton tablecloth, I savored the simplicity and happiness of the moment.

As we drank what was left in our glasses, Kieran asked, "What time do we have to leave for the boat?"

We were taking a night cruise on the Seine.

"Seven," I said casually. "What time is it?"

Tim looked at his watch. "Seven ten!"

If we needed to get the kids out the door in five minutes for school, they'd take at least ten. If we needed to get out the door to go on a night cruise in five minutes, they took three. We flew into our long underwear (*Paris, we're catching on to you!*), and any other layer that would fit under our coats, ran to the metro, then ran from the metro to the dock.

We made it just in time. As we were boarding the boat, the Eiffel Tower lit up in dazzling lights, as if someone had just plugged it in. Apparently, a light show happened on the hour—but I preferred to believe it was Paris's gift to us.

We awoke the next day, December 31, to our last full day in Paris. The following day, the first day of 2014, we would be boarding a train to Bruges. But this day we were headed to Montmartre. The kids really loved art, especially when they could watch the artists create their pieces, and what better place, tourist trap though it was, than Montmartre?

After a metro ride and a walk, we made our way up to Sacré-Coeur. After stopping at the giant blue Wall of Love, with "I love you" written in 250 languages, and seeing how many we could recognize, we walked around Montmartre. The kids each found their favorite artist and purchased a small piece of art as a souvenir (all three bought a rendition of the Eiffel Tower). After, we sat at a café partway down the hill where each kid enjoyed a bowl of *chocolat chaud* and Tim and I sipped *cafés au lait*.

Mae went from a high to a low when she got mad at her brothers for making fun of how slow she was drinking and stormed off. She went about ten yards and stood against a wall. When I tried to approach her, she glared at me, moved farther away, and sat down in a huff on a stoop. Mae often would turn on a dime and get really mad, essentially hijacking the family. *If I'm going to be in a bad mood, I'm bringing you all down with me.*

A man walked by with a small dog on a leash, which paused a few inches from Mae and looked at her. Mae looked at the dog, but her frown stayed. If a cute dog couldn't turn Mae's mood around, recovery might take a while.

With time, physical distance from her brothers, and some piggybacking, we made it back to our flat. I made a dinner from provisions I'd bought locally with my best French and sign language, both met with a conviviality and warmth that lifted me, and then we ventured out on our final night for the elusive flower-shaped ice cream.

Rain was falling, but the kids didn't care. Tim had to piggyback Mae again, but it was our last night and our energy was high. We arrived to find the shop not only open at 7:45 p.m. on New Year's Eve but also the friendly young woman at the counter confirmed that they did, indeed, do the flower shape. All three kids got their elusive treat, and we got very cute pictures—little faces wet with rain, jacket hoods up on their heads, little ice cream flower petals in front of their "We got it!" smiles.

We arrived back at our flat—five wet, happy campers.

That night in bed, my mind already moving on to the Bruges portion of our trip, I paused to think back on our past few days. The trip had not started that well, but it had turned. Despite being frustrated with myself that my attitude might have been a factor in those early negative experiences, I also offered myself some grace; I was beginning to comprehend that keeping my eyes always up ahead (*ahem, Bruges*), or on a prize, would also ensure that I missed meaningful moments along the way. A journey is a journey; that is the prize. An upward trajectory was a bonus, and a flower-shaped ice cream waiting at the end, a gift.

Chapter 17

IT'S THE LITTLE THINGS

I wasn't sure what *porteros* usually did, as I had never lived in a city, let alone a building with a doorman, so my knowledge was gleaned from movies—but our *portero*, Antonio, cared an awful lot about keeping the stairs clean. As far as I could discern, his principal concerns as a *portero* seemed to be making sure the door of the *ascensor*, elevator, remained closed and mopping and polishing the stairs—this impression due less to keen observational skills than to my limited ability to speak Spanish and actually ask him.

Antonio's wife, Lucía, sometimes joined him at work, usually in the early evenings, even though they did not live in our building. The desk in the lobby had a small room off the back that she and Antonio came in and out of, she oftentimes in a bathrobe and rollers in her hair. Lucía was as difficult to understand as Antonio, but just as nice to the kids and to me and Tim. Every day when we returned home from school, Antonio— Lucía too, if she was there—would greet the kids warmly, patting them on the head, cupping their cheeks, smiling, and saying what I assumed were kind words. Antonio also was patient with my lack of Spanish comprehension, for which I also was grateful.

He might not have been so gracious if he knew the few roles I assumed his job consisted of.

When we'd left for our Paris and Bruges trip, Tim had tipped Antonio for Christmas and given him and Lucía a box of See's chocolates from Tim's recent trip back to the US. When we walked back in the building off the plane from Bruges via Paris at about 8:30 p.m., exhausted, Antonio was just finishing his work-day, as usual.

The kids and I waved hi and went straight to the elevator, happy to duck conversation, but travel-weary Tim stayed to talk with Antonio. (Tim was always a good sport in these kinds of situations. Unlike other people, who were already riding up the elevator.)

About ten minutes later, Tim walked into the flat with a smile as big as the glass of red wine he was holding in his right hand. In his left hand, he held something wrapped in tin foil; he opened this package to reveal a bunch of sardines.

"Lucía made these special for us!" he said in disbelief. He was happy to eat these sardines on his own, knowing his seafood-avoidant wife would not join him, specially prepared for us or not.

This wasn't usual, for Antonio to give us a friendly gift like this. Either our tip had been generous by Spanish standards, or the Spanish didn't tip their *porteros* at Christmas.

About four days later our phone rang—a rare occurrence, so our first reaction to it happening was always, "Oh shit! Is the elevator door open?"

Tim answered, and I heard him talking on the phone in Spanish.

"That was Antonio," he said after hanging up.

I was already thinking about the last time we'd used the elevator and deciding we couldn't have been the ones who'd left the door open.

"He wants me to come down," Tim said.

"Why?" I asked.

"I asked him, and he said, 'Just come down.'"

We exchanged looks. Anxiety creeped in.

As Tim went out the door, I couldn't help but feel our luck had run out. A neighbor had finally had enough of our stampeding down the stairs every morning, or the running footsteps above them, or the crying and yelling below them. They had called the owner of our flat and we were being evicted. The rational side of me said, *That can't happen, you signed a lease. Except the lease was all in Spanish, and you have no idea what is in it, idiot, or what rental law in Cataluña is. Maybe landlords can kick you out for whatever reason: Two weeks' notice. Get out.*

The doorbell rang. Confused as to why Tim would ring the doorbell, I opened the door to find Antonio, holding a yellow cake. With a wide, warm smile on his face, he held out the cake, saying something in Spanish while wagging his finger and holding his stomach. Then he said one thing I did understand: "*muy caliente*"—very hot. This cake was from him to us, and either it was hot and would burn our stomachs or it was spicy and would give us indigestion.

Smiling widely and nodding, I took the cake—and as Antonio backed out to the elevator, I gave as many *gracias*-es as I could.

Tim came into the flat from the service elevator two minutes later.

"Lucía just made that for us!" he said, grinning.

"She did? Why?" I asked in grateful disbelief.

"I have no idea, but she said it just came out of the oven, so it's hot, and it's best to eat it while it's still warm. And she said we can serve it for breakfast, with milk."

I was touched by the simple gesture; Tim clearly felt the same.

The kids had already brushed their teeth, but Tim and I were beginning to understand that the small moments were actually our big moments in Spain. So, we called the kids out of their rooms, and they oohed and aahed with big smiles over the surprise cake and the kindness of Antonio and Lucía. Savoring the kids' joy over the gesture and something as simple as cake, Tim and I cut a piece for everyone, and we all bellied up to the table and dug in.

The cake resembled an unfrosted Betty Crocker cake but had the consistency of cornmeal and tasted sweet, with a hint of lemon. Homemade—just for us. *Un regalo para la Navidad.* A present for Christmas.

Mae ate it for breakfast the next morning, with milk, before stampeding down the stairs. Eviction would wait for another day, and maybe we had someone in our corner helping to push out that day, despite our lack of elevator etiquette.

Chapter 18

THE SPANISH WAY OF SPORTS

$\mathcal{T}$im and I both played Division I sports in college—Tim soccer, me lacrosse—and we both had success on our teams, including some national championships. Our siblings played Division I sports, our nieces and nephews were playing Division I sports. We had a fair bit of experience in the sports world.

One thing our college sports experience did not prepare us for, however, was being a parent in the youth sports world. Mainly, how to deal with the parents who brought to the sideline a level of intensity that they seemed to think was necessary to ensure success for their child, a level of intensity that seemed to be indirectly proportional to their own experience playing sports. The way we dealt with it was by . . . not. We distanced ourselves from these types of parents, sat far away from the parents who seemed to cheer only when their son had the ball—"Go to goal, Alex!" They seemed to also be the ones who always thought the refs were idiots.

A pleasant realization that had dawned on me as we flew over the Atlantic on our way to Spain was that we would not have to deal with these crazy parents or be around their attitude of "my nine-year-old is destined for greatness, and I'm going to give him

every opportunity money can buy so he can try for that greatness"
for a whole year. I suppressed a small smile as I had this thought,
hurtling toward Spain, our jet stream vapor floating lazily back
toward the land of crazy parents.

Spain, as it turned out, was a country of even higher expectations and higher commitment at the youth sports level. Though
when I say "youth sports," in Spain that really meant youth *soccer.*
Which only meant boys' soccer. No other sport seemed to exist,
and if it did, it didn't seem to count. Just like girls' sports.

The local *fútbol* club that Kieran, and by proxy Patrick, joined
was called Penya Burniol. Finding that club had been no easy feat.
If you wanted to play *fútbol* in Barcelona, you had to knock on
the doors of local clubs to see who would take some Americans.

Tim had driven around club to club with another American
dad from our kids' school who was looking for a club for his son.
Penya Burniol had agreed to take our boys, who would be the
only Americans aside from the one other already there in a club
of more than three hundred boys. Upon signing up, they'd been
given physical exams and an ECG, at the expense of the club.
They'd also been given game shorts, pregame shorts, a pregame
polo shirt, a sweatshirt, a track suit, and a rain jacket.

Practices in Spain were efficient and intense, and concentrated on ball handling and distribution. At Kieran's age Spain
still kept the teams to seven players on a smaller field, as opposed
to the American teams at his age, which had already transitioned
to eleven players on a full field. Spain focused on teaching kids
this age how to hold on to the ball under pressure, how to find
the right pass, and how to build out of the back, as opposed to
the American strategy of playing the long ball to the athletic, fast
kid up front who will run onto it and hopefully score. Kieran's
Spanish team played in a division within the city that had about
twenty other teams. There were ten divisions in the city of Barcelona alone, just for his age group. *Fútbol* was serious business,
and big business.

About a third of the way through the season, Kieran's team had a so-so record. A WhatsApp message was sent out to the parent group of his team that said some of the parents had met with the club to discuss the coach. (*We're unhappy with the coach? We didn't know!*)

Marc, the coach, was fired (*What?*) and we had a new coach starting Thursday. This new coach, Enric, had coached in the men's Third Division of La Liga—another indicator that youth *fútbol* was serious business. Unhappy with the coach? He is fired midseason and replaced with a professional.

Being an American was a disadvantage. US soccer sucks in Europe's eyes, if the Europeans even take the time to watch American soccer. Now Kieran the American would have to prove himself all over again to a new coach.

We had made friends with the dad of the American kid who had already been with the club when Kieran joined. Tom was fluent in Spanish and learning Catalan, so he understood what was happening in the club much better than we did. He said he'd just had a meeting with the club director because his son had barely played in the last game. His son's team, the lowest team in his age group, had had two "A" team players guest-play, and his son had barely gotten on the field. Tom wanted to understand the philosophy of what had just happened.

He was told by the director that the club had three goals: win, win, and win. The coaches got paid more if they won. And having "A" players play in that game was better for Tom's son, the director explained. His kid was the worst on the team, said the director, and if the team had lost, the players would have blamed the worst kids on the team. So not only did having those A players help ensure a win, it also ensured that his son wouldn't get blamed for a loss.

Meanwhile, Patrick was only going through the motions. He told us he wanted to play, yet he seemed lost out on the field; his attention wandered. He was a good kid and a good student—he wasn't goofing off. How much of his indifference came from a lack of interest, how much from not understanding Catalan, how much from wrong placement as far as skill level? We couldn't tell. But we were bothered and worried that he wasn't having a good experience.

At one away game, Tim watched Patrick play in his usual unfocused way. He moved where the ball went but hovered around the action instead of getting *in* the action. He sat out the first quarter then played the second quarter. He didn't start the third quarter but was subbed in partway through. The team was down 2–1. The coach pulled Patrick out of the game that same quarter, and Tim overheard him say, in Spanish, "We need to win. This is too hard for you."

Tim decided then and there that we wouldn't put Patrick through this experience any longer.

On the way home from the next practice, we asked Patrick, "Are you enjoying *fútbol*?"

"Yeah," he said as he scootered next to us.

"This is a much longer season than soccer at home," Tim said. "You've already played a full season of soccer if this was the US. If you want, you can be done with it now."

"Really?" Patrick's head swiveled our way. "But you already paid for the whole season. You'd lose money." Leave it to Patrick to do what we wanted him to do and worry about an issue like payment instead of doing what he would rather do.

"We want you to enjoy it, and if you feel like you've had enough, we are fine with that," I said. "Do you want to be done?"

"Yes," he said sheepishly.

"Then it's settled. On to bigger and better things. Let's find a new activity for you."

That same week, Kieran strained a muscle in practice. The assistant coach took him into the clubhouse, where they checked him out; according to Kieran, they were very kind and concerned, and when Tim came to pick him up they explained to him that Kieran should rest for four days, no activity; then they filled out some forms, handed them to Tim, and said to take Kieran and those forms to see the club doctor.

The youth club had a team doctor? If we weren't traveling to Rome in the next few days, I would have absolutely taken him to the team doctor, the doctor in me intrigued about the experience. But Kieran healed on his own and missed only one practice in the process.

When he returned to practice that Thursday, Enric, the coach, said to Tim, "*No puede jugar este fin de. Está flojo.*"—He can't play this weekend, he's "*flojo.*"

Tim didn't know what *flojo* meant and had to ask another team dad. In this context, *flojo* meant "weak." Strange, since he was fine. We thought the truth was that Kieran was getting benched for missing a practice.

At the game, Enric ended up playing Kieran in three of the four quarters. Guess he didn't seem too *flojo* after all.

During a corner kick at that game, Enric yelled out, "*¡Killian! ¡Dos!*" Kieran, whose name Enric couldn't pronounce, cut toward the ball as it sailed across. Next corner kick: "*¡Killian! ¡Dos!*" Apparently Killian wasn't following the *dos* plan because Enric yelled louder, "*¡KILLIAN DOS!*"

It was becoming apparent that Kieran didn't know what play *dos* was.

A final scream across the now-silent field: *¡KILLIAN! ¡DOS! ¡DOS!*"

Killian was pulled from the game.

He sat, head down. Two minutes later, he got up and walked to the coach. Kieran stood with one leg out to the side, both his hands grabbing the end of his jersey—a pose of anxiety only his mother could read. Enric gesticulated as he talked, bending over to Kieran.

I could only assume Kieran had the *huevos* to ask Enric what he was meant to do during *dos* and now Enric was explaining— hopefully in Spanish, not Catalan—and Kieran was hopefully understanding.

Times like these were when Kieran's Spanish took hold and his skin thickened. He listened to Enric. He nodded.

Enric put Kieran back in the game.

Another corner kick, and: "*¡Killian dos!*"

I turned to our friend Oriol, another dad on the team, and asked, "*¿Qué es dos?*"

"I have no idea," he said.

The ball sailed across; Kieran cut in and one-timed it out of the air into the goal.

Oriol turned to us with a grin. "*That's* what *dos* is!"

I liked watching Kieran's games. But the boys were required to be there an hour and a half before game time for one hour of pregame talk—in Catalan—and a half-hour of warmup. That was the cue for the parents to head for a *café* or beer, irrespective of time of day—or, if it was an away game, to sit there and partake at that club's clubhouse. (Since our club was downtown and didn't have a stadium or clubhouse, the parents went to a bar across the street.) We always felt bad leaving Kieran for an hour of pregame talk that he mostly couldn't understand, but he was passionate about *fútbol*, so he swallowed his medicine without complaining. Tim and I could see his resilience and perseverance building through these experiences, because of his love for the game.

As much as Kieran didn't like sitting through his Catalan lesson, I didn't like bludgeoning the other parents' language for an hour and a half, so I often elected Tim to take Kieran and be there for the pregame instead—yet another example of Tim being a better person than I. For an away game, Kieran and Tim would be gone for most of the day. For a home game, Patrick and Mae had to haul on scooters with me for the start of the game and then be bored off their gourds for several hours, entertaining themselves by putting cones on their heads and arms and legs.

After making it through the parents' pregame, we still had the weird gender lines to contend with. At games, women sat on one side of the bench, men on the other. I liked to watch games with Tim. Since soccer was his sport and I had never played, I liked to ask him questions and discuss Kieran's play. If I sat with the other women, I had to make small talk—badly, in Spanish. So, I usually broke the rules and sat on the guys' side. I don't know what *las chicas* thought of this. I hoped I wasn't offending them and they were just relieved not to have to make small talk at a first-grade level with the American.

With their dedication to attending their sons' games and their insistence on firing a coach mid-season for poor performance, one would think these parents would be as fiercely overbearing and competitive as their US counterparts—but not so. Granted we missed the nuances because of our level of Spanish, but we were in the know enough to feel the vibe, and the vibe was different. The *fútbol* field wasn't the site of insane parental involvement or pressure. Sure, the games were intense, and parents might yell at the kids on the field during a game—they might even yell at other people's kids—but as soon as the final whistle blew, that game was in the past and the parents all gathered for a *cerveza*. A bad game did not ruin a perceived scholarship years down the road. College soccer didn't even exist in Spain. If you were serious about *fútbol*, the path was youth club to professional club. And athletes and athletic ability weren't revered to the degree they were in the US. As one Spanish person told me, "Sure, they can play *fútbol*, but what else can they do?"

When Messi, who lived close by us, was in the park playing with his son, parents and kids didn't swarm him. When Sergio Ramos from Real Madrid posted a stupid comment on Twitter, Catalans were merciless about how dumb he was. The Spanish didn't deify professional athletes the way Americans did. *Fútbol* might be like a religion in Spain, but the Spanish don't often go to church.

Still, I knew enough to know I didn't know enough. We would have needed a few more years in Spain before we could have understood the youth sports culture well enough to knowledgeably compare Spanish versus American parental attitudes and actions.

Since we weren't fortunate enough to have a few more years, and we would eventually need to face the American youth sports culture again, we could at least import a page from Spain's playbook: At the kids' games back in the US, instead of separating the men from the women, maybe we could have the parents who thought their nine-year-old was destined for a scholarship on one side, and the rest of us on another.

Chapter 19

TRUST US

A few months earlier, Tim had been introduced by an
American expat to Pascual, a Spanish entrepreneur who
was looking for someone to help him run his latest startup. After
a few meetings, Tim started consulting for Pascual, a wonderful
human being full of heart and ideas. After a few months, Pascual
approached Tim about staying another year to be the CEO of
the startup, with the idea that a year later Tim would transition
the company to the US, where the company's market share was
focused anyway. So we would get another year in Spain, and for
sure head home after the second year.

The opportunity was great for Tim, work-wise, and would
allow our family to stay in Spain an additional year. Though I
had been grumbling my way through our day-to-day, my heart
knew something my brain was slow to catch on to: I wanted to
stay for another year, explore what my heart understood, and give
my brain the time it needed to catch up.

Tim and I had several conversations about the kids and
whether staying was the right move for them. But we knew it
was, 100 percent. Here, they were dealing with challenges they
wouldn't have at home—what it felt like to be the outsiders, to

need to break in, fit in, and what it meant not to. Here, they were the kids who couldn't speak the language and were learning what it meant to push themselves because they needed to. They were encountering more disappointment than they would face at home, but also having more experiential wins than would be possible there. Who else their age could say they'd gotten themselves out of a Russian bully's headlock or been cursed at in Catalan and understood it? They were also traveling places they would never have gotten to see if we'd stayed in California.

What we danced around and then confronted was the knowledge that the kids probably didn't want to stay. We knew staying was the right decision for all of us, but we had never been the "because I said so" kind of parents. And even though it would've been easier to just tell them, "We're staying, trust us, end of story," it wasn't how we operated.

As we were figuring out how to proceed, what did feel right was giving Kieran, the oldest, the respect of letting him in on our thought process, so we wouldn't surprise him with a decision.

"Kieran," I began, "we think your Spanish is doing so amazing here—"

"Let me guess," Kieran cut in. "You want to stay another year."

Tim and I tried not to look at each other, shocked.

"Yes, we're seriously considering it," I admitted. "Pascual asked Dad to run his company for one more year here. Then we'd move back to California. Dad would keep working for Pascual when he got back home. It would be great for Dad. But for us as a family, we think it would be a great opportunity too. We like it here. You all have good friends here. Your Spanish will *rock* after another year. But how do you feel about it?"

Kieran thought about it. "Well, if I went home, I'd miss my friends here. But if we stayed, I'd miss my friends back home." Home never had been Spain—home had always been California. "It wouldn't be fair to my friends who think I'm coming home. Plus, the food is so bad here. That fish they serve at lunch is disgusting. And school isn't hard enough. If we stay another year, I'll be so far behind everyone, especially in math, and I won't be able to catch up. And the patio here is too small. You can't even play a game. At Spring House there is a field to run around on. I'd rather just go home." He looked down, not meeting my gaze. Then looked up, brow furrowed. "And how do I know that next year you won't say the same thing, and next thing you know we're here for five more years and we never go home?"

Kieran got up and started to walk away. I was so sad, and surprised by his lengthy list, and unsure of what to say, I let him. Then I got up and went to our bedroom and lay down on our bed. Kieran's reaction had made me feel worse than his reasons had. He hadn't thrown a fit or cried. He'd just been resigned. And then retreated.

A few days later Kieran said to Tim, "Have you made up your mind yet? I just want to know if we're staying or going."

A few days after that, out of the blue, he restated the reasons why he didn't want to stay. Falling behind in math, it wasn't fair to his friends at home. What would they say if he didn't come back?

Including Kieran in our thinking had been a mistake, and now being in limbo was causing him to be miserable. He was like his mom: Give me black or white, no gray. And we could clearly tell which decision to him was black and which was white.

Even Mae, who was still in the dark, must have sensed our faltering because a few times that week, she brought up California. I would say something like, "You have such a great group of girls in your class. It would be cool if you could be with them in class again next year."

"But I'm not," she'd say—and then, when she got no validation from me, she'd say again, "I'm not, right?"

Mae for sure wouldn't want to stay. She had her best friend, Elly, our neighbor, to get home to. Elly, who was five years older.

Elly, who would be entering sixth grade next year, and when has a sixth grader ever preferred to hang out with a first grader instead of her fellow middle schoolers? But I wasn't going to lob that bomb.

Patrick was our wild card. He could be psyched about staying—he had fallen into a good posse at school, and he tended to roll with everything—or he could say no thanks, I want to go home. You just never knew with that kid.

On a gray Saturday morning in February, with a *fútbol* match for Kieran and a birthday party for Patrick in San Cugat (*San Cugat!*) on the docket, we called Kieran into our bedroom. Tim and I were lying on the bed on top of the covers, and we asked Kieran to lie down with us.

We had learned our lesson, so we got right to the point. As we told our eldest son we had decided to stay in Spain another year, tears welled up in his eyes. He wiped at them, and when that didn't work, he put a pillow over his face.

This was squeezing my heart, but I kept talking, because what else could I do but get through my speech? I knew our decision was making him sad, but we couldn't change course now.

"Dad has a great job here, and we want Dad to be happy, and staying here with this job is good for him." I had consulted with the counselor at school as far as how to help the kids with this change, how to avoid "because I said so" parenting, and she'd suggested focusing on one thing that might make each of them happy about staying. So I continued, "And staying another year will be great for your soccer. We're really lucky that you have great friends here and great friends in California. We are going to go home this summer and you'll get to see all of them, and then come back and be with all your friends here. How great that you get to have two sets of such great friends! And then only ten more months of school and you'll be home again. None of your friends in California will forget you. You don't stop being friends with someone just because you're not there."

Kieran got up from the bed, eyes red, face expressionless.

"How are you feeling?" I asked gently.

"A little better," he said and walked out.

A little better than what?

Feeling like an HR department calling in the next round to be fired, we brought Patrick and Mae into the room, secretly hoping Patrick's reaction might be positive and his enthusiasm might temper Mae's reaction. Peer pressure.

As they lay on the bed with us, we stuck to the counselor's advice and focused on reasons why they might want to stay in Spain. Patrick kept breaking in with, "Okay," and wanting to get off the bed. "Wait, we're not done," we said, and we explained a little more.

Patrick got up to leave.

"Wait." And we explained a little more, gently.

"And we'll go back home to California for the summer," I finished.

"I refuse to come back to Spain! I am not coming back!" Mae yelled. So much for peer pressure. "Maybe if you said we are coming back to Spain for one day, or two. But I refuse!" And she stormed out. Patrick, using his sister's eruption as a diversion, got off the bed.

"Wait, Patrick," I called after him. "How do you feel about all of this?"

"Good!" he said as he walked out of the room with a spring in his step.

Tim and I looked at each other, both of us deflated and dejected—due to Mae's and Kieran's reactions and how seriously short our parenting skills had fallen. We didn't know best. Maybe we should have gone with the "because I said so" method after all.

As happens, life had to go on. All five of us got on the metro to head to San Cugat and Patrick's friend's birthday party, all of us—except Patrick—dismayed for our own reasons.

When we arrived at the friend's grandparents' house where the party was being held, we discovered a backyard that appeared to go on forever—such a refreshing view compared to city streets. As Tim and I chitchatted with other parents, we could see in the distance, past a hill, a trampoline and a grass tennis court. A table with a big spread, complete with Nutella sandwiches on white bread, chips, olives, Doritos, and Fanta, stood behind us as we looked out at the kids rolling down the hill and shooting each other across the yard with NERF guns.

After about half an hour of letting all three of our kids have a good dose of yard, which they hadn't seen in months, the four of us left Patrick with his buddies and made our way back to the metro station. Kieran and Tim had to be back for Kieran's *fútbol* match.

I was thankful we'd had this happy diversion from the big news of the morning. Patrick would be content for the next few hours, and Kieran was setting off to do something he loved.

As was the case for us with all parties in San Cugat, shortly after we got home from dropping off Patrick at the party, Mae and I had to turn around to start the journey back to pick him up. The day was gray, drizzling off and on, as we made our way back to the metro station we had walked out of not so long before.

"Can we get some gelato?" Mae asked.

"There isn't anything open on a Sunday," I said, "but we'll have dessert tonight after dinner."

No response.

"Hey, remember that new frozen yogurt shop that opened up last summer back in Menlo Park?" I asked cheerfully, trying to improve the emotional undercurrent. "We'll have to go there a few times this summer when we're home, for sure."

"Wait," Mae said, looking up at me wide-eyed, incredulity in her voice. "We'll be home this summer?"

"Yes, of course! You'll get to play with Elly, bike around the cul-de-sac—"

"*Yes!*" Mae interrupted me, doing a big fist pump.

I had just told her that morning we were going home that summer. But obviously the news hadn't registered with her. She was probably so blown over that we were staying that she hadn't heard the rest. I was, unfortunately, familiar with this phenomenon from work; when a doctor has to convey bad news to a patient, the patient often stops hearing anything that was said after "there was an abnormality on your CT scan."

Mae looked at me—fish-eyed, but clearly in a better state of mind—and asked, "We're definitely going back this summer?"

"Yup," I replied.

I returned her fish-eyed look with a half-smile and said, "Because I said so."

Chapter 20

TEA AND TRADE-OFFS

laudia had invited me to tea. I didn't really know what "tea" exactly meant or entailed, other than we'd most likely be drinking tea. It didn't matter to me; I was just happy to be getting time with Claudia. With her busy work and life with four kids, it was hard for us to find time to spend together—as just the two of us, as couples, or even as all eleven of us. Even so, my friendship with Claudia had deepened over the months; we had become very good friends.

Trudging up the hill toward Claudia's house for tea, staring down at my running shoes as I went, I thought about how an American friend said she thought Claudia was the best-dressed mom at LIS. Claudia always dressed in a fashionable way that maintained professionality, even at home. She would not be answering the door in yoga pants, sneakers, and a puffy jacket. But I couldn't make it up to Claudia's house in a nice outfit without ending up with blisters and pit stains. Yes, the clothes I wore, often, were a very American look—but as my sister pointed out to me, "You *are* American." It was a trade-off I was learning to accept—getting to go places but having to look very American in order to get there.

Claudia never commented on my clothing, but she did still occasionally comment on my needing to speak more Spanish. I knew she wanted me to practice my Spanish with her and Tomás, but my two tenses and basic vocabulary made it very difficult for me to have the level of conversation I wanted to have with close friends. This nagged at me—would language be a barrier to our deepening friendship?

Claudia buzzed me in through the gate, and I walked past the first of three modern houses stacked in a deep row before ringing the doorbell for her home.

"*Hola! Hola!*" Claudia greeted me—big smile, impeccable clothing.

We exchanged kisses, and I entered their spotless house and moved through the foyer to the bright, modern kitchen.

"*¿Quieres una infusión?*"—Do you want an herbal tea? Claudia asked, knowing it was what we both drank.

"*Sí, gracias.*" I dipped my head in a yes.

"*¿De qué tipo?*"—What type?

I interpreted our start in Spanish to be a signal that she expected me to try in Spanish. But I knew my Spanish couldn't get much past tea-level. And I wasn't willing to make that trade-off; deepening our friendship was more important to me.

"Do you have something like mint?" I asked.

"*Sí, ¿menta poleo?*"—Yes, mint tea?

"*Perfecto.*"

"Would you like me to take your tea bag out or leave it in?" Claudia asked, hopefully not hearing my sigh of relief that she seemed accepting of our conversation continuing in English.

I knew there was a proper way to do tea, and I knew I didn't know what that way was. Claudia and Tomás had lived in London for many years, so I knew she knew. "I just leave mine in," I said. "I doubt that's the proper way, but—"

"Me too," Claudia said with a big smile, handing me a white teacup and saucer. "*Infusión* isn't 'proper tea' anyway. Come, let's sit." She directed me back to their living room.

We walked back to the sunlit room with its floor-to-ceiling windows looking out to their small yard and small pool. Not a pillow out of place, not a toy in sight, with twin four-year-olds and two older boys living in that house. On the low coffee table sat a plate of cookies and chocolate, neatly arranged.

"Please, help yourself," Claudia said, pointing at the chocolate.

She and I shared a fondness for—some might say addiction to—chocolate. There were squares of Lindt chocolate on the plate, a mix of digestive biscuits, and what looked like the Spanish version of Pepperidge Farm cookies. My addiction tended to rear its head in the evening; I didn't need chocolate in the middle of the day. But I did take one, as I'm not totally uncouth or unaddicted.

I had had a situation nagging at me, so I took this opportunity to run it by Claudia. I was hungry for her opinion, and our conversation being in English opened the door to having a deeper, more meaningful discussion with her.

I had been hemming and hawing about taking a two-week trip with an American friend, Deb, to walk the Camino in the spring. I had told Deb the trip would be fun, but I hadn't committed to going. Recently, Deb had put the big push on, and last week I had finally said yes. We would need to start looking into plane fare and hostels soon. But Tim was now working full-time at Pascual's startup, and I would be leaving him with all three kids, for two weeks, to do this trip. Plus, we were staying another year; I could walk the Camino next year, a thought that gave me some relief. Which made me think I should wait.

"So, you are going to commit to doing two weeks with this person and you don't want to really do it?" Claudia asked after listening to my explanation of the situation.

"Well, I want to do it, but the timing isn't great," I said.

"And do you want to go with her?"

"I really like Deb," I replied, "but I'm totally happy pushing it off 'til next year."

"The Camino is serious," Claudia cautioned me. "It is intense. You do not want to be doing it for two weeks with someone you are only so-so doing it with."

"It's not that I don't want to do it with Deb, I like Deb . . . it's that I don't feel the timing is right. I would feel much better not burdening Tim with going right now. But I've been dragging my feet. I've been halfway committed for several months, and I just said yes last week."

"This is easy," Claudia said matter-of-factly. "You tell her no. Why would you do something you don't feel okay doing? You explain the timing is not good and you can't go."

Claudia was very decisive, and the world was black and white for her. We were very much kindred spirits in this way. But for this discussion I wished my EQ twin, Tomás, were there to weigh in. He would have understood the sticky awkwardness of backing out of my promise to travel with Deb, would have thought through it out loud, and, though he would have arrived at the same conclusion as Claudia and I did, probably would have come up with a softer landing than "you just tell her you can't." But Claudia fit the mold of some of my best friends back home—bold, strong-minded, resolute—and that resonated with me.

As I walked home with the kids after pickup from school that day, looking down at all our scuffed and dirty sneakers moving across the tiled cement sidewalks, I laughed again at how different Claudia and I appeared, at least when it came to wardrobes. But my necessary footwear for hoofing it up and down the mountain with my family, and the clothes that went with that footwear, didn't bother Claudia. And more importantly, today I felt more confident that she wasn't going to let my poor Spanish slow down our friendship (though I wasn't under any illusion that I wouldn't continue hearing from her that I needed to improve my Spanish).

I couldn't help but share her disappointment in me when it came to my language skills; I felt like I was cheating, speaking in English with her. I knew my Spanish would improve far more rapidly if I kept trying with her. But I was making a trade-off: my Spanish progressing at a slower pace for the sake of a great friendship.

That was a trade-off I was willing to make.

Chapter 21

BIRTHDAY PARTY, MEDITATION REQUIRED

*I*n the years leading up to Spain, my fuse was often short with the kids. Maybe I was irritable from the stress of work or the stress of raising three young kids; or perhaps it came from feeling torn between my obligations to my job and my family and having the sense that I wasn't doing a good job at either. Whatever the cause, my patience was lacking. And I was blessed with having good insight into my behavior—not only did I wallow in guilt after every time I blew up at the kids, I actually was aware beforehand when the epinephrine-fueled explosion was about to occur. But rather than step away from the rising anger, I allowed the blow-up to occur each time, leading me to wallow in the guilt yet again.

After enough of these exhausting (to me) and possibly scarring (to my kids) outbursts, I turned to meditation, with the simple goal of trying to even out, not blow up so often, and hopefully become a better mom in the process. Over the years, I felt minor shifts in the way I moved about life—almost more in the absence than in the presence of something. The way I would have responded before but didn't this time; my ability to detach myself from an emotion, to almost be impartial. Perhaps there were more serotonin-infused moments of calmness in my life and fewer epinephrine-fueled blow-ups after I started practicing meditation. But that didn't mean I was fully *tranquila*.

On the first Sunday of March, Mae and I headed out to her friend's sixth birthday party. Martí was one of the kids whose company Mae had really enjoyed since our very first months in Spain; she was excited for the party.

The email said to drop off your child for lunch and tea, from 12:00 to 5:00 p.m. Surprisingly, an end time. Back home, the invitation would be from 12:00 to 1:30 p.m., maybe 2:00 p.m., no drop-off. (*What secret sauce are you drinking, Spanish parents?* I wondered. *It's not your yummy* gintonics, *because I've had plenty of those, and I still wouldn't host a five-hour birthday party for my child.*)

While Tim took the boys to Kieran's *fútbol* match, Mae and I rode the metro over to San Cugat. Fucking San Cugat. Because it was a Sunday, most lines weren't running. Which meant we couldn't go to our nearest metro stop, we had to walk to the larger one ten minutes away. Six minutes too long with a five-year-old and a birthday present in tow. Then we had to switch trains in Sarrià.

After about twenty minutes on the second train, we got off at the last stop in San Cugat. The day was bleak and cold. We were in a residential area: lots of apartment buildings, not much action, definitely no taxis. Once again, we had to walk. Mae was a willing participant because she was going to her buddy Martí's party. I was guessing she would be less enthusiastic on the reverse commute.

As we walked there, holding hands, I recognized my mood reflected in that gray day: I was irritated over the long trip to the party. I recognized my mood, but instead of staying separated from that emotion, as meditation had taught me, I just swapped it with another one—anger. At myself. Why was I wasting this time with Mae being frustrated rather than enjoying being with her? She was in a good mood, we had nothing else going on, nothing that needed to be done but walk to the party, holding hands. What was my problem? And then I chastised myself for being so angry. And then I laughed at myself for the absurdity of this mental conversation, and how well I was doing with my meditation practice.

Once we found the house, we were welcomed by Martí's parents—Brazilian mom, Spanish dad. Fernanda bent over on a knee, welcomed Mae with a kiss on each cheek, and told her in a kind voice that she could find all her friends upstairs. I took Mae's jacket and she went up the stairs—not in a rush but not unsure of herself either. Fernanda invited me back to the kitchen, where some other parents were gathered. I knew none of them well but was acquainted with several from the halls of school.

I used to be good at small talk. Tim said it was still a forte of mine. But I found it exhausting now. And that was what this birthday party circuit was for a new family in a new country. At our school, every kid invited their whole class to their birthday party, so every child always got many invitations. Which translated into many opportunities for standing around with a bunch of adults you didn't know, making small talk. A chore in my eyes—but the Spanish, I now understood, experienced it as a pleasurable part of life. You met new people. You got to know one another over a glass of rioja. At noon.

The smell of barbecue wafted into the kitchen from outside. Fernanda told me her husband was cooking steaks. She asked if I would stay for lunch.

My American social etiquette went into overdrive. You don't accept a last-minute invitation to a lunch you weren't invited to in the first place. They were just being nice.

Except they *were* nice, they weren't just *being* nice. The invitation was sincere. This was a celebration, a time to be with friends and family, and "friends" could include new friends. This random assortment of parents was all staying for lunch. That was what you did here. But this calm, serotonin-induced insight was negated by the burst of epinephrine brought on by Fernanda's invitation. *I can't stay for lunch! I can't stay for the whole party! That's five hours!*

I declined a second time, a third time.

My internal arm-flapping fit was interrupted when one of the Spanish dads, Gerard, engaged me in conversation. Shortly into our small talk, he ascertained how Mae and I had gotten to the party. He attempted to hide his shock. *You took the train? And then walked?*

I suppose it would be like hearing that a family took a bus and then a taxi to get to a birthday party back in California when the rest of us had just driven the fifteen minutes in our cars. Of course you would insist on making the next commute totally painless for that family. And that's what Gerard did. He insisted on driving me home. He left his Russian wife at the party and drove me the twenty minutes back to my flat. And he insisted on driving Mae home afterward too. He was going back to the party, of course.

Since Tim had recently mastered Zipcar rentals, I told Gerard my husband was running other errands and was tacking on Mae-pickup to that list, but thank you.

At 4:20 p.m., Tim set off to get the Zipcar from the parking space in the public garage where a car was waiting for him. The boys were in their bedroom, playing on screens, and I was left sitting at our IKEA dining room table, looking out the windows at the gray sky reflected in the pond six stories below me, epinephrine safely washed out of my system.

What was my *problem*? What *was* my problem? A group of kind, fun people sitting around having steak and wine? Oh no, don't invite me to stay for *that*. I hadn't learned from my epiphany at Javier and Sonia's that my best life was a fully present one, one where I just sit and enjoy. *Tranquila.* All these years of meditating and I was still the trapped bird, ramming into windows.

Tim didn't respond to my texts when I asked if he had gotten Mae, and he and Mac walked in the door about an hour later than I expected them.

"Where have you guys been?" I asked as they came in.

"Well, you know how it is at these parties," Tim said, unwrapping his scarf and taking off his coat. "You can't just get in and get out. Gerard's wife is a pusher. She's hilarious." He shook his head with a smile. "She made me have a beer. And they were all sitting around the table, so I had to sit down. It was actually nice. There were like ten adults there, the kids played. We sat around talking. Marti's parents are really nice."

Tim didn't even meditate.

Chapter 22

SHOWER CAP MASSAGE

*S*ome people like facials, some like pedicures, I like massages. We had been living in Spain for several months, and the gym we belonged to offered massage services. I was at a point where I felt comfortable enough with my Spanish that I could bungle my way through a massage. You didn't talk during most of a massage, how bad could it go?

I showed up for my appointment, and the good news was that the women at the front desk seemed to agree I was supposed to be there. A young woman—in all black and perfectly made up, like all women who worked there or worked out there—showed me to a small room. She introduced me to another woman in black, who I gathered would be doing my massage. This second woman ushered me into a dimly lit room with a massage table in the middle, a cabinet off to one side, frosted glass walls on two sides, a few plastic chairs lined up against one of them, and a table with some oils on it. Not really the same overall experience as a massage in the US, where you might be offered the use of a sauna, a steam room, or showers, and could expect to wait with your feet soaking in hibiscus-infused cucumber water while gentle music relaxed your frayed nerves. No, here you showed up and were directed straight to your massage table, albeit by gorgeous women.

After the masseuse left the room, I took off my jacket and set it on one of the chairs. As I did so, I looked at the table. A fitted white sheet lay on it, nothing else. As I went to take off my pants, I thought, *What is going over the top of me?*

I looked around the room. Not a sheet in sight. *How about a towel? A robe?*

Nope.

I'm supposed to take off my clothes and lie naked on the table, nothing to cover me? Does the masseuse really want to walk in and see my bare ass? Or am I supposed to keep my bra and underwear on? Hard to believe that would be the case in a country where most women go topless on the beach.

And so I opted not to undress; I would wait and clarify when the masseuse arrived.

As I waited, however, my old friend appeared—that panicky feeling that overcame me when I needed to explain something but didn't have the ability to do it in Spanish.

What I wanted to say: "I'm sorry, I didn't see any towels or a sheet. Do you want me to undress and lie down? Everything off? Or is there supposed to be something to cover up with?"

What I did say, in Spanish, when the masseuse came back in the room: "*Lo siento. No veo unas toallas o sábanas. ¿Me quieres removar la ropa?*"—I'm sorry. I don't see some towels or sheets. Do you want me to word-doesn't-exist-in-Spanish my clothes?

Masseuse: "*Sí, claro, desvístete.*"—Yes, of course, undress.

She glossed right over my "there are no towels or sheets."

"*Y ponte esto.*"—And put this on.

She handed me a small plastic bag with what looked like a paper shower cap inside. I took it and smiled as she walked out of the room, as if having to lie totally exposed on a table while wearing a shower cap wasn't something totally new or extremely strange to me. The door closed, and I opened the bag to find not a shower cap but a paper G-string. Oh, so making me lie naked without a covering on a table was normal, but God forbid I'm not wearing underwear while I do it?

I rapidly undressed, put on my new underwear, and hopped on the table as quickly as I could. I was embarrassed enough that my ass was hanging in the breeze; I didn't want to have to walk to the table while the masseuse was in the room. She didn't have to see my front *and* my back.

Soon after, the door opened. "*¿Lista?*"—Ready?

"*Sí,*" I mumbled to the headrest, and then I felt a sheet being placed over me.

What? Where did that come from? Why not leave the sheet out for me to get under while you were out of the room? Why make me lie here naked and then *cover me up?*

The massage was good not great, but it landed squarely in the tally column of "Things I Cannot Learn in Spanish Class." These were the experiential lessons that were making my time in Spain unique, oddly fulfilling, and left me craving more. Though they were sometimes difficult and sometimes involved a paper G-string, I couldn't have these experiences unless I showed up, took a risk, exposed myself.

And so, after my massage, I walked out through the gym doors and into the sunny park confident in the knowledge that in order to fully live this life, I needed to put myself out there. Bare ass and all.

Chapter 23

JA JA HA HA

When it came to clothes, my life in Spain was very much like my life in California: a perpetual risk-benefit analysis. I never shopped, because I hated shopping, and because I hated shopping, I never had enough clothes, or any clothes that I felt were up to date. And so I would need to shop but wouldn't go, because I hated shopping.

What this inevitably led to was a shopping trip that was forced upon me every five years. Tim would be so sick of this endless "I have no clothes, but I won't go shopping" whine-fest that he would arrange—*he would arrange*—a shopping outing for me with one of my best friends, Jen, who was more of what someone might call a normal woman, and she had excellent taste.

The endless loop persisted in Spain—I needed clothes, but I wouldn't go shopping. And my predicament was *worse* in Spain because we had only brought one duffel bag of clothing each for the entire year, all four seasons. Some women can't even pack for a week-long vacation in one duffel bag.

Since Claudia was an impeccable dresser, when she suggested we go shopping at some of the boutiques around Galvany, I took her up on her offer. As much as I hated shopping, I would do this and get some QT with my good friend.

After success at one particular boutique, where seemingly every label simply read "MADE IN ITALY," Claudia and I decided to grab "*un café*" and ducked into a bar on the corner. Drinking *café* was something I had had to adopt in the past few months, as almost any daytime socializing is done over *unos cafés*. My struggling Spanish plus me not drinking *café* equaled an awkward social situation.

Bars aren't quite the same in Spain as they are in the US; Spanish bars also serve as the place people eat breakfast and take their morning *cafés*. This one was tiny, with two tables in the corner of the windows and seating for four at the bar.

After we had drunk our *cortados*, I asked Claudia about one of the many nuances of the language that were constantly out of my reach.

"So, when I read '*ja ja ja*' it's the equivalent of 'ha ha ha,' right? My head keeps wanting to actually pronounce the 'j.'"

Claudia peered at me with a look that said, "I may have overestimated you."

"Never mind that one," I said quickly. "So *la cuenta* means bill, but am I right that you don't use *la cuenta* when you want the bill for coffee?"

"Well you could," Claudia responded. "But for something like *café*, you might say '*¿Qué te debo?*'"

This, I knew, meant "What do I owe you?" Claudia, like all Spanish, used the informal form of the word "you," not the polite/formal form you would think you would use when you don't know someone, like the gentleman who'd served us our *cafés*. I also knew that Claudia's family called her "the German" because she was so direct and no-nonsense. What I didn't know was if "*¿Qué te debo?*" was the German speaking or if it was how any Spanish person would ask for the bill.

Not recognizing when to quit, I pressed on with Claudia.

"Sooo . . . Tim was told by someone at work that when you order a beer, you say, *'Ponme una cerveza.'*"—Give me a beer.

"Noooo!" Claudia exclaimed with a reproving look. "You wouldn't be that rude! You would say a *'por favor'* in there at the very least."

Qué te debo isn't too blunt but *ponme una cerveza* is? Where was the line between informal and ending up with a spit mixer in your beer?

"Try it—you ask for the check," Claudia said, pulling me out of my uneasy confusion. She nodded toward the gentleman behind the counter, a few steps away from us.

His back was turned to us. I waited, hoping my confidence would build so that I could pull off this apparently not discourteous way of asking for the check.

Claudia gestured in his direction, urging me on.

I summoned my inner Claudia. *"¿Disculpe? ¿Qué te debo?"*

No response. I glanced at Claudia and caught the tail end of a slightly pained Germanic expression that had just passed over her face.

"Not good, huh?" I asked.

"You were so polite!" she said, laughing. *"'¿Qué te debo?'"* she said in a singsong way, imitating my voice rising at the end. She turned to the barkeep. *"Qué te debo."*

A command, not a question.

"Dos setenta ocho," he responded immediately.

Claudia might have been a smarty-pants partner at a private equity firm, but I would venture to say that as the person who'd made the executive decision not to engage in Spanish with her, I was the smarter of the two of us. Our friendship was not just surviving but thriving, and I attributed that partly to the fact that we didn't ever have to converse in Spanish.

From there on out, whenever Claudia said, "You really need to be speaking in Spanish to me," I replied, *"Ja ja ja."*

In my head, of course. Not out loud.

Chapter 24

PLEASE PASS THE ANCHOVIES

*S*ometime in December, I had gotten a WhatsApp from a good friend back in California, Ed. He'd started out as my mentor in my emergency medicine residency at Stanford, and then he'd become good friends with me and Tim. Tim and Ed were similar in how genuine and easygoing they were, though Ed may have had Tim slightly beat in the laid-back department. Ed had gotten married and started a family later in life, and we loved both his wife and his little girl.

The WhatsApp only said, *Don't leave the country in May. We are coming to Basque Country*. Ed had extended family in País Vasco, or Basque Country, in northern Spain, and we'd heard wonderful stories of the trips he had taken to see them over the years.

We didn't need any convincing to join them. The trip came at a good time: Life had been hectic with the end of the school year approaching, planning logistics for our flight to the US and back to Spain again, and always trying to stay on top of daily life. A trip with friends would be a much enjoyed getaway.

A note of small importance: If you want to go somewhere warm and sunny, never invite the Breens to join. Tim's grandmother used to say we were bad luck. Whenever we visited her in

Hawaii, rain. That year: Paris, rain; Munich, rain; Bruges, rain; Canary Islands, rain; Italian Riviera, rain.

País Vasco? Rain.

We met up with Ed, Julia, and Danele, their adorable spitfire of a three-year old daughter, at a big drafty house we had rented on the French side of Basque Country, in Saint-Jean-de-Luz. The Breens were now veterans at dealing with Airbnbs, but Julia may have been just a bit displeased to find ants in the kitchen and worn-out linens stacked on the beds for us to make on our own.

The large old house had a pool out back that we adults thought was too cold to swim in, though the kids proved us wrong. Another lesson I had collected along the way: Europe is not California. In almost all our travels this past year, it had been too cold to enjoy sea or pool. Summer was when that would happen. As our Spanish friend Oriol had said when I complained in May that it was still chilly: "June. That is when summer will come. In Spain we are sometimes late, but we are never early."

The rambling house was home base for exploring Saint-Jean-de-Luz over the next couple of days. In cloudy, chilly weather, we played on the beaches of Saint-Jean-de-Luz and Biarritz, a seaside town that was a glamorous resort for the French back in the early 1900s. We took a train from the tiny town of Sare up into the foggy Pyrénées, where an enduring love affair with Basque cake was begun; we ate some of the best cake I've had in my life.

We then said goodbye to Saint-Jean-de-Luz and drove to San Sebastián, a gorgeous beach town on the Bay of Biscay. It is also home to three of Spain's three-Michelin-star restaurants, but our rag-tag group stuck to the *pintxos*, the food for which San Sebastián is famous.

Pintxos are essentially any type of food that is served on a toothpick. At many restaurants, multiple types of *pintxos* were laid out on a counter facing the street; you ate what you wanted while standing on the street at the counter, and you were charged based on the number of toothpicks on your plate.

After enjoying the day in San Sebastián we drove west along the coast to Mutriku, a small Spanish fishing port where Ed's family had lived for generations. Ed's extended family all lived within walking distance of each other, in meadows high above the Atlantic. We stayed at Ed's cousin Nerea's house, while Ed and his family stayed at another cousin's house just down the road.

Nerea and her husband, Mikel, were gracious and welcoming when Ed introduced us, and showed us right to our small flat, downstairs from their house. We had arrived late, around 9:00 p.m., but Nerea told us they wanted us to join them for dinner. Not late for them.

Since Mikel ran a several-generations-old family anchovy business, and since we were there in one of the two months of the year when anchovies were fished, we had fresh anchovies—a very special treat, for some. As previously mentioned, I am not a seafood or fish eater. I sometimes make myself try certain types of mild fish (because it's good for me, not because I'm trying to not be so obstinate), but anchovies would never make the cut. And unfortunately, a mother's taste in food is passed to her children: If she doesn't eat fish, it's unlikely she'll make it for her kids.

What was served that night was breaded anchovies, with their little tails sticking out of the breading, and a salad with tuna on it, typical for Spain. There was also Spanish tortilla—like a potato omelette—and bread and red wine.

Tim was in heaven; I was sweating. Because I was not going to offend Mikel—whose blood had anchovies swimming through it, and who had painstakingly filleted each individual anchovy, breaded it, and cooked it—and because I wanted to show my appreciation for him welcoming us so warmly, I would eat one. So I cut that little breaded anchovy into as many pieces as I could, put a bite in my mouth, tried not to breathe, stuffed some bread in with it, and then took a big gulp of red wine. Repeat. All while trying not to look like a child attempting to fake out her parents. I drained a whole glass of wine in my efforts to put down one little anchovy.

The kids knew they were being served fish that night and had already said they weren't going to have any, despite our protestations. When the moment came and Nerea asked them if they wanted any, the answer being so obvious to me, Mae and Patrick somehow felt my eyes burning into them and answered yes. Kieran must have had some superhero forcefield around him, because he didn't feel my eyes penetrating his skull and answered no.

Much to my surprise, Mae took a bite of the anchovy. She didn't like it, but she tried it. Kieran ate the salad with tuna. And he knew the tuna was tuna. Patrick just ate bread.

At some point during the dinner, Mae came over to my seat and whispered in my ear, "I don't want to eat any more. I tried the chicken part around the fish, but I didn't like it." She thought the fish was wrapped in a chicken nugget. But kudos to her and Kieran. And me too. I had to admit feeling proud of myself, even though my wine-to-anchovy ratio had been three to one. And even though what I accomplished was something we asked of our young children every day: *Just try it.*

After dinner, I took the kids down to bed while Ed, who had come to visit, and Tim stayed and devoured all the anchovies, happier than kids with plates full of real chicken nuggets.

The next day, while another family member of Ed's took Julia and me on an excursion—a visit to a tiny town with a tiny chocolate shop from the 1800s—Mikel and Nerea spent the morning preparing the midday meal and for the arrival of Nerea's three siblings and their families.

When Julia and I returned with our handmade chocolates, many of the families were already there, setting up folding tables in the garage due to the iffy weather. The lamb, whose body Tim had helped Mikel carry in from the trunk of his car that morning, was cooking in the outdoor oven, and paella simmered in large pans in the garage. Homemade paella. A true treat to almost anyone but me. Since I didn't eat shellfish *or* pork, I only liked paella if it was vegetarian. Which meant it wasn't true paella.

As we stood in the unfinished garage around the paella pans, newspapers strewn under the simmering meal, I took in the experience from afar. Here was an extended family preparing a lunch that would last four hours. Our kids were playing tag and doing art and holding kittens with Ed's cousins' kids, making friends only the way kids can do. We were drinking local *txakoli*, the wine of País Vasco, while looking out across a grassy expanse to the Atlantic Ocean and its whitecaps far below, while paella cooked in the garage. Tim and I were trying to talk in Spanish while people laughed at our attempts, all the while helping us with our Spanish. Three generations of family, sitting around enjoying each other's stories at folding tables set up in the garage, as unpretentious as one could get, with a dog roaming around, kids running in and out. Never once did anyone, of any generation, check their phone—not even the teenagers. No one was even taking *pictures* with their phone (I was the only one doing that). Life was slowed down and about family. Everyone seemed content and present.

As the paella was being made, fresh anchovies were passed around. Mikel graciously handed one to me first. After he went to get more, I turned to Ed and handed it to him. When Mikel returned, he was confused as to how Ed already had one but luckily didn't quite connect the dots.

I couldn't hide my dislike of seafood when it came time to sit down to eat, however, because I was seated, and paella was served to everyone. It's not like I could say, "Thanks, but I'm just going to have the salad," because this course was paella. And there was one big *langostino*, jumbo prawn, sitting on my plate.

Tim, luckily, was to my right, and I stealthily passed the giant shrimp, beady eyes and all, to him. Iker—one of the family members who was seated across from me, a wonderful guy—was not afraid to tell me to just try everything and kept checking in on how I liked each dish. He laughed when he saw that I had passed the *langostino* to Tim. At least I could be totally forthcoming about the *txakoli*.

I learned several new vocabulary words while staying with Ed's family, one of which was *tiquismiquis*. This is what Ed's family began to call me when they gathered I didn't like *atún* (tuna), or *langostino*, or any seafood, or lamb. In the kindest translation, it meant picky. Nerea, having surmised I was *tiquismiquis*, had roasted a chicken for me and the kids in the outdoor oven. I was grateful for her thoughtfulness and embarrassed by my near-juvenile idiosyncrasy.

When the dessert course came, I forgot about that embarrassment. There was cake, chocolate, and two types of locally made ice cream, all exquisite. Something was said and a few people laughed; I asked for a translation.

"They said that apparently you're not *tiquismiquis* when it comes to dessert," Ed explained, chuckling.

After dessert, the kids, including ours, walked down the road to Iker's family's house. Nerea and Mikel suggested that we go for our own walk, so Ed, Tim, and I joined them while Danele and Julia went home for Danele's nap.

After about an hour, we ended up at one of the other cousins' houses, and then beer was brought out, and we found ourselves sitting outside on the side porch in the late-afternoon sun, enjoying a Basque beer and speaking in Spanish. Ed's cousins would laugh when, after they'd talked to me for a few minutes, I'd say, "*No entiendo nada*"—I understand nothing.

I laughed too, though I was only partially kidding. Tim had a much easier time being part of the conversation.

As we sat in the sun, I could sense Ed's pure contentment, his joy in being with his family and friends, in his relaxed and smiling quietness.

I shared that contentment, but I also couldn't help but wonder how the kids were faring. I knew they were in good hands, playing with Iker's family. But we had been gone for a couple of hours. Would one of them want to go home? Were they comfortable enough to ask where the bathroom was?

When we finally walked up to Iker's house, he greeted us with, "The kids aren't ready."

Huh?

"They need ten more minutes," he said.

I needn't have worried. Our kids were happy and apparently involved in a project with all the cousins, who had been raised by each other's families. My kids were in the proverbial village.

We went into Iker's backyard and picked lemons and oranges while we waited. Finally, the kids let us see what they had been doing: an arts and crafts project for the adults, even wrapped in wrapping paper.

The kids were having such a good time they didn't want the day to end, but it somehow had become nine o'clock at night. Time for us to go home to bed.

When we reached Nerea and Mikel's house, they asked if we would like to join them for dinner. Spain! We declined, with many thanks, and went down to our part of the house, where we fed the kids some light snacks and immediately afterward hit the hay.

The next morning, we had a short drive back to San Sebastián to fly home. And—wouldn't you know—it was a beautiful sunny day. The Breens were leaving town!

Even without sun, the trip had been fantastic. Being with Julia and Danele and Ed, and Ed's family in Mutriku, had been a gift. As had being reminded of how important it was to sit back and enjoy. We didn't have to find contentment; we didn't have to create it. Contentment was right there, in the moment. Behind our phones, underneath our busyness. Right next to the anchovies.

Chapter 25

UNDERWHELMING FIREWORKS

*T*he Catalans, and the Spanish in general, seemed to have a love affair with fire and fireworks. National holidays, Barça games, Messi scoring a goal—all called for fireworks, heard loud and clear from our flat. These fireworks weren't the type we were used to—big displays watched from afar, well planned and executed by someone with experience and a license, to the oohs and aahs of people sitting on blankets safely far away, fire trucks at the ready. Some of the fireworks we had witnessed in Spain were more of the "light a stick in your hand and run and throw it" variety. Hopefully not at someone. The kind of fireworks that were a no-go for us Californians, who were used to living with constant mindfulness of wildfires, or for those of us who work in an Emergency Department, who knew fireworks could mean blown-off fingers or worse.

As our summer departure for the States loomed near, we spent as much time with our Spanish friends as we could, especially *la familia* Alemany—Tomás and Claudia and kids. Our second to last night in Barcelona fell on the summer solstice, *Sant Joan*, a big celebration in Cataluña. (This was marked by, yes, fireworks. The holiday is literally called "The Night of Fire.")

We spent the afternoon and evening at Claudia and Tomás's, eating, drinking homemade sangria, watching the kids playing in the pool, and talking about parenting and our families, our go-to discussion—which of us had overreacted to what kid issue, what was the latest request from our parents that had gotten us worked up, what would the kids, as adults, be saying about us to their therapists.

As night fell, pops echoed up from the city below us. The fireworks were beginning. Tomás had gotten sparklers, something that evoked memories for me of many childhood summer nights. The kids ran around on the street next to the house, their shrieks and laughter followed by the sparklers' trails of light in the darkness.

Tomás then pulled out his small arsenal of fireworks. We trusted Tomás, and his parenting was stricter than that of many of the other Spanish parents we knew. I didn't think I would have to hover over the kids to make sure fingers didn't get blown off though I was painfully aware that injuries were still a possibility, regardless of how safe someone tried to be.

After Tomás had shot off a few successful fireworks, we saw some teenagers run over to the giant dumpsters on the corner and throw something in. They were trying to blow up the dumpsters with fireworks! *Not* something reminiscent of my childhood, and sure to blow off more than just fingers if anyone got too close. Tomás tried to yell at the teens while we quickly gathered the kids and went back to the house.

We had to say goodbyes at the end of that evening, but these goodbyes were easy; we would be seeing our friends again in less than two months, when we returned for part two of our adventure.

Sitting in our home in Menlo Park that summer felt surreal. So much to process about the preceding year. So much to think about in the upcoming year. And five short weeks to pack everything in and enjoy Menlo Park.

Those weeks included many trips to favorite eateries and lots of playdates and reconnecting with friends, both for the kids and the adults. We even got Patrick into a camp for two weeks with his best friend. We watched the Fourth of July fireworks extravaganza with good friends, and I laughed to myself as we sat on a blanket safely far away from the source of the professional display—so different from our experiences in Spain, where at any moment we might need to run for safety.

We weren't spending our entire time in the States in Menlo Park; we saved the last part of it for a trip to a dude ranch in Idaho with my parents and sister and her family, followed by a visit to DC and then the Outer Banks in North Carolina for beach time with Tim's family. After a week at home, Tim said he was glad we would be in Menlo Park for such a short time; being home felt strange and temporary. I agreed. We were both looking forward to seeing our families but then getting back to Spain; we felt like outsiders in our hometown. I hadn't expected that.

When we ran into a friend or acquaintance in Menlo Park, the same question always seemed to arise: "Oh my god, how was Barcelona? Did you guys just love it? You haven't missed a thing here!" This seeming need to live vicariously through us, the conjured amazing life we *must* be living—spontaneous weekend trips to Lake Como, swims in the azure seas of Greece, long, carefree lunches and even longer cocktail hours where our kids must just disappear—took me by surprise and made me uncomfortable. While we were extremely fortunate to have spent the past year in Spain, our experiences were decidedly without the glitz and glamour people wanted to attach to them. And if I were honest, the year had also felt like a continuous uphill climb (in fact, it literally was most days). But being honest with myself again, my discomfort mostly came from worrying how it would be received if I admitted how hard I had found this past year to be. Who gets the chance to live abroad and then complains about how difficult the experience has been? An ungrateful person? An entitled one? Someone who is unhappy?

But at least sometimes in those reflective moments I was also able to see the ways I had been enriched during the climb: I had gathered wonderful friends, learned Spanish, overcome adversity, slowed down, grown. I was finally appreciating that living in Barcelona hadn't been an uphill climb, it had been an uphill adventure.

But if I had responded to our friends' questions with this explanation and revelation, I would have been met with blank, even surprised, stares. So I responded simply, "It's been an amazing experience."

Not fireworks, but the truth.

Chapter 26

OBSERVATIONS AT THE
END OF YEAR ONE

*I*t seems to be a fitting time to share some of my observations about Spain, the Spanish, and living in Spain. No offense is intended, and any offense given can squarely be blamed on my being an American, and the clueless, entitled snarkiness that comes from growing up as one and believing that we are the center of the universe.

1) Compared to Americans, the Spanish have figured out how to suffer a lower incidence of lung cancer while smoking more than we do. This should be investigated by the CDC and FDA.

2) Spanish people aren't modest. They don't use towels so much in the locker room. And they apparently don't believe in bathing suits, either, because I have yet to see a tan line on any woman in that locker room.

3) Spanish people aren't afraid of germs. I watched a toddler who was sitting apart from his mom on the bus sneeze, with copious amounts of snot coming out of his nose. The lady behind him, who didn't seem to know the mom or the kid, leaned over with a tissue and wiped his nose. The mom in the seat across the aisle said a very casual "*gracias*," as if this weren't the kindest and bravest stranger in the world, and went back to looking out the window as the other woman put the snotty Kleenex into her purse. That raises "it takes a village" to a whole other level.

4) There is no such thing as coffee "to go" in Spain. You will never see a Spanish person walking with a coffee in a to-go cup, or walking with a coffee, period. Or food, for that matter. Drinking coffee is a social time, a time to relax. Coffee is not an object; it is an experience to be enjoyed.

5) The Spanish know how to do time off. If there's a holiday toward the end of the week, often they will take the extra day in between the holiday and the weekend to make it a four-day weekend. The extended week-end is called *puente*, the bridge. America needs to build more bridges.

6) Pedestrians in a crosswalk may or may not have the right of way. Even though the green man flashing is tell-ing you it's safe to walk across the crosswalk, the car with the angry driver that stops one foot from your leg begs to differ. To drivers in Barcelona, a crosswalk is merely a pretty zebra pattern painted on the street for their appreciation.

7) No one in Spain is in a rush. You will never see someone walking fast, or dashing across the road, or maneuvering to get in front of people as they get off the metro. Never. Either the Spanish are perpetually late or they all leave a lot of time to get somewhere. Either way, they don't seem to be bothered by it.

8) So let me point out that while number 3 might be gross, and number 1 is clearly bad for them, it's obvious that the Spanish have a good way of life. They love their family and especially kids. They enjoy life (5) and seem to live in the moment more than Americans do (4). And they're not stressed about getting from A to B (7). You won't find them ramming into windows—they are relaxed, they are *tranquilo*, savoring life with a coffee in hand (and not in a to-go cup).

Chapter 27

HERE WE GO YEAR TWO!

*Y*ear two, we were told, would be even better, easier, than
year one. Year two, you were no longer rookies. You weren't
surprised when a shop was closed in the middle of the day, for no
apparent reason, when shops on either side of it were open. Spain's
maddening inefficiencies and bureaucracy no longer felt personal
or deflating; you had come to expect these things. You knew
enough of the language that you could enjoy more independence
and accomplish more in your day-to-day life because you could
communicate better with bus drivers, *porteros*, butchers, and
coaches—at least theoretically.

We had chosen to move out of Turó Parc to a spot closer to
school, and, as it happened, with fewer expats—an area called
Sarrià. Centuries earlier, Sarrià had been its own village, outside
of Barcelona, with its own church and market. But Barcelona
had grown and grown and eventually swallowed up Sarrià, and
now it was an old village within a city, with its narrow streets, old
cathedral, and fiercely Catalan residents.

Our flat was part of a modern-ish (for Sarrià) complex, with
a large grass area (grass!) and a giant swimming pool in the center
of the six brick apartment buildings making up the complex. After

having lived six floors up in Turó, with no access to the outdoors other than leaning out the back window to hang laundry and the kids having to go down six flights and out across a street to get to trees, this flat, and the pool and grass, felt like a godsend. On top of that, our new flat had a *terraza*, a patio, that overlooked the pool and grass and would serve as our warm-weather dining area and an extra room for many months of the year.

When we'd been home over the summer, the fact that I could get up from the couch, walk a few steps out the back doors, and be in a backyard had put me in a constant state of gratitude. We hadn't had access to the outside without considerable effort for a year. We were taken aback by how much we had missed access to the outside when we lived in Turó. A *terraza*, even one two stories up, would be game-changing for us.

We arrived in Barcelona a few days before school started, bringing all the favorite foods we had bought at the Trader Joe's in California along with us. (Setting foot back in Trader Joe's that summer for the first time in a year had been overwhelming. I'd gone to look for natural peanut butter, an elusive product in Spain, and quickly become mesmerized looking at shelf upon shelf, the sheer profusion, of peanut butter jars. And then it had dawned on me: *all* the jars were natural peanut butter. In Spain there was one jar of peanut butter to choose from, and that one brand was loaded with sugar. No choice, no problem. I didn't outright cry from happiness at my overwhelming abundance of choice as I stood in front of ten shelves' worth of natural peanut butter that day in Trader Joe's, but I would be lying if I said my eyes didn't mist over a little.)

When we returned to Barcelona, Patrick was happy about seeing his friends back at LIS and transitioned to the new flat like a knife through creamy peanut butter. Kieran, however, was holding a grudge: He was still mad that we had come back for another year, despite the fact that he had three good buddies at LIS. And Mae? She had no qualms about letting us know how unhappy she was about returning to Spain.

Mae and her best friend, Elly, had overlapped for only one week in Menlo Park that summer, and Mae had been the happiest girl in the world that week. My heart had ached when they'd had to say goodbye to one another, even knowing how unlikely a friendship between a sixth grader and first grader seemed. So for Mae, the return to Spain was bitter. But which was the lesser of two evils—telling her, "Sorry, Mae, this is our life, we're in Barcelona for another year" or "Mae, Elly is a sixth grader and will be moving on from a friendship with a first grader very soon—you'll need to make new friends"? We opted for the former, which allowed her to blame us and complain constantly that her life would be so much better if she were back in California with Elly.

I took those first few days back in Barcelona before school started to get my bearings in my new part of town. Since food shopping was hyperlocal, I needed to find my new local meat person, my new local produce person, and my new local chicken person. Though they didn't want to come, I took the kids with me. Would they rather sit in the flat and play *Minecraft*? Absolutely. Would shopping have been easier for me if they did? Absolutely. But with Tim working, this was going to be my new life: stay-at-home mom.

Would I prefer to be back in the Emergency Department working? No. I had pondered that question many times the previous year when I struggled through our new daily routine. But even as I struggled—even though I was frequently irritable, irritated, and frustrated—I never once concluded that I would prefer to be back in the ED working. I didn't miss it.

That didn't mean I was doing a great job as a mother who wasn't working. But I was at least more aware of that and working on it. I was continuing with my meditation; I was trying to appreciate what our daily life was, other than "hard." Spain had forced me to slow down—because I couldn't communicate, because I had to walk everywhere, because of lack of access to efficiencies like I had back in the US—which, I was beginning to understand, was good for me. In slowing down I had the time to not only notice what was around me and what I had but also *appreciate* what was happening in that moment.

So, instead of playing *Minecraft*, the kids went with me on an outing to the Sarrià market. We walked up the main street of Sarrià, Carrer Major de Sarrià, a wide pedestrian street that cars sometimes drove down. I had yet to figure out when a car could come through and when the road was purely for pedestrians. The street was lined with three- and four-story buildings, shops under and residences above. Shoe shops, *farmacias*, the "chino" store, more shoe shops, more *farmacias*, the baker, a meat shop, café, bar, bar, bar, hair salon, bar, *farmacia*.

As we walked, soaking in the sights and sounds of our new part of town, Kieran said, "Mom, you know how year two is supposed to be better?"

"Yeah," I said, pretending I didn't know what was coming next.

"Well, it isn't."

Since this was only our first week back in Spain, I chose to respond by saying, "Oh look, kids! That looks like a good place to get baguettes!" I would ignore Kieran's negativity until it became a larger problem.

Tra-la-la! Isn't year two great?

Maybe the gods were preparing me for how hard my role as stay-at-home-mom-with-working-spouse-in-a-foreign-country was going to be—building my endurance. Because that same day, when I needed to cajole the kids out of the pool so I could prepare dinner upstairs, it was Mae's turn. She was not an independent swimmer yet, and as she clung to the pool wall at my feet, she looked me in the eye and said, "I'm going down to the deep end to drown, and then I'm going back to California."

Then she made her way down the edge of the pool, hand over hand, away from me.

Chapter 28

A SPANISH MOMENT

fter we landed in Barcelona, it took us only two days to visit *la familia* Alemany again. By the first week of school, we already had gotten the families together twice.

The Saturday before school started, my friend Alba invited her son's good friends—Kieran, Guillem and Jaime—and their families to lunch on the beach. They lived a few towns north of Barcelona, in Premià de Mar. Patrick already had a birthday party to go to that day, but the party was at a waterpark north of town, so the plans fit perfectly.

Kieran woke up Saturday morning and, not knowing about the plans for that day, said, a bit spitefully, "What are we going to do today?" As in, *I already know I'm in for a boring day, so just tell me that we're going to the* amazing *market so we can stare at all the* amazing, *dumb vegetables and dead fish for hours.* I chose to overlook his attitude, channeled all the compassion I could muster, and explained the plans—which, of course, changed his attitude immediately.

Claudia and Tomás were lending us one of their cars, so we cabbed it up to their place and hopped in their Volvo SUV—a tight fit by American standards for a family of five, but luxuriously spacious by European standards. And really, after a year of no car of our own and using rental cars that could have doubled as clown cars, the Volvo did feel luxurious.

We followed *los* Alemany out of Barcelona and dropped Patrick off at the waterpark—he didn't even say goodbye as he ran off with his buddies—then we drove a bit farther north to Premià. Alba and Manuel lived a few blocks back from the beach. Premià was still urban enough that the homes were all connected townhouses on city blocks.

Once Guillem's family arrived, we all walked a few blocks to a restaurant on the beach. It was slightly more substantial than the typical *chiringuitos* that were a mainstay in Spain. A *chiringuito* seemed to be almost a temporary structure—a small bar plopped right on the beach, set back from the water, usually with a cement patio filled with plastic tables and chairs. Every beach had a *chiringuito* for your midday *cerveza* and crisps or *café*. This restaurant we went to had a lengthier menu than most *chiringuitos*. But we still ended up with typical lunch fare, starting with crisps and *las aceitunas*, olives, which the kids—not mine—devoured (*Who knew kids liked olives?*). Then came lunch, consisting of *croquetas* (fried balls of ham, fish, or chicken), *calamares* and *chipirones rebozados* (squid two ways), *jamón serrano y jamón ibérico* (thin slices of cured ham), *pan con tomate* (tomato rubbed on toasted baguette), *patatas bravas* (fried potatoes with a red sauce), *ensaladilla rusa* (cold salad with mayonnaise, peas, tuna, potatoes, and eggs), and more *aceitunas*. I also ordered what I would call a "normal" salad, one with lettuce. I only had one choice: iceberg with olives and carrots on top. And I didn't like olives.

Manuel explained to me the reasoning behind the seemingly small beers that people always ordered. Why, I had wondered, since they were consumed in great quantities in Spain, were *cervezas* not served in steins or big pints like in Germany and England?

"There are *cañas*," Manuel said, pointing to one of the small glasses with beer, "and *jarras*. *Jarras* give you more beer, but they get warm fast. So just order a few *cañas*."

I got it. Beer gets warm fast here in the summer. Drink your cold beer in a small glass, then order another small cold beer. Don't be a dumb American and order a *jarra* only to get halfway through before you're drinking warm, gross beer in the Spanish sun.

After a few rounds of *cañas*, we walked along the beach back to a spot in front of Alba and Manuel's block, and everyone took a swim. The September Mediterranean was like bathwater. I had forgotten how salty the sea there was, and how well you could float in it.

After our swim, the women dried off and sat on the beach, catching up about our summers and what lay ahead for school and the kids, and the men stood on the edge of the ocean, discussing men things. The kids played in the water or on the beach, and I realized I was becoming *muy española* because I wasn't really even keeping an eye on them; I assumed the men were doing it. Even though I had been told not too long ago that Spanish dads were the worst at watching kids around water. Last year I hadn't even let Patrick go to that pool party for that reason, and now here I was, dropping Patrick off at a waterpark and barely paying attention to what my other two were doing in the ocean while I talked with my *amigas*.

Tim and I were learning that a recipe for family happiness in Spain was to not always do things as a nuclear family, which was our instinct. Instead, it often made more sense to incorporate going to the beach (or festival, or lunch) with other families, to avoid time constraints for whatever activity was planned, to be *tranquilo*, and to give the kids free rein to be kids, preferably with other kids. I knew Patrick was in his element—freedom with his friends at a waterpark. And I had proof of concept right in front of me, with Kieran and Mae running around with their friends, laughter and screams and other fun kid noises trailing after them. If they weren't beginning to enjoy year two yet, today they were doing an incredible job faking their happiness.

Eventually the parents made their way up to the *chiringuito* at Alba's beach while the kids kept swimming and running around. We ordered *cafés*, not *cervezas*, this time. Drinking coffee at the beach felt odd. But why not. We sat around talking easily for another couple of hours, only pausing to buy ice cream en masse when the kids swarmed us asking for treats (an idea planted by one and adopted by all).

I felt caught between two worlds at that *chiringuito*. My only obligation was to make sure we picked up Patrick at a certain time. Other than that, nothing to do but enjoy. Yet only a few weeks earlier I had been immersed in my American life of buzzing here then there, perpetually strapped for time. I hadn't fully shed that go-go lifestyle. But sitting there with the warm breeze and ocean mist, soaking in the smiling faces of my friends and the shrieks of laughter from the kids, I could feel that part of me cleaving away. What felt right was breathing, enjoying, laughing, *being* with my friends. Contentment was infectious. This was how my friends and the Spanish in general lived their lives; you worked hard, but family was of the utmost importance, and weekends were for family and friends.

"You have to pick up Patrick, no?" Claudia asked me.

Ironic that the German would remind the American, who was enjoying her Spanish moment, that she had something she needed to do.

Chapter 29

INTERNATIONAL RELATIONS

*M*y second year, I wanted to take my Spanish to another level. I had been motivated the previous year and put forth the effort, but the means to the end were wrong. The first few months, with zero Spanish background, I'd enrolled in a language school that offered courses right at the kids' school. Easy-peasy. All the expats took classes there. I had learned some Spanish, but I was disappointed by my slow progress. I had taken four years each of Latin and French in high school. I knew the old-school way of learning a language, and for me, that worked. Teach me the basics of grammar, teach me the verbs and the conjugation and the vocabulary, let me plow ahead. But the Spanish class at the kids' school had been experiential—you "discovered" grammar as you deciphered pictures and practiced conversations. I could see how this might work over the long run, but for someone who wanted to learn as much as I could in the next three to six months, I needed the mechanics of the language.

I had stuck out that first class until the second semester, and then I'd switched to having a friend give me some lessons over *cortados*, with a lot of supplemental independent study. But I'd gone home this past summer feeling I was way behind where I wanted to be. Everyone back home had assumed I would be fluent after one year of living in Barcelona, a city whose official language wasn't even Spanish. Even though I wanted to say, "Cut me some slack, they speak Catalan!" I could just as easily have said, "I can't even hold a conversation with my best friend's kindergartner."

Now that we'd returned, though, I planned to hit the ground running. By October I was enrolled in an intensive Spanish course at Kings College: three hours a day, five days a week, for as long as I could take the intensity and commitment. All Spanish, no English. Drinking from the firehose. After taking an online test and speaking to the director, Kings determined my level and assigned me to a class.

My first day of school, I was put in a small classroom on the second floor with four other women and a female teacher. The classroom was tiny and grungy, with one wall of windows looking out to an oddly sunny alley. The room was only big enough to hold a few tables set into a square, so we all sat around the square facing each other.

My teacher was warm and all smiles—which was a ruse, because she set upon torturing me by trying to get me to talk. Immediately. She began class by asking me a few questions with a big smile. I stumbled through my answers, sure that my fellow four students were cringing for me. I knew I'd been assigned to the wrong level—a concern that was confirmed when Miss Smiley moved on to someone else, and they didn't stammer or turn red or bluster as they gave their answer.

At the first break, the tall and willowy young woman with heavy-lidded eyes whom I had pegged for American because of the way she carried herself—there's a certain confidence or boldness Americans have, even in situations where they shouldn't—told me not to worry, everyone felt they were in the wrong class the first day. The class got easier, she said. She *was* American (*I knew it!*).

Her way of looking at you from under those heavy eyelids made you feel like everything was going to be okay, and that she was possibly stoned. I aspired to be this twenty-something-year-old one day, albeit a sober version, because she was so at ease speaking in a second language—no embarrassment or hesitation about making mistakes.

That was the last time I spoke English at Kings. Not that I had a choice.

Within a week, I was making myself overcome my own inhibitions, learning to speak without as much fear, convincing myself that no one was judging me. I saw that, more or less, we were all at the same level. Some people were more fluent; some people were better with grammar but not spontaneous conversation. People came and went from the class as the weeks went on, but a core group of us long-haulers remained—the possibly stoned American, Chelsea, who was an au pair to a Spanish family for the year; the young Korean woman, Jia, whose Korean-accented Spanish I had trouble understanding; the young German guy, Tobias, who was taking engineering courses at the university for the year (in Spanish).

And then there were the Russians. Dasha looked like Selena Gomez but spoke in a Russian accent. She was always hungover and flirted with our new teacher, Santiago. Tania had been a doctor in Russia but was now in some kind of management position. As in most of my Spanish conversations, I spoke with my classmates in broad strokes, big picture only. Not because I wanted to but as a result of knowing so few words. So Tania may or may not have been in management. The word "pharmacist" also entered the conversation at some point—so, as I did most times when conversing in Spanish, I made a leap and concluded she was a manager of pharmacists.

Judging Tania's age was difficult. She was younger than me but older than the au pair, the German, and her Russian comrade.

Old enough to manage pharmacists. She was well put-together, wore nice clothes, and always came to class fully made up. Based on how I typically dressed for class, she probably assumed I was recovering from the flu the entire time she knew me.

As an American, I assumed we were the center of the universe. So when I came to find out that I couldn't converse with my friend from St. Petersburg in English because she didn't speak that language, I fleetingly questioned whether she was educated enough to manage pharmacists. But her friend didn't speak English either, nor did the Korean woman. Sure, the German did, but that was because we had occupied his country in the 1940s.

Tania and I began to take our coffee breaks together. The professional woman and her poor, sick friend in sweats would walk to the local café down the block and discuss topics that all new friends discuss over *cortados*, except with 5 percent of the vocabulary that most people can speak with. And mostly all in the present tense. Except when we began learning the *pretérito perfecto*. Then we were able to expand our conversation to include events that had happened in the very recent past. Anything that had happened in the very distant past we weren't able to discuss, because the *pretérito indefinido* was next week's lesson.

Chapter 30

HALLOWEEN HELL

*M*y mom had called me earlier in the week to tell me about an episode of vertigo she'd had. (As resident physician in the family, I'm either consulted before anyone sees a doctor, to find out whether they need to, how worrisome whatever is happening is, and what they should be asking the doctor, or I'm called after, to see if I agree with what the doctor said and plans to do.)

I had never really liked dealing with vertigo in the Emergency Department; the patient never really got a singular, distinctive moment of relief. Usually, after I gave them medications and let them sleep it off, they woke up after several hours, groggy and better, an ungratifying resolution (for me) and perhaps an unsatisfying one (for us both). There are some physical "maneuvers" that can work in resolving vertigo, like the Epley maneuver—twisting the patient's head this way and that, moving their torso here and there—but I'd never found great success with those maneuvers when I was working. Luckily, my mom's episode was over, so I didn't have to explain how to do the Epley over the phone.

"Tell me what your day-to-day is like now that you're in a different part of town," she asked after filling me in about the vertigo.

That wasn't hard. It was almost always the same. Life that fall had become routinized and insular. And I didn't mind one bit. I told her how I walked the kids uphill twenty minutes to school, holding their hands, then turned around and walked partially back down the hill ten or so blocks to the metro station, rode three stops to the Gràcia station, walked about nine blocks to my language school, mangled Spanish for three hours, reverse commuted to the Sarrià station, then walked six blocks home, where I would eat a quick lunch, then meditate for fifteen minutes out on the sun-soaked *terraza*, then change into workout clothes and walk a block to the gym to work out, then come home and quickly shower and dress to go walk the now fifteen-minute walk (since the kids weren't with me) up the hill to school. Then we would all walk home (holding hands!), the kids telling me about their day until we reached our flat, where I would prepare them a snack and then take them to their activities or hang out and start making dinner. And trips to various shops to make a single dinner were also squeezed somewhere into the day, always.

As I told my mom about these routines, a slight sense of frustration and embarrassment crept in. Frustration that I could actually live this habitualized existence anywhere, and I was doing it in a foreign country where there was so much to explore and get to know. And embarrassment that I was wasting this precious gift of living abroad. Couldn't I skip the gym and go get lost in the streets of El Born instead? Go find a cool new shop in Gràcia? But I knew that what I wanted and needed in my life right now was routine, and to circle the wagons around my family, hold them close. That brought me peace and contentment much more than surprise and adventure did. And I was hanging out with Claudia whenever we both could and having get-togethers with my other *amigas*. I wasn't a total hermit.

Though Zoé, a mom of one of Mae's friends at LIS, liked to point out that I was. She had invited us on several outings so far that year, most of which we had declined, not feeling any need or desire to un-circle the wagons. Zoé, an Argentinian, and her husband, Carlos, a Catalan, had become good friends with some expat parents in Mae's grade, and that group went out together quite a bit. We'd managed to become friends with Zoé and Carlos despite our lack of desire to socialize as often as they did.

Zoé, with her long blond hair and blue eyes, perpetually perfect lipstick, tight-fitting jeans, and heels, liked me—but she couldn't hold back her comments on how I didn't care enough to dress femininely and never went out. "Oh, that's right, you're fragile," she would say with a wry smile when I explained why we hadn't joined for some outing. Despite our unglamorous and unsocial reputation, we were invited to their All-Soul's Day party. My inclination was not to go. But then I thought back to the frustration I'd felt about my regimented life when I talked to my mom—and realized that it would be a fun party for our whole family—and accepted the invitation.

It was a beautiful fall afternoon when we arrived at Zoé and Carlos's for the party. The boys, Tim, and I were dressed in red and wearing devil horns, and Mae was dressed as an angel—we were the "Family from Hell." Zoé and Carlos lived in a penthouse flat, and the party was out on a rooftop deck that encompassed the entire top of the building. Barcelona's skyline was in full glory in the setting sun. The kids scattered once we stepped outside, each knowing someone from school. Mae had almost her entire posse there. Gorgeous Zoé, dressed up as a flower child, greeted us with kisses and made sure we knew where the drinks were.

I settled in on a couch on the deck with Tina, another American who had come to Barcelona around the same time as us the previous year. She and her husband, Scott, were from Denver, they had a daughter Mae's age, and we had gotten to know them fairly well, as Americans with same-aged kids at the same school do. They were very funny people, but you never knew what might come out of their mouths. They were part of the group that hung out with Zoé and Carlos, a crew we had mostly enjoyed from afar—from within our wagon circle—during our time in Spain.

But apparently that's not how our behavior appeared to others. Or at least to Tina. I was enjoying our conversation that evening— she was quick-witted and funny—but then the conversation flipped upside down and she proceeded, with a tipsy slur, to lay out all the reasons she and Scott didn't like us. She did so with a matter-of-factness that didn't fit with the emotional content of what was coming out of her mouth. She called us "social maneuverers," always looking for someone better to talk to. Tim was "a salesman," "always working a room." We snubbed them.

On the one hand, what she was saying was extremely hurtful. But she was so off the mark in describing me and Tim that her criticism didn't penetrate. The conversation felt surreal. Tim was the furthest person from a guy who works a room, and anyone who knew him well would have spit out their drink if they'd heard Tina saying that. I almost choked on my *gintonic* when she said we always wanted to talk to someone better. Did she see the lengths I went to avoid talking to anyone at all at drop-offs?

Some people would have gotten up and left, or thrown their drink in her face. Me? I just sat there in stunned surprise. I watched her mouth move. I looked around. Up felt down, down felt up. What was happening?

Finally, the world steadied enough for me to stand up and leave without soaking her with my *gintonic*. I had lost what little desire I had for being social, even though according to Tina I was probably walking away to find a person higher on the social ladder to talk to.

I found Tim and gave him the one-minute version of what had just happened. We went and found Zoé and Carlos to say our thanks and goodbyes. Zoé gave me a hard time for being unsocial and leaving so early, and if we had actually been the kind of people Tina had described, I would have casually and inconspicuously thrown her under the bus. But we weren't, so I didn't.

The next few days I felt off balance, like I was experiencing an episode of vertigo like my mom had so recently described over the phone. I had chastised myself for living too insular and habitual a life, and so we had ventured out beyond our wagon circle—but when we did, we'd been met with a berating for being social opportunists. I felt like I needed to lie on the couch and do the Epley maneuver on myself, to right my spinning world.

I had gone through something hurtful that was making me question myself and my values. But I knew who I was; Tina didn't. And after this experience, I felt even more confident in the comfort I found concentrating on my family—that never felt wrong. If a routinized existence came with that approach to life as well, so be it. A quiet existence, anchored in a focus on my family, worked for me.

With that determination, my life righted itself over the next few days. Still, the resolution did feel a bit like treating a vertigo case at work—gradual and unsatisfying.

Chapter 31

A BENEVOLENT UNIVERSE

Every day as the kids and I made our way up to school, Tim already off to work, we jig-jogged from Avinguda de Josep Vicenç Foix, behind our flat, to the top of Major de Sarrià, Sarrià's main pedestrian thoroughfare. We passed through the narrow corridor along the side of Sarrià's church, Sant Vicenç de Sarrià, at the top of Major de Sarrià, and then continued up the side roads to the top of the hill to school.

Though the trek was still all uphill, as it had been the year before, the journey didn't feel so "uphill" anymore. Every day we took the same route—Patrick, Mae, and I still in some hand-holding configuration, Kieran next to or in front of us—passing by the Italian café, several *farmacias*, a Tae Kwon Do studio, a flower shop, and several more cafés before the neighborhood became more residential on the last push up the hill.

The Halloween debacle a few weeks earlier had thrown me, but a silver lining was that it had pushed me to do more self-reflection in the quiet moments as I walked the kids to and from school every day. And I was finding that I was more content with my life, less critical of myself, not wondering if I should be having more of an adventure. Being focused on my family had never felt better or more right. It's like the universe had sensed my wobbliness after Halloween, reached out and steadied me, and said, "I got you."

Today, I was looking at the Tae Kwon Do studio as I came out of my thoughts. Seeing the studio reminded me that—speaking of focusing on the family—I needed to get the kids signed up for a winter activity. Back home, I had not been a fan of the various martial arts outfits around town. We had tried a few over the years, and while we liked the principles they espoused, we couldn't help but feel some of the owners had lost sight of those principles in their quest to make money; we seemed to pay for more belt tests than the kids had rightfully earned. I was not chomping at the bit to give this Tae Kwon Do shop a go, but since it was on our path home from school and the kids had expressed interest, I decided to let them give it a try.

And there entered our life one of the best things to happen to our kids while in Spain: Sabon.

"Sabon" was the name the kids' young instructor introduced himself with on the first day of class, and that would be how we would address him for the rest of our time in Spain. I never found out his real name (I knew Sabon wasn't it, but that was as far as I got). Nor did I find out if Sabon was the Catalan term for a Tae Kwon Do instructor (or was it *castellano*, or Korean?). That was not a conversation I foresaw having a satisfactory ending, thanks to my limited *castellano*.

I could picture it easily:

"*¿Sabon es una palabra catalana? ¿O coreana?*"—Is Sabon a Catalan word? Or Korean?

"*Es coreana.*"—It's Korean.

"*Sí, pero ¿es cómo una persona coreana dice la palabra también, o cómo un catalán dice la palabra coreana? ¿Cómo una americana dice Sabon?*"—Yes, but it's how a Korean person would say the word also? Or how a Catalan would say the Korean word? How would an American say Sabon? (And of course I had yet to learn the conditional tense; I was unable to say "how *would* an American say that," so instead I'd say, "how *does* an American say that," further confusing the issue for the person I *would* be asking).

Because this type of questioning was usually met with a blank stare—due to my grammatical mistakes, or perhaps just because the questions themselves were perceived as uninteresting and dumb, I was never sure—I generally quit before I even started.

Whatever the genesis of "Sabon," he was young and handsome, with dark brown hair and warm brown eyes; he emanated quiet confidence and commanded respect but radiated caring and thoughtfulness, along with that special Spanish warmth towards kids. Twice a week, the kids eagerly showed up in their white uniforms and belts to follow his instructions, their enthusiasm for his lessons easily overcoming the language barrier.

Sabon spoke zero English. Kieran's comprehension and speaking were already very good; Patrick's comprehension was great, but he was shy about speaking; and Mae—well, if she was learning Spanish, we couldn't tell. The boys had a leg up on her there; not only did they have *fútbol* in Spanish and Catalan, they also had mainly Spanish friends at school. Mae's school friends were from New Zealand, the UK, and Iceland; she was immersed in English. But she had to know *some* Spanish, because she was learning Tae Kwon Do without any English.

If Sabon had been an instructor in the US, I would have taken the time to show him our gratitude, explain how fortunate we felt that we had found him and he was a part of the kids' lives. But since my Spanish was barely passable, I couldn't and didn't. One of many regrets.

If Sabon embodied respect and confidence that winter and spring, then lightheartedness and joy found its human form in Diego.

One weekend afternoon, as the five of us were walking back to our flat, we left busy Major de Sarrià—storefronts on the street level and flats above, motos zipping past in the street, men standing smoking on the corners, women walking by with their shopping carts in tow—in favor of a quieter side street. At this time of day, all the side-street shops had their metal gates down and few cars or motos were zipping past; much more relaxing.

As we walked, something to my left caught my eye. Tim and I took a step back to peer in through the open "storefront" and saw a large studio with art everywhere. It wasn't a gallery, but art covered the walls, as if on display.

"¡Pasa! ¡Pasa!"—Come in! Come in!—a voice from within called out.

And for the second time that early winter, our life was changed by a teacher. Diego, the owner of the studio, was a handsome young artist from Colombia, warm and engaging, with crazy curly hair, warm brown eyes, a smile from here to the corner, and nice clothes that were a bit rumpled and askew, befitting an artist. Our kids immediately took a liking to him. Diego asked them about their interest in art, and they were not shy in answering.

Everywhere we went in Europe, our kids were fascinated by art. Not art as in museum art, but the ever-present graffiti art we saw in every city, and the artists working in the plazas and streets. Inevitably, those artists held their attention far longer than any historical or architectural lesson we could hope they would absorb. We always ended up buying a small fortune's worth of awful art from street artists. (I'm looking at you, painting of dolphins jumping out of what could be the Amazon River, with jungle behind and a sci-fi moon above, everything in an orange and purple glow, created by a street artist with spray paint and a blow torch on Piazza Navona in Rome.) But I couldn't begrudge the kids their choices. Art is in the eye of the beholder, and buying that art made the kids supremely happy.

Diego was an accomplished artist who believed in giving back by teaching art. By the time we walked out of his studio, we had lined up weekly lessons for all three kids, not knowing that we had just arranged for one of the best experiences our kids would have in Spain.

Diego had two rules: 1) you only spoke Spanish; 2) you never said anything bad about yourself. He said, "I never want to hear, 'My drawing is bad.' I want to hear, 'I'll try harder next time.'" This was even before "growth mindset" was all the buzz. He wanted to know what the kids were learning in their humanities class in school, because he wanted to blend that into their art lesson. The kids gave him blank stares. Tim explained to Diego the kids had no humanities class (and were clueless as to what one would be). So Diego took it upon himself to mix in Spanish culture and fables while they created art. The lessons had the potential to be dry for the kids, but Diego, as it turned out, was a boy trapped in a man's body, so the kids had a ball and were unaware Diego was infusing them with culture and art—in Spanish, no less.

One time when I came to pick them up, I heard their laughing and yelling from half a block away. I found all four of them, Diego included, with notecards stuck to their foreheads, mythical creatures drawn on the cards. They were pointing at each other and yelling, obviously in a fierce competition, Diego's warm and bellowing laugh the loudest of the four. They couldn't care less that I was there.

Another time, I walked in to see a similar setup except everyone was bent over laughing at Mae, who was doing some kind of boogie with her butt sticking out. They were all, including Mae, laughing so hard that once again I was inconsequential. Apparently, Diego's rule that day was that if you spoke English three times, you had to spell your name in the air with your butt. Mae had spoken too much English.

Another day, the kids walked home with three amazing oil paintings of apples. Tim and I were stunned by how good they were. Way better than I would expect my kids to produce; way better than I would expect *any* kid to produce.

"That stuff's easy," Diego said with a shrug. "I can teach anyone how to do that."

The kids' art had taken off and so had their Spanish.

A few months into the kids' lessons, Diego hosted a gallery debut, showcasing his students' work. Little did we know that our three kids were his only students who were children.

Our kids were thrilled to be a part of the night. They were full of excitement as they dressed up to head out for the debut later than they usually went to bed. You couldn't have put a price on the pride they felt seeing their paintings hung on the wall and their names listed on the sign out front of his gallery announcing the showcased artists.

A few weeks later, Diego asked if he could borrow Patrick and Mae to do some work for him while Kieran finished a painting he had been working on. The kids would have killed me if I said no; I brought them to the studio.

Diego sent a video that afternoon of Patrick and Mae, in their dirty smocks, busily and happily painting a dark color in the background of a very large canvas, with a pencil drawing of a girl Diego had already sketched in the middle. Diego wasn't giving them busywork; he was actually having them do work on one of his paintings, a painting that was going in an exhibit. In the video, as the kids painted, Diego yelled out, "*Cool Mae!*" as he sometimes did to her, intentionally trying to spook them—and he succeeded, because they jumped (not ruining his painting in the process, luckily). Mae turned around and gave him the stink eye before resuming her painting, unfazed by his puerile antics. She had seen this behavior before.

That painting was *La Menina*, Diego's reinterpretation of one of the ladies-in-waiting in Diego Velázquez's famed painting *Las Meninas*, which hangs in the Prado in Madrid. After taking a trip to Madrid a month or so later and seeing *Las Meninas* hanging on the wall in the Prado, we bought *La Menina* from Diego. The happiness that painting brought me and Tim, and the happiness that creating that painting brought the kids, was worth every penny we spent on the kids' art lessons and the painting itself. It was worth *more than* every penny, in fact. Diego was priceless.

We felt extremely fortunate having Sabon and Diego in the kids' lives, and for the experiences our kids were having in Spain. That *we* were having in Spain. Focusing on my family absolutely felt like what I was supposed to be doing. And my days no longer felt like wasted opportunities; I was more gracious with myself and more comfortable with however my days went, whether they were comprised of the same old Spanish class–and-gym routine or an early-afternoon glass of wine with my *amigas*. I was appreciating and soaking up whatever the universe was sending me. And the universe had sent us Diego and Sabon.

"I got you."

Chapter 32

MY BAD, BARCELONA

*I*n November of our second year, we finally took a trip the kids had been asking for: London. Mainly because every kid in their school talked about Hamleys, the famous toy store. Our kids were the only kids in school who hadn't been to Hamleys. Apparently. We had good friends from Menlo Park, Michael and Courtney Becker, who had moved to London two years earlier, and the last time we'd spoken they'd said, "Come stay with us!" So of course we did.

From the moment we touched down in Heathrow, we became privy to a secret: Life was easier in London. People spoke *English*. We could order food without conferring for ten minutes beforehand on what to say. We could get in a cab and arrive at a destination without worrying we had communicated the wrong directions. The kids were beside themselves at being somewhere where they were able to speak without thought or effort.

It hit me then how hard the previous year must have been for them. Every single trip we had taken had been to a country that spoke a language other than English, and at the end of each one we'd returned home to a country that *also* spoke a language other than English. The only time they'd gotten to speak English on a trip that whole year, in fact, was our short visit home in the summer. And so life, all of a sudden, was almost simple. Ah, London!

Our home base, Michael and Courtney's house, was a beautiful five-story flat in South Kensington. We had our own floor. And Courtney made the guest quarters nicer than any hotel, with every amenity you could possibly need. I had slight feelings of guilt and shame comparing what Courtney had provided to what I typically did for friends and family who came to visit us. And she and Michael cooked breakfast for us each morning, too—scrambled eggs and spinach and toast and bacon and sausage and fresh fruit, and the world's best pancakes. Courtney said the secret was the coconut oil, but even using that supposed key, I have not been able to replicate her pancakes. My kids are always quick to tell me, "Not like Mrs. Becker's."

We had planned visits to an extravaganza of tourist attractions every day so we could see London while also getting out of the Beckers' hair; they still had work and school and activities and life. We wasted no time in getting started on the list.

Our first stop was the Tower of London to see the crown jewels. The kids knew about the crown jewels only because we had watched *Johnny English*, in which Rowan Atkinson, incapable British spy, let John Malkovich steal the crown jewels right from under his nose. When we got to the Tower, the ticket lady said it was closing in one and a half hours. She said it about seven times. But she didn't know the Breens, who can whip through anything historical in under an hour. Yup, thanks, we know, one and a half hours. Toodle-loo!

After we confirmed that the crown jewels were indeed there and saw a few Beefeaters, we reluctantly made our way to Hamleys. Courtney told me the store was the same as a Toys "R" Us but crammed into four different levels with employees doing a ton of demonstrations. A kid's dream, a parent's nightmare. We tried to persuade the kids that European children were wowed by Hamleys because they didn't have Toys "R" Us. But the kids were relentless, so into Hamleys we went.

Courtney was right. The store was no better than what we had back in the US, and damn those employees, they were professional toy-pushers. The kids left with a big and small toy each, and Tim and I left with happy kids.

The next day, after another amazing breakfast, we went to Buckingham Palace. Another reason London felt like a dream? It was the only city where for sure a family of five could fit into any cab. Love you, London.

After getting our fill of the outside of the palace (*Look, kids! The Arc de Triomphe!*), we cabbed over to Covent Garden. After we had meandered around the shops, the kids laid eyes on people having burgers and milkshakes and wanted some of that action. Turned out the source was a popular American chain we hadn't heard of yet, the Shake Shack. Tim and I bought the kids their burgers and then got salads from Pain Quotidienne, a French chain, for ourselves. A decidedly un-British lunch affair.

Next up was a show in the West End, *Charlie and the Chocolate Factory*. Patrick and Mae tried to lie down on the way there, exhausted from staying up late with their friends and being dragged around London, but we got them to the theater and in their seats in time for the play's start.

Partway through the show Kieran whispered to me, "Mom, I feel like I have to throw up."

I sat there and weighed my options—and as I did, I saw Kieran start to nibble on his Willy Wonka bar. As we say in medicine, "a tincture of time" is sometimes all that's needed. We stayed put, with no ensuing vomiting.

After the show, Patrick and Mae reported they liked it, but Kieran said, "I've read the book three times and saw the movie once. It was okay."

Would Tim and I have picked *Charlie and the Chocolate Factory* as the show we'd see as our West End experience? No. Had we been catering to the kids, trying to make it a good experience for them? Yes. Was I mad? Yes. Should I have laughed instead? Yes. Could I? No.

Being *tranquila* was still a work in progress.

Back with the Beckers after the show, we headed out to a pub for dinner. Close to South Kensington as we were, the restaurant served updated, hip pub food, not just fish-and-chips pub food. The number of dishes on the menu I could eat overwhelmed me. My giddiness was tempered by my realization that I'd been living a very (self-imposed) restricted culinary life in very Catalan Barcelona, land of olives and ham and strange seafood. Eating oh-so-yummy sticky pudding drove that realization home.

And when the Beckers took us to their neighborhood park the next day, Saturday—a park for which only residents had a key, and whose grounds offered a whole city block of just grass and trees—our kids just ran. And ran. And rolled around and ran. And when Michael and Courtney then took us to a "real" park, which was grass and trees and *fútbol* pitches and playgrounds as far as the eye could see, I felt nothing but envy. This wasn't even Hyde Park. I was pretty sure Barcelona didn't even have this much grass within its whole city limit.

I couldn't help but think, with no small amount of disappointment, *Barcelona, what is your excuse?*

After our fill of parks, the Breens went on one last touristy adventure, recommended to us by Tomás and Claudia ("Yes, it is super, super touristy," they had said, "but it's also very, very fun!"): a speedboat ride on the Thames. The ride came right at dusk; the buildings were lit up, and the boat played James Bond music as it made sharp turns. The kids loved every high-speed, water-spraying twist and turn.

Afterward, we rendezvoused with the Beckers at a Lebanese restaurant for dinner. I almost cried when the falafel and hummus were served. Now my disappointment turned to anger. Why was it so easy to have such good and varied food in London and not Barcelona? Why didn't Barcelona have so many different choices of ethnic food? Continuing on with my hissy fit . . . why couldn't you even get a decent salad in Barcelona? Why, when you walked into any corner store in London, did you get ten choices of everything, but in Barcelona your only choice was trans fat or an insulin spike?

The next morning was travel day, but we snuck in a quick trip to the Natural History Museum while the Beckers went to school. Saying goodbye was tough. We loved their family and were grateful for how they'd opened their home and lives to us. We hoped we could reciprocate if they visited us in Barcelona. We did not have an extra floor on which to host an entire family, of course, but I felt sure that if we could show them one quarter of the hospitality they'd shown us, they wouldn't regret coming.

At Heathrow, a woman asked Mae where she was from. Mae replied, "California."

"But we're living in Spain right now," I clarified.

Looking at me, Mae said, "We're just *visiting* Spain."

The trip to London and speaking only English days on end had rejuvenated all of us, but it had also had the unintended consequence of shedding light on some of the shortcomings and difficulties of living in Barcelona. I'm guessing by Mae's reaction in the airport, I wasn't the only one who had compared London with Barcelona and felt Barcelona had fallen short. Maybe London and all things English, accessible, and easy made the kids' homesickness more acute. And that made me angry . . . at Barcelona. If you can be mad at a city. Which I definitely was.

I had read that anger is an empowering emotion. I was feeling pretty powerful. But I remembered also reading that empowerment keeps you in the anger, preventing you from looking deeper. So as we flew home, I looked deeper—and I saw that while I was frustrated, I was not necessarily angry. And certainly not at Barcelona; it was just my easy target. If I were honest, I was frustrated with myself, for many well-tread reasons—that I couldn't communicate as well as I wanted to, that I wasn't as adventurous as I could've been in exploring my adopted city, that I was so (self) restricted food-wise. Barcelona is renowned for its food. Just because it isn't renowned for the type of food I craved wasn't its fault.

So I made a silent apology to Barcelona and disembarked from the plane knowing I had more work to do on myself. But that didn't mean I wouldn't curse under my breath the next time I saw only one uninspired salad on the menu, and no sticky pudding.

Chapter 33

SWEET NAVIDAD

*T*he lead-up to Navidad 2014 was similar to the lead-up to Navidad 2013: lots of travel. After London, we took a freezing whirlwind of a trip to Dublin in early December, which we wrapped up with an afternoon spent exploring the town of Bray and cozying up to the fire in the local pub, trying the beers on tap and allowing the kids their first taste of Guinness. Patrick was the only one of the kids to like the deep brown ale, and I could envision him, with his easygoing but slightly closed personality, thriving in his early twenties in Ireland.

After Ireland (and pressing right up against Christmas), we embarked on another quick trip, this one to Budapest. After spending the requisite hours planning the trip, I had lunch with *mis amigas*. We were talking about our Navidad plans, and when I said my family would be taking a quick trip to Budapest before our bigger trip to Southern Spain for Navidad, they all smiled and said, *Qué bien*—How great. Then Carmen added, "Budapest is fantastic, but you know what? You should instead go to *Praga*. Praga is a better city."

"Well, I think it's a little too late," I said, as I tried to calmly sip my *cortado*. "We have our flights and stuff already."

"Okay, then you should take the train from Budapest to Praga for a few days," she said. "It's maybe a few hours by train."

My stomach sank. So much time and effort go into trip planning; who wants to hear that after all the time and energy you spent planning, you booked a trip to San Jose when you should have gotten tickets to San Francisco? When I got home, I looked up the train from Budapest to Prague. Seven hours? The train from Budapest to Praga was *seven hours*? Okay, well, we definitely would *not* be going to Prague—and now I felt like we were going to the runner-up city.

Over the next few days at school, however, as people chatted about where they were headed for Christmas holiday, anytime I mentioned our plans to an expat, their reaction was: "We love Budapest! It's fabulous!" And if I dug deeper, asking how Prague rated versus Budapest, they all said Budapest over Prague any day. What in the world?

So at least we headed into our trip feeling more confident.

We never made it to Prague, so I still couldn't compare, but Budapest did not disappoint. Fantastic Christmas markets. Thermal baths—complete with old men standing in their Speedos in frigid temperatures drinking vodka before noon. Great food—the kids tried goulash, and Kieran loved oxtail soup.

At the airport, as we waited to board our plane back to Barcelona, we struck up a conversation with an American expat living in England who had just traveled from Prague to Vienna to Budapest. I asked how she had enjoyed Budapest.

"I liked Prague better," she said.

Well, there went my theory that only the Spanish preferred *Praga* to Budapest.

After we got home from Budapest, during a meditation, a memory from childhood came to me. It wasn't a memory of an event or place but a memory of a feeling, how something or somewhere or someone had made me feel as a child. It was a feeling of happy curiosity, of independence while feeling safe. I wondered what our kids would remember from our time in Spain. The specifics, like gladiator school in Rome or drinking a Guinness in Bray? Maybe not—especially Mae, who was only six. But if she had good experiences, those would shape her; the feeling of them would color her fabric. If she had lots of unhappy experiences, lots of memories of her mother yelling, she might not remember *why* Mom was yelling, but the shame or guilt or hurt or sadness would weave into her fabric, too. I found that thought affronting. I committed to redoubling my efforts to entwine as much happiness and love into my children's everyday lives as I could. When they went to therapy later in life, it would be because they needed help extricating themselves from my smothering, inexhaustible love.

On the day of Christmas Eve, or *Nochebuena,* we got together with *la familia* Alemany in the late morning at Parque Santa Amelia, a park a few blocks from our flat. Like most parks in Barcelona, it was sandy, with a playground for the kids, and had a small café with outdoor seating. But Santa Amelia, unlike many Barcelona parks, was large enough to offer small grassy areas and a little pond—in other words, large enough that the kids could run around without being underfoot. (Of course, that did not stop one of the six kids from coming up and saying, "I'm hungry" or "I'm thirsty" every few minutes as the four of us attempted to enjoy our *cafés* and each other's company. Tomás would tell the child in question, "Cay-mon, you just had breakfast! You can't be hungry already!" But after that child leaned into him and pleaded and pleaded, Tomás would pull out his wallet, hand over enough euros for all six kids to get some crisps and Fantas, and send that child off with a kiss on the head.)

Claudia and Tomás asked about our plans for that night and the next day. I knew they felt awful that we were alone for those two special family times, and if they weren't going to be at his family's place or hers continuously over the next forty-eight hours, they would be having us over to their house. But we didn't feel lonely, spending Navidad with just the five of us.

Claudia and Tomás then asked if we had gotten the traditional sweets for *Nochebuena*. Not only had we not, we didn't even know what the traditional sweets were. So we got an education on the traditional Catalan *dulces* for *Nochebuena*.

That afternoon, Claudia texted and asked if someone was free to meet her at our building's gate—she was out there in her car and had something for us. Tim went out and came back minutes later with a platter full of all the Catalan *dulces* Claudia and Tomás had described at the park, as well as a message: "If we can't be with you on *Nochebuena*, at least you can celebrate the right way."

Gifted with such kindness and love, we headed into our *Nochebuena* dinner with full hearts. I made spinach lasagna, and we ate by candlelight, looking at the twinkling lights on our two-foot-tall plastic Christmas tree from IKEA. We were used to a large live tree back in California—the pine smell greeting you when you came in the house, lots of ornaments on the branches. Tomás and Claudia had laughed at how pathetic this fake tree was when they had been over a week earlier and had offered to give us some ornaments to liven it up. But this pathetic little tree with IKEA's pink, lavender, light green, and yellow Christmas lights and our homemade paper chain—well, it was fine.

We tried the chocolate *turrón* from the platter of *dulces* Claudia and Tomás had given us. We ate some of the *polvorones* and tried to say "Zaragoza," as Tomás had laughingly instructed us to do, since it is difficult to pronounce this town's name with its "r" and two "z's" with your mouth full of *polvorones*. We saved the rest of the *dulces* for Christmas day.

In Spain, *Nochebuena* is significant; that's when relatives visit, presents are opened, and the big meal is consumed. Christmas spirit resides in that night. But you couldn't take the American tradition out of these Americans, so we saved our present opening for Christmas day.

The tree looked a little happier in the morning. There were lots of small gifts under it, thanks to my mom, who had shipped two boxes' worth of presents for the kids.

Tim and I tried our best to stick to the "go in a circle, one person opens at a time" rule, so the small number of presents wouldn't be opened in four minutes. The strategy worked, to an extent. Wrapping paper flew off of art supplies, books, games— enough that the kids were happy. We ate our favorite homemade French toast for breakfast, and the day floated by with talking to Tim's family, me making carnitas in the kitchen, the kids on screens, the kids drawing and playing with their presents, all of us eating the *polvorones, turrones, neules,* and *mazapanes* that *los* Alemany had given us the day before.

We ate by candlelight again that evening, and we asked the kids to remember the presents they had gotten—a form of gratitude, but also a way to make sure they wouldn't forget some of their gifts, since they were all kind of small that year. By the time we reached Mae, the exercise had petered out.

After dinner, we did an hour-long FaceTime with my sister and her family and my parents, who were all together, which we capped off with a jam session by the five cousins, our nieces playing violin and clarinet, our kids playing the wooden spoons and drums we had bought at the Christmas market in Budapest. At least we got to spend time with our relatives, albeit digitally.

After we said our goodbyes, we dug into the *pomodoro* that I had bought, a large Italian spongy cake that looks like an upside-down lamp shade. And though it wasn't quite the hit I was hoping for, we dipped the slices into the thick hot chocolate I had made—which no one liked but me because it was too thick and too chocolatey (who were these people?)—and ate cake and chocolate soup.

As we wrapped up dessert, Kieran started lip-synching, standing on the couch, this time (he did this quite often) to my personal holiday favorite, "Last Christmas" by Wham. I loved that side of Kieran, not being afraid to put himself out there. We decided to do a lip-synching contest, as we were sometimes known to do.

Patrick opted out and wanted to judge. I got up on the couch and gave "Last Christmas" my all—but still lost. Kieran sang to "Uptown Boogie" and Mae to "Mr. Roboto," complete with robot moves. Of course the boys criticized her moves as she was singing, and so she stormed off the couch and into her bedroom, slamming the door. And thus ended our Navidad.

I hoped, as I got ready for bed, that what had blended into Mae's fabric this Navidad was the love of family and friends, togetherness, and happiness—not anger and an overwhelming sentiment that her brothers were complete poop-heads.

Chapter 34

GET DOWN FROM THAT TREE

One lazy afternoon a few weeks before Christmas, over *cafés* with Claudia and Tomás, we'd discussed places Tim and I still wanted to travel to and which one we might pick to visit over the upcoming Navidad holiday. Southern Spain was on our short list. Claudia and Tomás said to us, "You have to go to Andalucía to see the real Spain." We took that seriously, coming from Catalans, and so plans were arranged. And on December 27 *la familia* Breen found ourselves on a high-speed train from Barcelona to Córdoba. From there, we planned to drive to Sevilla, Granada, and a few smaller towns. In total we'd be spending ten days in Andalucía, the southern region of Spain—home of tapas, bullfighting, and flamenco.

Córdoba was just a one-night layover so we could pick up our rental car the next morning and drive to Sevilla; we wouldn't be exploring the town until the back end of our trip. We were quite the vision that first night after disembarking from the train, walking through town from the Córdoba train station to our hotel—Tim carrying a huge duffel bag, everyone else with backpacks and carrying or wheeling some form of luggage or riding on said form of luggage, and at least one child kicking a soccer ball down the street. What a circus. We had been like this in Paris, in Bruges, in Rome, in London . . .

In the morning we had exactly enough time to eat breakfast and have Tim walk over to the train station to get the rental car before needing to hit the road. As we rode down the hotel elevator, we read a bulletin on the elevator wall advertising the hotel bar's breakfast option:

Desayuno en Cafeteria
2,50 €
Café + Zumo Natural + Bolleria o Tostadas

The bar had a wall of windows looking out to the street and park beyond. For a quick breakfast before Tim had to run and get the rental car, this would work. Plus we couldn't argue with the price—it came to just under $3 for coffee and fresh-squeezed OJ and either a chocolate croissant or a tostada—a piece of toasted bread about the size of Patrick's head—and the kids' meal came with hot chocolate.

After our most nutritious breakfast, which the kids would continue to have some version of for the next ten days, Tim walked to the train station to rent our car while I attempted to pay. Andalucía is infamous for its dialect; we had been told that they chopped off the second half of every word and also spoke very fast. Add to that my mixing up *castellano* with Catalan—a language most definitely not spoken in Andalucía—and I was going to face a rough ten days.

It had begun the previous night, as we tried to find our hotel:

Me: *Perdone, ¿dondé está avinguda Fray Albino?*—Pardon me, where is Fray Albino Avenue?
Stranger: Blank stare.
Tim: *Avenida.*
Me: (said a tad acerbically) What?

Tim: *Avinguda* is Catalan. They don't speak that down here. *Avenida* is *castellano*.
Me: (said to myself though I may have said it out loud) Yeah, I'm not an idiot, I know they don't speak Catalan here. What I don't know is what fucking words are Catalan and what words aren't!

I let the kids go across the street to the park while I settled the bill for our *desayuno*. I saw them scamper up the orange trees that were set back a bit from the busy road. And then chuck oranges at each other from the tree. I attempted to ask the waiter if it was okay for the kids to be "picking" oranges, and though I didn't understand much of what he said, I resorted to my time-tested strategy of reading body language to fill in the large gaps of my understanding. I took his occasional nodding as he spoke to be consent for the orange melée.

I half expected to see someone go up to the kids and tell them to stop. Every stranger in Spain seemed to be a caring parent to a child they didn't know. Every time a stranger interacted with my kids, whether telling them to tie their shoes or asking, "Why are you wearing shorts? It's too cold!" my tenderness towards Spain grew. Though I still felt a bit like I was outside looking in. Maybe I needed to be able to wipe the snot off the nose of a kid I didn't know before I'd feel fully enveloped in this familial way of being that I loved and envied. But I couldn't bring myself to do that yet; apparently my love still knew some bounds.

After successfully paying the bill, I grabbed the kids and we hooked up with Tim in the rental car. We were on our way!

Just an hour and a half later, we found ourselves in packed Sevilla. I knew southern Spain was crazy town at *la Pascua* (Easter), but the city was also swarming at this time—Navidad and *el Dia de Reyes*, Three Kings Day, the more celebrated holiday of the two in Spain, which takes place about two weeks after Christmas.

After finding our Airbnb and dropping off our luggage, we walked the teeming streets of Sevilla and found a restaurant open to a side street with people spilling out, eating their tapas and drinking their *cañas* in the street. Tim pressed his way into the bar and ordered whatever he thought might work for the family. The bartender wrote the order in chalk on the bar, and when Tim changed or added an item, the bartender crossed off the tally and wrote down the new sum.

The only food on the menu wall that had anything to do with a vegetable was *berenjenas con miel*, fried eggplant with honey. At least I didn't blame Spain for my lack of options anymore; I accepted the problem laid solely at my feet and my being *tiquismiquis*. And I also accepted the unpleasant truth that being *tiquismiquis* meant this could be a long trip for someone who mainly wanted vegetables, with many *cañas* needed to get me through. Starting at lunch.

I had booked a flamenco show in advance of the trip, and so a few hours after lunch we were seated in a darkened theater in one of only two rows of seats surrounding three sides of a low stage—a very intimate venue. The show started with just a singer and a guitar on stage in a spotlight. To my Western ears, the singing sounded Middle Eastern. This made sense later in the trip when I learned that Spain and the Iberian Peninsula had been part of the Islamic empire for centuries, which heavily influenced the food, music, art, architecture, and language of Spain. Had I been exposed to some history or religion books instead of having my nose in science texts most of life, I might have not been surprised by the singing.

Soon a female dancer joined, and the guitar played, the man sang, another clapped his hands and stomped his feet, and the woman danced with her eyes closed. It was a very powerful experience. Mae, who was seated on my lap, turned to me—incredulous and wide-eyed at the possibly inappropriate dancing she was witnessing on stage before her—and whispered in my ear, "Are her parents here watching?"

The next day, we visited the famed Alcazar, the palace built in the 1300s, a mind-blowing age by American standards. The colors and intricacy of the Moorish architecture were both breathtaking and like nothing I had seen before. Between the ancientness of Sevilla, the beauty of the architecture, and the powerful music we'd experienced the previous day, all of which I had never before been exposed to, I was acutely aware of my American provincialism.

We explored some of the winding streets of the Barrio de Santa Cruz, and by the time the dinner hour rolled around—the American one, we weren't even close to Spanish dinnertime—the kids were spent and famished. We purchased subpar sandwiches at an unimpressive sandwich shop just to get some food in their system before letting them enjoy their first gelato of the trip. While the kids were ordering, Tim's CTO, José Luis, who lived in Sevilla and commuted to Barcelona and had been so helpful in planning our stay, texted Tim suggesting that we meet up.

In minutes, José Luis was there with us in the gelato shop. Knowing that he had for sure not eaten dinner yet, and also knowing that Tim hadn't gotten to taste any real Sevillan food yet because of his picky family, I suggested that the two of them go out and get a drink and bite to eat. José Luis asked why we wouldn't come along, and I explained we were American and would turn into pumpkins shortly. I also knew the kids wouldn't have interest in choices like fried squid, pork cheek, or fresh anchovies. The kids were happy to go back to the Airbnb, and Tim would be thrilled to have José Luis show him Sevilla and eat like a local.

Walking away through the crowded streets back to our Airbnb—Patrick, Mae, and I navigating the crowds as a hand-holding threesome, Kieran alongside—I thought of José Luis gladly and willingly taking Tim out to show him his hometown and my heart softened, just as it did when I thought of strangers watching out for my kids. This openness and welcoming kindness the Spanish possessed created a pang of yearning in me to experience life like that, too.

The next morning we ate at the tiny bar right under our flat. The interior was narrow and lined on one yellow-painted wall with pictures of the Virgin Mary above brown-and-green tiles halfway up the wall; on the other side, behind the bar, was a small shrine to Jesus complete with burning candles. The bar was filled with locals whom we bellied up to the bar next to; we filled said bellies with *cafés* and freshly squeezed orange juice and tostadas before walking to la Catedral de Santa María de la Sede, the fourth largest church in the world (originally a mosque).

The cathedral may have been home to the tomb of Christopher Columbus, but the kids' only interest lay in playing in its courtyard, el Patio de los Naranjos, darting among centuries-old orange trees growing in a pattern throughout a courtyard paved with intricate brickwork. Tim and I absorbed the gorgeousness while the kids ran through it.

After we had reached the Breen daily maximum on culture, it was time to leave Sevilla and drive to one of the Pueblos Blancos, White Towns, of southern Spain. A young couple who worked for Tim, Pablo and Anna, had invited our whole family to visit them and Pablo's family over the holidays.

An hour and a half later, we pulled into the tiny town of Olvera, Pablo's hometown, whitewashed houses in every direction.

We parked our car and walked up the steep hill to our Airbnb, our own little white house with a red-tiled roof.

The caretaker, Frank, who was originally from England, showed us into the house. The door opened to a dark and very chilly kitchen and dining area. It was a cold day outside, but inside was colder. Maybe the house hadn't been opened in a while. Frank joked that he didn't know we had kids—"I only made up one of the bunk beds!" Silent groan inside me, thinking of having to make up two more bunk beds, one of my favorite chores.

As Frank showed us the room where Tim and I would sleep, he pointed to a floor heater and said, "That doesn't work, but the one in the den does." Noted. He then showed us up to the rooftop terrace, where we looked out over the red-tiled roofs of a whole town of whitewashed houses and then the green hills beyond. The jacuzzi we had read about on Airbnb sat empty. Frank said, "Oh, it's not clean. Or filled. Obviously. It's too cold for a jacuzzi!"

I was beginning to think this flat wasn't meant to be rented out in the winter. When we made our way back to the den, which would be Kieran's sleeping quarters, it dawned on us that the little heater in that room was the heater for the whole freezing flat.

I turned to Frank. "I just want to make sure I'm understanding correctly." I pointed to the little floor heater. "Is this thing the only source of heat for the house?"

"Yes, that's right," he said. "I told the owners to tell you this place isn't winter-ready. It really shouldn't be rented in the winter."

Tim and I couldn't make eye contact with each other.

"Oh, and one more thing," Frank said. "It's very old plumbing here. No toilet paper down the toilet. You have to throw it in the bin, and then take that out to the garbage."

Perhaps in an effort to calm my shell-shocked mind from the grenade Frank had just lobbed at us, I thought back to a conversation I'd had years earlier with my cousin Bill and his wife, Chrissy. We had concluded that there was something defining about a person in the way they handled their luggage being lost by an airline. Bill and Chrissy were of the opinion: "It's just luggage." The perspective I landed on after reviewing that conversation in my head was that lost luggage was a mere annoyance compared to an Airbnb that was not ready and had no heat, and whose toilet you couldn't flush toilet paper down.

That night we got lost on our way to meet Pablo and Anna for dinner. When we pulled into a gas station to ask for directions, Kieran hopped right out and asked the attendant before Tim and I could ro-sham-bo for who would go ask.

Kieran's comfort with speaking Spanish lifted my spirits, as did getting to spend time with Pablo and Anna—at least enough to carry me through another round of *berenjenas con miel* as the only vegetable option on the menu. The kids tried *rabo de toro*, bull's tail. At least some members of my family weren't acting like an obstinate four-year-old about food. And so, more out of shame than interest, I tried an olive, big girl that I was, as we caught up with Pablo and Anna. I once again felt myself warmed by their generosity of spirit as Anna chatted with the kids, genuinely interested in what they had to say, and the four of us laughed at the small-town Olvera stories Pablo shared.

We arranged to meet with them again for breakfast in the morning, and I didn't die from trying an olive. A successful evening overall.

We arrived home to find that all the groceries we had bought in Sevilla and put in the refrigerator had frozen solid. Red peppers? Frozen. Cucumbers? Frozen. Milk? Frozen. We went to bed hoping to not turn into frozen cucumbers ourselves.

After meeting Pablo and Anna at Bar la Piscina for yet another breakfast of tostada, we followed their recommendation and rented bikes for the Via Verde—a rails-to-trails system that wound its way through much of Spain. Back in California our kids had biked everywhere—to school, to friends' houses, to practice. But Barcelona was a city, and one on the side of a mountain, no less. Our kids did not get to bike. So we were all excited to get on the Via Verde and be able to bike with abandon.

We drove an hour to the town of Coripe to meet the bike guy. He pulled in with his van and five bikes, and we were almost off and riding before I remembered to ask for helmets. He said there weren't any. Not apologetic, just the way it was. The Spanish way: safety not high, or anywhere, on the priority list. So off we went down the dirt trail of the Via Verde, feeling so liberated to be on bikes, no cars allowed. I smiled at the shift in my attitude; the lack of helmets didn't faze me like it would have last year, or any time in years past. We biked past olive orchards; through pastures with goats and sheep, their bells bong-bonging as they walked; and past mesas with vultures flying above. It was a much-needed, hair-blowing-in-the-wind nature adventure for our city-bound family.

That afternoon, we joined Pablo and Anna at Pablo's family farm, located a few minutes outside of town. The farm was perched on the hillside and had a beautiful view of Olvera and all its white houses across the valley on the other hillside.

Pablo taught the kids how to pick olives from the olive trees and gather eggs. The kids loved climbing up the orange trees Anna pointed them to and exploring the rusted tractor sitting to the side of the barn. As we all stood in amazement watching two pigs sprint lightning-quick around their pen, Pablo pointed out that pigs are actually very fast animals; the ones we normally see just aren't given the space to run, he said, so it's impossible to know what fast animals they are. (Or impossible because we never saw pigs.)

We left Anna and Pablo feeling very appreciative of the adventures we'd just had, and for their unselfish desire to provide them for us.

We arrived back at the Airbnb to find that the jacuzzi had been filled by Frank and heating all day. We gratefully plunged in—and found that it was a few degrees below comfortable. Only Tim and Mae lasted past a few minutes, and Tim only because he is a great dad. I stayed in for less than a minute, not wanting the water to chill the warmth that Pablo and Anna's kindness had kindled in me.

Tonight was the big night. Not only was it *la Nochevieja*, New Year's Eve, but Pablo had invited us to join his family's celebration. The worry about how the kids would fare tonight—sitting around a table for hours with strangers, way past their bedtime—was offset by the anticipation of partaking in one of the most well-known Spanish traditions: stuffing twelve grapes in our mouths at the stroke of midnight. And we'd be doing this with a family who would be graciously opening their house to us for this deeply traditional family time.

Pablo had invited Tim to join him and his dad at a wine cellar that late afternoon—another great outing, but Tim didn't return home from it until nine. Tim wasn't concerned about the timing, however, because Pablo and his dad had just left too, and knowing the Spanish, the party wouldn't be starting until ten.

Or so we thought. As we were getting ready, Anna texted Tim, *Where are you? We're all sitting around the table waiting for you!*

Exchanging astonished glances with one another was getting stale on this trip, and would have wasted precious time, so instead we rushed the kids out to the car, socks and shoes in hand, embarrassment running high—until we opened the door to Pablo's parents' house, at which point embarrassment overflowed. Twenty people were inside, sitting around a very long table, and as all forty of their eyeballs came to rest on us, the room suddenly fell quiet.

Normally I would be tripping over myself, apologizing profusely for holding up their family celebration—"I'm so sorry, I can't believe we're so late! I'm so embarrassed! Thank you so much for having us!"—but all my stupid brain could produce in Spanish was, "I'm sorry; nice to meet you," as we met Pablo's parents and the other family members, who miraculously seemed to forget or forgive within mere moments that these strangers had been the obstacle to starting their family celebration.

Pablo ushered us to the far head of the table, where he and Anna sat down with us. The room was narrow and cozy, made cozier by the Spanish chatter of Pablo's family floating around us. Behind us were large windows with cream-colored drapes; the table before us was set with white china on a rose-colored tablecloth, giving the room a festive feel.

As soon as we sat down, dish after dish of food was carried out of the kitchen by Pablo's family—pheasant eggs with potatoes, *lomo* (cured sausage), Manchego cheese, Spanish tortilla (potato omelette), breadsticks. At one point, Pablo's grandmother, who was seated across the table from Patrick, reached over and served Patrick a piece of tortilla, as a good grandmother would. Patrick didn't like it, but he smiled politely and gave me a look of *what do I do?*

"*¡Hombre!*" Pablo said to Patrick. *¡Tienes que comerte la tortilla si quieres ser grande y fuerte y jugar bien a fútbol!*"—Dude! You have to eat the tortilla if you want to be big and strong and good at soccer!

Patrick again gave a polite smile and then pushed his fork into the tortilla.

I leaned over and whispered, "Patrick, don't worry, I'll eat it."

Immediately, Patrick's dark brown eyes welled up with tears and he sat back in his chair, exhausted and uncomfortable. He was also probably hungry, despite all the food. He took after his four-year-old mom in that way.

I ended up eating way more tortilla than I wanted.

And then Anna announced that the meat course was coming out. Holy *comida*, that whole table of food was just the first round! Platters of lamb chops and beef and chicken and baby clams and prawns and all manner of food, all prepared by Pablo's mother, came out amidst the warm Spanish banter and clinking of wine glasses. The kids ate a bit, but they were on fumes and just needed bed.

That course was followed by a shot of warm *caldo de pollo*, chicken broth.

And then, before we knew it, bowls of grapes were being passed around. It was a few minutes before midnight. Everyone counted out their twelve grapes. The idea was that if you stuffed a grape into your mouth for every bong on the clock as it struck midnight, prosperity would follow in the new year. Twelve bongs, twelve grapes.

"*¡Tres, Dos, Uno!*" everyone shouted, and then we were all stuffing grapes in our mouths as fast as we could as the clock struck midnight.

It turned out these were not seedless grapes. Mae, sitting on my lap, was still chewing grapes and spitting out seeds five minutes later. Meanwhile, everyone sang out, "*¡Feliz Año Nuevo!*" and toasted with champagne and wine.

Enveloped by warmth and family love, we all got up from the table and exchanged *Feliz Año Nuevo* and kisses on the cheek.

Soon after, we had to say our goodbyes. The kids could last no longer. I was not equipped to impart in Spanish to Pablo's family the appreciation I felt for their generosity in opening up their family gathering and *Nochevieja* feast to us. I hoped my eyes would communicate what my *muchísimas gracias* could not, especially to Pablo's sweet mother, who had done all the cooking and had been so gracious to us.

As our hostess bent down and gave Mae a big hug, she said to us, "*Las puertas de nuestra casa siempre estarán abiertas para vosotros.*"

"She says her home will always be open to you," Anna said, translating her mother-in-law's Andalucian accent for us.

I felt my heart ease and expand, bathed in this family's warmth.

The next morning, after hugging Pablo and Anna goodbye and giving them our heartfelt thanks, and after one last round of tostadas, at Bar la Piscina, we set off for Granada. We drove through a gorgeous countryside of mesas and olive orchards, the sun high in the sky, the kids singing to a song on the radio together—harmony, sweet harmony—holding on to the good mood from our visit with our friends for as long as possible. But as happens with family trips, it wasn't long before the next thing on our list was upon us.

We arrived in Granada with ten minutes to spare before our tour of the Alhambra, one of the few activities I had planned in advance of our trip. We actually didn't want a tour; our preference would have been to see this monumental historical site the Breen way—as in, walking around and looking at whatever was of interest to three elementary school kids until they could last no more. But all entrance tickets had been sold out way in advance, and the only way for us to get into the Alhambra by the time I went online had been via a tour.

I had paid for an English tour, but after chatting with us ahead of the tour and ascertaining that we all spoke varying levels of Spanish, our guide told us our tour was only going to be in Spanish, but he would translate anything into English that Mae and I needed him to. I guess we could have complained—I had reserved an English tour—but Spain had gradually worked its magic on us and we were *tranquilos*.

"How long is the tour?" I asked.

"Two and a half to three hours," the guide said.

Very much longer than the Breen way. The kids would never last that long in English, let alone Spanish. Tim and I placed bets with one another on how long Mae would last. I wondered how long *I* would last.

The guide's Spanish was clear and I understood about 75 percent of what he said. The Alhambra had been built in the 800s as a fortress and then added to over the years under Islamic rule, then Christian rule, until it became a huge, gorgeous enormity of palaces, gardens, and mosques. I loved expanding my world, learning and absorbing this beautiful architecture and color and symmetry that I had never been exposed to before. I didn't know what the kids were absorbing, but I hoped the exposure was leaving an imprint on them even if they didn't remember specific details.

Kieran was understanding everything the guide was saying. Mae and Patrick had tuned out, but they hung in there, which surprised us. When the tour went out to the gardens, we finally bailed. The kids had done amazingly well and the weather was cold; we felt good about closing the book on our cultural experience for the day.

That afternoon, after the kids had played *fútbol* in a plaza and we enjoyed a long, leisurely lunch of *cañas* and tapas, we drove back to Córdoba for our last day and a half. The next morning we ate a buffet breakfast at the hotel, which even had a kids' table replete with sugary cereals, hot chocolate, and gummy worms. (How is it that America so handily tops the charts of childhood obesity?)

After breakfast, we walked over to see the Mezquita, the famed and ancient mosque-turned-church that was the only attraction on our to-do list in Córdoba. The ticket window was closed until 3:00 p.m., however, so we had a whole day to kill.

The fact that we were *tranquilos* about this delay revealed once again how Spain had influenced us. We ended up at the Córdoba zoo—probably the last place Tim and I would have chosen to pass the time, but the kids enjoyed themselves so much that their repeated thanks for taking them there changed our mood.

On the way back toward the Mezquita, we stopped to watch a shepherd tending his sheep and goats next to the river, then headed off to find a lunch spot. In town we came upon a small plaza with two bars and outdoor seating, the tables filled with people soaking up the sun and the gorgeous day. Kieran saw boys playing *fútbol* in the plaza and asked if we could eat there. My body really wanted some vegetables, and not of the *berenjenas con miel* variety I knew I would find on the menus here, but—liking the idea of a cold beer in the bright sun—I relented and all three kids ran off to the group of boys and asked if they could join in.

Soon enough, Tim and I were sitting in the warm rays sipping our *cañas*. Patrick begged off early from the *fútbol* game and wandered over to a tree. Mae continued to play in "goal," a short wall with rocks demarcating the posts, and Kieran was in heaven showcasing his *fútbol* skills and chattering in Spanish.

After a few minutes of blissful relaxation and maybe forgetting I had kids, Mae ran up and reminded me that I did, saying, "That lady is going to call the police if Patrick doesn't come down from the tree!" I looked over to see him up in the branches and an elderly woman, hands on hips, looking up at Patrick, who wasn't making any moves to come down. Patrick wasn't one to be disrespectful, so Tim went over to understand what was going on.

Within six seconds, he and the woman were both laughing, so I knew everything was fine. Turned out she was just worried that Patrick was so high and thought he was in danger of falling and breaking something.

Again, that warmth permeated me. Things were right in the world when a grandmother showed care for a child she didn't even know. I looked down at the table with our small plates of fried bar food and *cañas* with the last few sips left in them, the sun reflecting off the metal table and hurting my eyes. It was so bright—the light, the warmth in me, the clarity of how good life felt right then.

I looked back at the grandmother and Tim talking, Patrick climbing down from the tree. I thought of Pablo's grandmother trying to get Patrick to eat tortilla. Of Pablo's mom hugging Mae.

Strangers no longer strangers, treating us so kindly and caringly. If a kid walked by with a runny nose, could I pull out a tissue and wipe it?

Luckily, one didn't walk by to test me. Instead I lifted my glass, turned my face toward the sun, and finished my *caña*, melting in the moment.

Chapter 35

TRYING NEW FOOD

$\mathcal{R}$esearchers tell us that a kid will be more willing to eat a food if exposed to it ten to fifteen times. Any mother who has the fortitude to prepare a vegetable ten different times, let alone fifteen, in the face of inevitable rejection should be more proud of herself for preparing that food that many times than of her kid's newfound tolerance for cauliflower. I always wondered: *Did the "ten times" mean the food actually had to enter the child's mouth ten times? Or did glaring at the food also get counted?* For my part, after my kid refused to eat anything I had prepared more than three times, I wasn't going to waste my mental or physical energy on said food anymore. Ten to fifteen times? That would probably mean cooking it thirty times to get it in my child's mouth ten times. And since Spain neither shares the same love affair with frozen foods nor obsession with efficiency that America has, I didn't have frozen peas that I could just stick into the microwave as my easy exposures numbers four, five, and six. And so my kids' breadth of acceptable vegetables became very narrow while in Spain.

That being said, I did, in general, subscribe to the notion that repeated exposures could bring about change, at least in relation to myself. I knew I could benefit from becoming more *tranquila*, from not being that trapped bird ramming into windows when friends invited me to sit and enjoy, and from being fully present as I did all this. And so, when opportunities arose to try to be more *tranquila*, I actually put that vegetable in my mouth rather than spitting it out on the table. And *poco a poco*, this effort was working.

An occasion to "try the new food" arose at Kieran's birthday party that year. We had given Kieran an experience instead of a party, since that was his preference, for his last three or more birthdays. For his eighth birthday, he'd gone to a San Jose Sharks game; for his ninth, the Globetrotters; for his tenth (a combo birthday and Christmas present), the lucky boy got to go to *El Clásico* in Barcelona for a Real Madrid–Barça game. This year, however, Kieran actually wanted a party so he could celebrate with his good friends. So we found ourselves navigating the ins and outs of scheduling and hosting a party in a foreign land.

Since Kieran was into rock climbing, we rented space at a rock-climbing gym, Climbat (*kleem-bot*, as the Spanish pronounced it). After Tim spent several minutes on the phone, in Spanish, with Climbat, we knew we had space reserved and the boys would have juice after. Tim had asked if we should bring our own food or cake. The answer was no—there would be *postres*, dessert.

No, we shouldn't bring in food? No, don't bring a cake? Not knowing what to expect, I told the mother of one of the boys who would be attending, "Feed him ahead of time; I have no idea if anything will be served."

When we arrived at the climbing gym, one guy was assigned to our group of fifteen kids. His first attempts at engaging the boys with climbing were worrisome and subpar at best. ("Do this ropes course. Now do it backwards.") After fifteen minutes, however, a group of young men showed up to help. They looked more like buddies that had been called in by our guy via SOS than people who worked there, but immediately they had the boys fully engaged and loving the competitions they had organized. The boys were happy climbing maniacs for the next two hours.

Watching how those guys connected with the boys reminded me of an interaction I'd witnessed in the Barcelona airport a few months prior. A young man in uniform, the equivalent of a TSA officer, was standing at attention as we walked through the body scanners, kids first. By the time I got through, the guy in uniform was talking to Patrick, smiling good-naturedly, and ruffling Patrick's hair. How often had I seen a twentysomething in the States interact so comfortably and warmly with a kid they didn't even know? Close to never.

Spain is all about family, and this often translates to older kids spending a lot of time around younger kids. Which translates to young adults, males included, being good with kids. Which may translate to dads placing family first. Weekends are family time. Dads are as present at school drop-offs and pickups as are moms. Seeing these good-natured young men at the party so naturally and warmly interact with our kids made me wistful that we, in the US, don't generally raise boys in a way that allows them to develop like this, into this.

After nearly two hours of climbing and playing, the guys ushered our boys into a brightly lit room with green linoleum floors, royal blue walls, and a few groupings of pint-size tables and chairs, a kiddie party room. Our boys didn't seem to mind, as the endless chatter and laughter continued inside. Before the boys sat in the kiddie chairs, the older guys made them all wash their hands. (Good with kids *and* responsible!)

As the boys jostled to use the sink, the guys bustled in and out of a side room, bringing out trays of Cheetos, crisps, and other assorted brown and orange snacks. Then they filled everyone's very large soda cup with juice, all the way to the top. And then came the bowls of olives. It was like sharks to chum; the olives got demolished.

When the boys seemed to be slowing down on the snacks, out came trays of donuts. These must be the *postres* the gym had talked about on the phone with Tim. But then Mae said, "I see a cake in there!" And next thing you know, as if donuts weren't enough, out came the cake.

One of the young men asked Kieran, "*¿Quieres tu canción de cumpleaños cantada en castellano, catalán, o inglés?*"—Do you want your birthday song in Spanish, Catalan, or English?

Kieran chose *castellano*, and the group of guys led the boys in a boisterous rendition of "Happy Birthday"—off key, out of sync, some in English (not everyone got the memo), and the rest in Spanish—as one of the guys patted Kieran on the head and tousled his hair. Kieran was a happy kid, beaming, surrounded by all his friends, a very different boy from the one who didn't want to be in Spain a second year.

Funnily enough, not many kids partook of the cake. I had seen this at other parties in Spain. Olives? Definitely. Donuts? Maybe. Cake? Probably not. My three kids plus three or four other boys dug into the cake while parents started drifting in to pick up their boys. We were happy to give the rest of the pastry to the guys helping out with the party, plus a tip—they had made the party a success.

Even though I didn't eat any olives literally, I did "try the new food" figuratively that day. I intentionally tried to relax and be in the moment rather than worry about what could or should happen. I knew going into the party that it might turn into a birthday party without a cake. What kind of mom would I be if, at the end of the party, no cake came out and Kieran looked up at me with questioning, sad eyes? A *tranquila* mom, albeit one with a resentful eleven-year-old with no birthday cake. When we showed up to the party and the one guy in charge seemed to be leading the activities somewhat lamely, we could have fretted, we could have asked management for more guys. But we'd chosen instead to let it run its course, to believe it probably would work out—and it had, beautifully.

Eating the new food was not comfortable. But I had tried, and I hadn't spat it out. Now for exposures numbers two, three, four . . . maybe by exposure ten I might actually pass for *tranquila*.

Chapter 36

YOU COULD LOOK BETTER

*S*usana and I were standing in the sun, waiting for the bus to pull up with our kids, who had been on a field trip. Had I known about the field trip before that morning? No. Had I signed a permission slip for this trip? No, because there hadn't been one. So I blamed Spain for me not knowing to pack Mae a brown-bag lunch for the field trip. And for not telling her she was going on a field trip.

"Why do all Americans dress so . . ." Susana looked me over. She was pretty, with long, curly blond hair, and always dressed fashionably. She had become part of my *amiga* group in this second year, and she was a lovely person with a good heart. When she asked a question like this, she wasn't judging me. Like many other Spanish, she just spoke directly.

"So . . . *casually*?" I finished for her, casting a glance down at my customary sneakers, Lululemon pants, and puffy jacket.

"So *athletically*," she said. "You're always wearing clothes for the gym."

The Spanish do not mind telling it like it is—or making eye contact. As a friend said, "Their gaze lingers," especially if they are men. As I had gotten to know a few Spanish people better and been more and more subject to this directness, this seeming judgment, I'd had to choose how to react. My gut took offense, but my mind told me, *They're not judging you, they're just being open*, and I tried not to take umbrage with whatever they had just said.

Susana's question about my clothes reminded me of my recent visit to the hair salon for my first-ever hair coloring. It's easy to brag when you can say, "I don't have to color yet," and you have hardly any gray. But when you say that and instead of hearing, "You're so lucky!" you get an eyebrow raise, it's time to make that first appointment.

In the past year, my hair had been collecting more and more gray. When I told the kids this was their fault, Mae liked to scare me and run off saying, "There's another gray for you, Mama!"

When I told my group of Spanish friends, "I think I'm going to get my hair colored," instead of hearing, "Oh, cool!" (the closest version to "You don't need to yet!" I could imagine in that moment), Claudia said immediately, "*¡Eso!* You are going to look so much better! Really. You will look years younger!" and Susana said, "I thought you were letting yourself go gray." No words minced there. But none were said with judgment or snideness, just candor and directness.

So, with the knowledge that my *amigas* were in full support of this undertaking, I walked into a hair salon and gave myself over to a stylist I had seen before and knew spoke English, confident I wouldn't end up with raven-black hair—my real fear in this undertaking.

Estel proceeded to give me a trim before handing me over to someone named Mari Carmen to color my hair. Estel spent about three minutes speaking to Mari Carmen in Spanish about what to do. I felt somewhat confident she was explaining to María Carmen the exact shade of brown I needed so I wouldn't walk out of there looking like a goth girl.

After Mari Carmen had applied the color and I had sat for the requisite amount of time, an older woman tapped me on the shoulder and signaled for me to follow her. She would be rinsing out my color. She also gave me a nice scalp massage and turned out to be the person who spent the most time on my head that day. After the massage, I was passed off to a young woman who blew-dry my hair. She asked me to lean forward and flip over my hair. That was new to me, and I wondered if this was her thing or a Spanish thing as I sat with my head between my knees, hot air blowing on my head.

After my blowout, Estel checked out my color and pronounced it a success.

I had to admit, I did look better without any gray.

As I was paying the owner of the salon, a well-put-together woman in her sixties, she said to me, "*Momentito; un poco de color*"—One moment; a bit of color—and signaled to a young woman. The woman proceeded to take a compact of makeup and put "*un poco de color*" on my cheeks, nose, and forehead.

Instead of feeling good, I felt slightly inadequate after this *momentito*. The message was, "You look good, but you would look better with makeup. Here's a little something to help." Open and direct, no mincing words.

Couldn't a girl just feel good for a moment having fewer gray hairs?

I walked out of the salon into the bright sun asking myself, *Where's a Spanish guy whose gaze will linger when you need one?*

Chapter 37

SHARK TEETH

W hen Patrick was two or three, he slipped and knocked his front baby tooth out on the edge of a wooden kitchen chair, root and all. Lots of blood. In that moment, I froze; even though I was an emergency medicine physician, I wavered on whether I should put a baby tooth back in. An adult tooth, no doubt. Jam that sucker back in there quick, root and all. But a baby tooth? My mind was blank. I placed an emergency call to our dentist, the one I had been going to since I was a resident, and Janet told me without hesitation to put the tooth back in.

When you lose a baby tooth as a kid, its root has disintegrated, and therefore the tooth becomes wiggly and comes out. The only thing the tooth fairy sees is the little tooth. But when a baby tooth is knocked out prematurely, the root comes out too. And the root is very long. I remember having a teenager come into the ED with an avulsed (knocked-out) tooth, and I just kept staring at that huge root and saying to myself, *There is no way in hell that thing is fitting back into that space.*

So with Patrick, on the count of three, I shoved that tooth with its root back in, and then I held it there as we tried to distract him with TV. After the initial shock, Patrick calmed down and let me sit with my fingers in his mouth for the next ten minutes. I did not want to move a muscle; if he was going through this pain, I was going to make sure I did everything I could do to ensure a clot would form around that root and it would stick. I will never forget how Patrick handled that emergency—one of the too many times when we would have to test his pain threshold, after which we'd walk away thinking, *That is one tough kid.*

Once the episode was in the rearview mirror, I read up on avulsed baby teeth, and the literature was clear that you in fact should *not* reimplant an avulsed baby tooth, because, among other reasons, doing so could cause damage to the growing bud of the adult tooth that was in there. We'd have to hold our breath for the next five or so years to find out what kind of damage I had caused.

Fast-forward four years, and Patrick was now growing shark teeth—as in, two rows of teeth, just like a shark. His adult front tooth was growing in fully behind his baby tooth. So this was the damage I had caused. His baby tooth was ever-so-slightly loose, but it would not come out, despite us pulling on it.

After a few months of that tooth stubbornly staying put, on Christmas Eve our first year in Barcelona, an accidental blow to the mouth by Kieran's elbow caused that stubborn baby tooth to fly out of Patrick's mouth and skitter across the foyer floor. We picked up the tooth and found attached to it a mummified little root. Instead of disintegrating, as it should have, that thing had calcified. It had planned to stay in there for the long haul.

After that night, Patrick was no longer a shark, but he did still have a fairly messed up set of front teeth.

That summer, when Pascual, Tim's boss, was visiting us in the US, he noticed Patrick's awkward front teeth and said, "Let me guess: a traumatic avulsion and it grew in behind the other tooth." Pascual happened to be a pediatric surgeon turned oral surgeon turned entrepreneur. The guy had serious credentials. He also had a heart the size of our living room. He said, "My daughter, Marta, can fix that. Go see her as soon as you're back in Barcelona. She'll put him in a retainer; it needs to be pushed forward or else it will do damage to the root." The *root*! Coming back to bite me.

Pascual's daughter was a dentist. I wasn't sure if she was an orthodontist; I didn't know a thing about orthodontia in Spain—maybe dentists did the orthodontia work? I also had no idea if our private insurance would cover a trip to one. But here was Pascual, offering up his daughter's services. As happened so many times in Spain, we summed up our options quickly and, operating on a bit of blind faith, went with the best one at hand: Marta.

After a few weeks of a failed non-retainer option, Marta put Patrick in braces just covering his top six teeth. He was thrilled to be one of the first in his grade to have braces. I wasn't as thrilled. Remembering my own experience with braces, I didn't recall my wires ever slipping out from the brackets and sticking painfully into my cheek. Yet this happened multiple times to Patrick. Each time, Tim would have to call Marta's receptionist and combat her desire to speak in Catalan to get an appointment. Then I would get Patrick on the bus and we would head down the hill to the office, where they would clip and reinsert the wire.

This process didn't take long; within ten minutes, we were back in business. But by the eighth episode, my patience was wearing thin. I had personally jerry-rigged the wire back into the bracket as many times as I had gone down the hill to their office. Tim was out of town for work, and the braces broke three times in as many days. With that eighth episode, I didn't even bother calling the office and trying to negotiate an appointment. We just showed up. All I could manage to explain to the receptionist in the brightly lit, modern waiting room was, "*Sus brackets rompieron.*" I was trying to say his braces broke, but I probably said, "His braces broke something."

Whatever, I thought. *We're here now and we're your problem.*

Except it quickly became my problem again, because Marta wasn't in until Monday, and it was Friday. Luckily, a dental assistant was able to clip the wire and feed it back through the brackets.

I was grateful she had helped us and attempted a fix, but I had zero confidence the wire would stay in place for three more days, as this was the same fix I was doing at home.

And the wire broke on Saturday. And again on Sunday. Each day, I put a headlamp on my head, picked up a bobby pin, and told Patrick to lie on the couch. Welcome to the dentist.

We had a follow-up appointment on Monday with Marta. I was prepared to say, while trying my best to hide the fact that I was d-o-n-e, "Any chance of taking these off? Now? Please?" But I didn't have to, because she looked in Patrick's mouth and said, "¡Un éxito!"—A success!

As we rode the bus back up the hill, looking out the window at the buildings going by and motos zipping in between traffic, I got lost in my joyful thoughts about how I wasn't going to miss this routine, and how I could finally retire my headlamp and bobby pin. But another thought interrupted my gleeful contemplations. In the midst of my frustration at the constant trips for broken brackets, I had almost lost sight of how generous Marta had been in taking care of us in the first place. I wondered how I could repay her, and Pascual, for their kindness in doing this for Patrick. Maybe when someone knocked their tooth out, I could be the person in their office who would jam it back into its socket. I'd do that for Marta.

The thought of jamming a tooth back in its socket made me think of Patrick all those years earlier, handling that awful experience like such a champ. I looked at this great kid sitting next to me and smiled at him. He looked at me and smiled back, flashing his new pearly whites—which were, just like us, side by side.

Chapter 38

SO . . . ARE WE HAVING WINE?

*I*t had been decided without me, by *mis amigas*, that we would be taking a girls' trip together. Even the date and location had been picked. Susana had grown up in Andorra, the tiny country nestled in the Pyrénées between Spain and France, and had offered up her place. The group going to Andorra for a weekend would be Alba, Carmen, Claudia, Susana, Lucia—a friend of Susana's and Carmen's—and me.

The trip sounded fantastic . . . but at the same time didn't. These were all Spanish women, and my Spanish was decent but nowhere near where it should be to enjoy a weekend away 100 percent in Spanish. Which it would be, because with five Spanish-speaking women, why wouldn't it be? Actually, the conversations would be in Catalan, because that was their primary language. I wasn't sure I was up for it; trying to keep up with the conversations, not to mention participating in them, would be exhausting. I loved spending time with these women, but I was going to have to be comfortable with being just on the edge of understanding. Participatory to an extent.

But Tim convinced me to go, and before I knew it, we were all traveling a few hours up to Andorra in Alba's minivan, a rarity in Spain. I sat in the back with Claudia, and from the get-go she yelled, "*¡Chicas! ¡Castellano!*" — Girls! Spanish!—each time they spoke in Catalan. As the weekend went on, the reprimand went from "*¡Castellano!*" to "English!" as they saw that I was on the outskirts of the conversation even in Spanish.

I was so disappointed that I still was not at a point where I was comfortable speaking Spanish with my friends. I had taken six weeks of Spanish classes, three hours a day, five days a week upon our return to Barcelona, but with a trip to Dublin, a family visit, and then the trip to London coming on the heels of those classes, my life had taken a decidedly English turn that had been difficult to recover from.

On the drive, I texted Tim to check in on the kids. He texted back: *Mae said, "I want Mom to come home and you to go away . . . forever."*

Well, at least I could start my weekend comforted by the knowledge that Mae was completely herself.

Just over two hours later, we arrived at Susana's home. The Pyrénées appeared like great walls rising straight up on all sides of Andorra. I was constantly looking up. So far it had been a bad winter in Europe for skiing, but there was snow on top of the mountains. You could only imagine how beautiful Andorra was as a winter wonderland.

The day started off with shopping—lots of it. It's tax-free in Andorra. Though not much of a shopper, I was content just roaming around with my friends, drifting in and out of stores. Sometimes Claudia forgot to say, "*¡Chicas!* English!" and my Spanish would allow me only partial comprehension of what was going on. Had we decided on stopping for a glass of wine, or on doing more shopping? I was okay with simply walking onward, happy to be there, and when we ended up at our destination thinking, *Oh, I guess we decided on wine.*

Susana had planned a surprise for us that evening; the only thing she'd told us ahead of the trip was to pack some very warm clothes, as we would be cold for about fifteen minutes at some point. That night at about eight, just as it was starting to rain—we hadn't eaten dinner and were late for the surprise—Susana asked the group if we were okay not returning home to get our warmer clothes and just going for the surprise. Perhaps if we had been standing outside in the cold rain making this decision, instead of inside a warm car, we would have decided differently. But up the mountain we drove.

As rain turned to heavy snow, Susana called someone at our destination. They told us if the car didn't have chains, we shouldn't risk traveling any farther.

As the snow came down, reality hit us: We had to turn around. And so Susana revealed to us the surprise—she had arranged for us to be transported up the ski mountain on one of the Sno-Cats that groomed the trails, then have dinner at the lodge at the top.

We were so disappointed for Susana, and for ourselves, that we brainstormed and said, "Let's take a cab up," thinking a local cab would be better equipped for the weather. After much trouble getting one, the six of us hopped in a cab that could take us to the top. But this cab wasn't any more prepared for the snow than the minivan had been. Maybe the driver had chains somewhere, but they weren't on the car. Maybe he had snow tires on, but guessing by how the car was handling, I'd say not.

We had all been laughing, but the car steadily grew more and more quiet as we made our way, slipping and sliding, up the dark mountain. Finally, at a steep section, it looked like the taxi wouldn't even have the traction to get up. Susana asked something to the effect of, "Maybe this car isn't going to make it?" to which the driver responded something along the lines of, "Why wouldn't it?" (such a typical Spanish male response) as he gunned the car over the top of the steep part.

Once again, I found myself in the uncomfortable position of having to be comfortable with not knowing exactly what was going on. Such as if we were safe.

We were all very relieved to get out of that car at the base lodge. Hanging over my head, and maybe over some of my friends', was the thought that we would still have to get back down the mountain after dinner.

I didn't want that thought to ruin the nice night Susana had arranged—but I didn't ruminate on it for long, since the ridiculous temperature outside soon turned my mind to trying to stay warm in -15°C winds while waiting for the Sno-Cat driver in just jeans and a coat—no hat, no gloves.

We were the only ones around, waiting at the base of a ski run, outside a locked building with one or two spotlights on, snow driving down. We all were somewhat in a state of disbelief, freezing and wondering what was next. Or maybe that was just me.

And then, through the blowing snow, we saw lights making their way down the mountain. Thank God—the Sno-Cat. When it pulled up, the driver handed us three red blankets, and we soon realized we weren't going *in* the Sno-Cat, we were loading into the metal basket at the *front* of the Sno-Cat. Salvation from the cold was still ten to fifteen minutes away.

At this point we were laughing, through chattering teeth, at how absolutely freezing we were—laughing at the absurdity and implausibility of finding ourselves, six moms from Barcelona, on the front of a Sno-Cat, headed up a mountain, in a snowstorm. When the wind wasn't blowing the moment was defused by wonder, the vehicle's lights illuminating the silent shower of snowflakes, the mountain quiet under its white blanket.

In ten minutes we arrived at the lodge. Surprisingly, other people were dining there, having snowshoed up or also having arrived by Sno-Cat. We ordered some wine and fondue as we began to thaw, and then proceeded to eat and drink and talk about life over the next two hours in the warmth of the lodge. Many of the conversations were just like ones I'd have with my closest friends at home—about life with kids, marriage, problems at school, ourselves. I always loved listening for the differences or similarities between life in Spain and life in the US. How the Spanish raised their kids, their attitudes toward school and toward sports, how they dealt with conflict, what was important to them in life. Most life issues seemed to have no geographic boundaries.

At one point someone said, "Look outside!"

The snow was blowing upward and sideways in the lights. The door next to us, which led out to a porch, blew open several times during the course of our meal; at one point my wineglass even blew over. Thank God we were going down the hill in a Sno-Cat—*But then*, I couldn't help but think, *we still have the taxi to contend with*.

But as is so typical with the Spanish, no one seemed worried. Either they "knew," or they were quite comfortable in the "not knowing." Carmen ordered a *gintonic*. The waiter brought shots of something yellow. Everyone was *tranquila*.

Finally, the last group of diners in the room with us got up to walk back down the hill. As we were now the last ones there, we thought we, too, should wrap up dinner. Susana called a taxi so it would be waiting at the base when we got down the mountain. As we walked out the door, the employee who was holding it for us counted out *"Dos, dos, y dos."*

Not until I saw the three Sno-Cats waiting did I realize he was telling us to pair off, two of us going into each vehicle. They apparently thought -15°C was too cold for riding on the front of the Sno-Cat, so we got to climb inside the heated cabs with music playing. So, this was how the better half lived!

Our caravan pulled away from the lodge and slowly made its way back down the mountain, the Sno-Cats falling into formation, one behind the other and staggered out to the side, grooming as we went down.

The snow had stopped, and at the bottom we discovered the road had been plowed while we talked through life's issues over drinks in the lodge, so our ride home was far less nerve-racking than the ride up had been. We arrived safely back at Susana's at 1:30 a.m.—the latest I had been up in months, a normal bedtime for most of these friends.

The next morning, we lounged around in our pajamas and ate fruit and cereal and yogurt. Despite the cold weather, we decided to rally and take a walk in the woods to a frozen lake. Susana said she had spent her youth exploring this forest and foraging for mushrooms. After we had driven to the trailhead and begun walking through the silent and crisp woods, I envisioned Patrick doing just this—idling his day away exploring and climbing and picking—and I felt down thinking of his and our very suburban life back in Menlo Park.

We naturally fell into pairs as we walked on the trail, and I chose to fall in with Alba. Her English was the worst of the group, yet she constantly tried to speak it so I could be a part of the conversation. I wanted not only to practice my Spanish but also to reciprocate the kindness she had always shown me. The effort was exhausting but gratifying.

By the time we had finished the hike, Susana's mom had called and said there had been a rockslide in some town on our route home. We had planned on leaving much later that day, but because weekend traffic would soon snarl behind the rockslide, we decided to leave right away. We stopped for a "quick" lunch on the way out—sandwiches, fries, and salad with tuna on it. I ate a tomato and cheese sandwich.

A *quick* lunch was, of course, a misnomer. We ate, then had pastries, then *cafés*, talking all the while. No one looked at their watch once.

The trip home was relaxed and enjoyable, if lacking the excitement of the trip up. We discussed different issues our kids were facing, everyone chiming in with advice and opinions. The only excitement of the journey was almost running out of gas, Alba being one of those people who doesn't pay attention to details and also never gets stressed about anything. So even almost running out of gas on the highway was met with laughter.

When I arrived home, tired but so thankful both to be home with my family and to have gotten my weekend with friends, the kids were keyed up with excitement. I just sat there with Tim on the couch, the kids alternating between wrestling, dancing, and smothering each other. I noticed a picture Mae had drawn on the white board—two girls with big sad eyes. One girl said, "I miss Mom." The other said, "I miss Mae." She must have drawn that when she told Tim she wanted him to go away forever. But in front of me were three very happy kids, no worse for the wear. And Tim was in pretty decent shape too.

I didn't know whether his time as a solo dad had been rough or not. But quickly assimilating my lesson from this weekend, I made myself comfortable in the not knowing.

Chapter 39

AND THE HEAVENS OPENED

I felt a dark cloud settling over me. Tim had to take a work trip back to California for eight days, and six of those days fell during *Semana Blanca*—White Week, or Ski Week. The kids were off school three-quarters of the time Tim would be gone. The cloud gathering was dread.

Back in California, when Tim had to travel I would drive the kids to the zoo or the beach, or call a friend and get the kids together to play, or take the kids to the movies, or take them out to lunch or dinner, or go to the pool, or hire a babysitter to relieve me for a few hours. In Spain, where I couldn't speak the language well, had no car, and wasn't confident venturing beyond my comfort zone (both physically and emotionally) without parent backup in case something (like leaving a kid on a train platform) went wrong, none of those things felt like options. *Mis amigas* were all traveling with their families. I was going to be sitting in a flat with three kids who were out of school and had nothing to do, with no one to help, in the winter. Dread.

And then dread turned to self-reproach. Hadn't I felt this same way over a year ago when we first arrived in Spain and Tim had to travel back to the US to collect our visas? And hadn't I been disappointed with myself then for merely trying to survive? And what was I doing right now but once again preparing to pace myself, not give too much of myself?

What would happen if I didn't pace myself? Would the world end? Or would the sun shine the next day? It's like I had forgotten the lesson I had learned over the past year—that extending myself was worth the reward. The dark cloud of dread seemed insignificant compared to the storm of dismay and self-reproach beginning to gather over me. Either way, a tempest was coming.

As most parents of young children know, patience is gone, dried up, by the end of every day. One of the early days Tim was gone, I told Mae that I didn't want to yell that night, that I needed her help not to yell, that I needed her to listen to me when it was bedtime. But when she was supposed to be getting in bed that evening, she was in Kieran's room, laughing, instead.

Normally I would have raised my voice and told her to get in bed. But because I was drained, I started by saying, "I told you I would try not to yell, but you were supposed to help me by listening to me. And so I talk like this, without yelling, but you ignore me."

The barometric pressure in the room was dropping quickly.

"So how am I supposed to get you to do what you're supposed to do *unless I yell at you like this? Get. In. Bed!*"

The lightning had flashed, the thunder had boomed.

I went to the kitchen fuming but simultaneously feeling horrible; I just had rained fury on my six-year-old. A few minutes later I heard her talking in her bedroom, which she shared with Patrick. The eye of the storm had passed; exhausted and defeated, I walked back to her room to find her standing in the doorway, lights on. She threw a sticky note at me and then turned to climb into her bunk.

I said through gritted teeth, "Get. In. Bed."

Lightning still slashed, but the crash of thunder no longer immediately followed; the storm was moving on.

When I got in the kitchen, I read the note. It said, "I just want Dad."

The thunder rumbled in the distance. The only thing left in the storm's wake was my guilt and sorrow—for my behavior, for my inability to do better. In the quiet and stillness of the room, I cried.

The first day back to school after the break—day seven, the second-to-last day of solo parenting—I dropped the kids off at school, and instead of feeling like the clouds had parted and the sun was shining down directly on me, specifically me, I felt incredibly gloomy about the previous six days. In my effort to make it through those days, I hadn't attempted to do anything that would remotely qualify as fun for the kids. I hadn't even played a board game with them.

As I came out of this thought, I was at the part of my walk back to our flat where I crossed the plaza in front of Sant Vicenç de Sarrià, Sarrià's church. I had been raised Catholic but since then had become a "fallen Catholic," as another fallen Catholic friend liked to refer to us, which meant we didn't go to mass anymore and lightning would probably strike us if we did. But I loved churches. I entered any I found when we traveled. Growing up I'd always found mass to be a time of meditation—or, more apt, of "not paying attention." As an adult, instead of listening to the homily or any part of the mass, I would find myself thinking about all sorts of issues in my life. I think I was drawn to churches now because they provided a place of quiet reflection for me.

Sant Vicenç de Sarrià was centuries upon centuries old. It sat at the top of the hill of Sarrià, overlooking one of the plazas, right where the main pedestrian road of Sarrià intersected a busy street with cars. Every day on our way to and from school, we walked through the narrow alley alongside the church and across the plaza. Instead of crossing in front of the church to walk down the narrow alley beside it now, I found myself walking up the few stairs in front of the church and entering. I pushed through the large, heavy wooden doors into a space dimly lit by various hanging lights and candles burning along the length of its walls, twenty pews on either side of the center aisle leading up to the altar, the memory-laden smell of incense filling my nose.

I walked about halfway up the middle aisle of the quiet, chilled church and ducked into a pew on the right. Two or three other people were scattered through the church.

I sat. Noises echoed in the quiet—a cough, a chair scraping the floor. I let my mind go where it wanted. It quickly settled on what a poor job I had done this past week, and how hard the week had been. Why, in this very privileged life I led, did I feel like I could only manage the bare minimum? That juxtaposition hit deep. I had made such progress in the past year, understanding that great experiences resulted from putting myself out there, even a little, and a full life was one in which I was present. That made my attitude of survival this past week, and the backslide that represented, even more disappointing—punishingly so. A few tears started down my cheeks as I rolled these thoughts over in my mind.

My tears were silent, but apparently my grief was not, because I looked up to see a priest slowly cutting across the pews toward me from the left side of the church.

He stopped a few feet away. "*¿Está bien?*" he asked, hands behind his back, slightly bent toward me.

I nodded yes.

"*¿Quiere hablar?*"—Do you want to talk?

I shook my head no.

This much I could say in Spanish, but in that moment I honestly didn't trust myself to speak at all. When I'm holding back tears, sometimes my brain feels I'm okay to speak and then words come out and my heart hears the shakiness of my voice, and then the heavens open.

So instead, I just nodded that I was fine, and as he turned away, I managed to say, "*Gracias.*"

I had never done that before—cried in public, let alone cried in a church. I wasn't sure if this was because I didn't usually have a church at my disposal when I was upset; perhaps it would happen more if I did. But this sadness had more layers and depth to it than just guilt for my past week's performance and disappointment in myself.

I sat with that thought for a moment and then decided it struck too deep, was too big, to grapple with in that church. So I got up and walked out the giant wooden doors, into sunshine that barely registered.

Chapter 40

DANCING, AWKWARDLY

$\mathcal{W}$e had received the bad news a few weeks earlier that my mom had been diagnosed with stage II non-small cell lung cancer. A chest X-ray turned into a CT scan turned into a PET scan turned into the diagnosis. She would need a lobectomy, in which part of her lung would be removed, followed by chemotherapy and maybe radiation. I spent a lot of time talking to my parents on the phone before doctors' visits and after, preparing them for what the doctor might say, preparing them with what questions they should ask, translating what the doctor had said, talking through options.

Around this time, I found myself wanting to make an appointment with a dermatologist to get my skin checked. I was in a higher risk category since my dad had had melanoma, so I usually got yearly mole checks, but I had missed the previous year's.

I surmised that this sudden urge to make a derm appointment was my way of working through my helplessness with my mom's situation. My focus on my health was a proxy for my inability to be there to help take care of Mom's. I felt the need to do something in the face of not being able to do much. *I gotta dance to keep from crying.*

Tim made the appointment for me online, since it would take him about a third of the time compared to me, given our differing levels of Spanish proficiency.

On the day of the appointment, I walked down the hill and into the hospital rehearsing what I might need to say to the receptionist, as I often do before a planned encounter with anyone: "*Hola. ¿Dondé está dermatología?*"

Der-mah-toh-loh-HEE-ya? Der-mah-toh-LOH-hee-ya?

I went with the former and was told that department was in the building across the street. I followed the signs for der-mah-toh-loh-HEE-ya up the stairs to a desk with two ladies behind it. I said *hola* and pushed forward my insurance card. Normally, I'm a friendly person, but not knowing how to make small talk in Spanish I now came across as the strong and silent type. Or just the silent type.

I perspired as I waited for a tirade of fast Spanish to be thrown my way, but the lady simply handed back my insurance card with a deli ticket with a number. A flashback to getting our *NIEs*.

I sat in the large waiting room full of people all staring up at a TV showing random numbers with a room number next to it. I wondered if I should yell "Yahtzee!" when my number appeared.

After ten minutes, my number appeared next to 209. I rose and walked down the hall past several closed doors until I found the one marked 209. I knocked and opened the door to a bright room with an examining table in front of me, a table laden with medical supplies to my left, and a man sitting behind a desk to the far left, with two chairs in front and a big window behind the desk looking out to the street and sunny day outside. I was thrown off to see an office in the examining room.

The man looked up, said, "*Hola,*" no smile, and then looked back down at his computer. He wore a long white lab coat, so I assumed he was the dermatologist. In the US, long white coats traditionally are only worn by attendings; short white coats are for med students and sometimes lab techs, pharmacists, or other healthcare personnel.

Since I had no idea if the coat hierarchy existed in Spain, I waited to see whether he would launch into my medical history or ask for my insurance card. He said, "*Buenos días*," again without a smile; I said *buenos días* back as I leaned over the desk to shake his hand. Everyone in Spain and most of Europe greets with a peck on each cheek. I was pretty sure this would be an inappropriate greeting at a doctor's appointment, but he did not seem comfortable with me reaching across to shake his hand either. This dilemma was not something we had discussed in Spanish class; my answer would have to come from living through it. (And asking Claudia, which I made a mental note to do.)

He asked in Spanish what the nature of my visit was. The website had claimed he was English-speaking.

I braced myself. "*Lo siento, ¿hablamos en inglés?*"—I'm sorry, can we speak in English?

"*Sí,*" he responded curtly. I explained, in English, about my dad having melanoma and my needing an annual mole check. I also said I was interested in knowing, as a forty-three-year-old, what I should be doing to take care of my skin. Up to this point, I hadn't done anything, and I thought maybe I should start.

"Well, we need to do an exam," he said, sounding a bit put off.

Um, yeah. What dermatologist doesn't do a skin exam when someone says they're concerned about melanoma?

"Please get undressed," he said as he motioned to the exam table.

I looked at the bare table. No gown there. A quick search of the walls only revealed more lab coats, no gowns. Was I supposed to put on a lab coat?

"Remove my clothes? Or is there a gown?" I asked almost haughtily, expecting a gown to appear. And him to leave.

"Remove your clothes," he said as he shuffled some papers on his desk. Not leaving.

Haughtiness dismantled, I considered that at least my previous massage experiences had prepared me for this moment. The Spanish comfort with nudity plus his indifference made me more comfortable with the decision I had to make, in a split second, as to whether he was a creepy doctor who wanted to watch me undress or this was just how exams were done in Spain. Another question to definitely ask Claudia.

I started taking off my clothes and saw nowhere to put them. *This isn't awkward at all*, I thought as I stood there with my skirt in hand. At least it wasn't my first experience in Spain with my ass hanging in the breeze. When I got down to my bra and underwear, he said, "You can lie down."

So, bra and underwear were the end of the line. Did this man think that women in Spain were immune to getting skin cancer on their boobs, that there was no need to check them? Not that I wanted him looking at my boobs. I had lost my interest in a thorough exam back at the words "get undressed" with him still standing there.

The survey of my moles took less than two minutes. When he finished he told me to get dressed and join him back at his desk, like nothing weird had just happened, because maybe it hadn't, and as I was working that out he said he didn't see anything suspicious and then gave me the name of some over-the-counter sunscreen to use. "Make sure you wear it when the sun is strongest, in the middle of the day," he admonished. "From noon 'til five."

Since when was the "middle of the day" between noon and five? Well, I supposed, in Spain, where people normally woke up at eight and went to bed at midnight, "middle of the day" would technically be considered noon to five.

On my way home, I stopped at *la farmacia* to get some of the sunscreen the dermatologist had recommended. On my way out the door—while rubbing sunscreen all over my face, since it was 3:00 p.m., "middle of the day"—I texted Claudia: *omg please tell me I didn't just have a very creepy experience.*

After I gave her a brief rundown, Claudia's response was: *totally normal.*

I wasn't sure why what I had just experienced should be classified as "normal," but at least I wasn't dealing with the other possibility. I pictured Claudia looking down at her phone in the middle of a partner meeting at her private equity firm and reading my frantic text; I hoped she found the interruption amusing. Dumb American friend's first experience with a non-puritan (i.e., non-American) doctor visit.

As I walked back into our flat and threw my keys on the shelf under the window, I wondered whether I would tell my parents that I had had a mole check, and all was well. I knew my mom would want to hear that good news—she would want to focus on my health as a diversion from her own. And I was taking care of my own health as a weak substitute for being with her and focusing on hers; I was dancing to keep from crying. Though after this particular experience, I needed to find a different dance.

Chapter 41

THE HILLS ARE ALIVE

*W*hile I was not a control freak like my sister or my mom, I was the presiding control freak in my nuclear family. But living in Spain had afforded me many opportunities to get comfortable not being fully in control. Trips were one such opportunity. Extensive trip planning allowed me a modicum of control, pre-trip, but once we were boots on the ground, my planning only helped so much and my sphere of control all but vanished. With the kindness of strangers and some luck, our trips generally went well. But there were things that could sabotage even a well-planned trip, as well as any illusion of control—like weather, sickness, or your own family members.

Tim had recently reconnected with an old colleague who was Danish but now lived in Switzerland. In the course of catching up, Tim had asked where that friend took his family skiing. When he passed that information on to me, he did not know I would be acting on the information almost immediately. We had a four-day weekend coming up and no plans. Now we were going skiing in Switzerland, using his friend's advice.

When I'm not in the mood to trip-plan, nothing happens. But when I'm in the zone, watch out. In a two-day span I planned three different trips, booking flights and hotels for Zurich, Marrakech, and Madrid.

I had an American friend in Barcelona who was still looking for a ski trip for her family a week before we left for Switzerland. I asked if her family wanted to piggyback onto our trip. I liked Anne and her family a lot, and Patrick was in class and friends with one of their daughters. The Danners were laid-back, not the type of family to attach themselves to our hips. Anne bought tickets the next day and booked a hotel next to ours.

We flew into Zurich, where we met up with the Danners to catch the first of four trains that would take us to Wengen, the town Tim's friend had recommended for a family ski trip. The Danners were a family of six, we were a family of five, and we had many large duffels full of ski gear and warm clothes. Our normal circus had doubled. With each successive leg the train got older and cuter and the scenery more stunning. I had grown up a *Sound of Music* lover, and though this was Switzerland and not Austria, it was still the Alps; I felt like I was getting my *Sound of Music* moment.

The train made its way past impossibly picturesque land-scapes of wooden houses, cows in fields with snowcapped mountains behind them, and stream-crossed fields before finally pulling into Wengen, a town tucked into the side of a mountain, hidden from the world yet connected to it by this impossibly old-fashioned railway.

Our circus unloaded and made its way down the hill, passing barns with an array of cowbells hanging from the doorframes and houses with flowers carved into the gabled roof rafters.

Our hotel was smallish—only twelve rooms, an old chalet converted into a hotel. Our attic room was complete with two small bedrooms, two bathrooms, two bars of Swiss chocolate awaiting us, and one balcony with a breathtaking view of the Swiss Alps.

We hadn't even been there a day and the kids were already telling me to quit my *Sound of Music* outbursts. I did my best to control myself and not annoy, and possibly embarrass, them further. At least with my singing.

After walking back into town and outfitting our crew of eleven with ski gear at a local shop, we enjoyed a big group dinner at our hotel before saying our goodnights, ready for a great skiing adventure the next day.

Before leaving the hotel the next morning, we first needed to celebrate Mae's seventh birthday. We had decided to save the present opening for back in Barcelona, so we settled for lots of hugging and happy birthdaying before heading downstairs to breakfast.

A glorious sun streamed through the dining room's thick-paned windows. When I laid eyes on the breakfast buffet, I was so thrilled that I thought, *Even if the trip ends right after this breakfast, I'll go home a happy woman.* Eggs, fruit, homemade bread, cheeses. The bread seemed fresher here. The butter looked creamier! The raspberry jam tasted sweeter! The yogurt was out of this world, and the muesli added to it? Heavenly! I was as euphoric as the birthday girl but kept my musings about cream-colored ponies and crisp apple strudels to myself.

We rolled our stuffed selves down the hill to meet the Danners at the ski shop where our rented gear was stored. From there it was just a few steps to the gondola, and soon we were on our way up the mountain.

One of the Danners' daughters saw a mountain goat as we ascended, severely testing my self-restraint about lonely goatherds high on a hill. Meanwhile, Anne, Charles, Tim, and I consulted a trail map and discerned that to access the mountain from the gondola, we had a choice of two blue runs or red or black runs.

My kids had been skiing only two or three times prior to Europe, and then once more on a recent family trip to Andorra, where we'd had them take lessons for two days. Their experience did not run deep. We chose one of the blue runs.

When we reached the top, Kieran and Patrick hopped on their skis and took off with the Danner kids, form lacking but speed intact. Mae started snowplowing heavily down the trail with Tim next to her. The run was a narrow connector, so no room for turns. Tim tried to slow Mae's momentum by holding his pole across her body, but despite this she fell a few times. By the time we reached more open terrain, she was in tears—and she wasn't one to cry. They had taken the run too fast, plus she'd realized by now that she was not able to keep up with the other kids. Add in a few falls, and she was embarrassed and frustrated. And done. After her last fall, she refused to get up. As she looked down at our group, fifty yards down at the bottom, she yelled, "I don't want them to wait for me!"

I sidestepped up to replace Tim where Mae was dug in, and as he skied down to the others, Mae yelled at him, "Go! I don't want you here!" Pure frustration. To me, she said, "I'm not skiing anymore! I'm staying here the rest of the time!"

Mae had hijacked our family moment and I felt an utter lack of control. It wasn't the first time, and I sighed, thinking it wouldn't be the last. But this wasn't a forcible situation, so I gave her a minute and just sat there with her, hoping her frustration would defuse, looking out over the snow-covered peaks all around us.

After a few moments I suggested we sidestep down together, out of skis.

No.

I suggested we slide down on our bottoms.

No.

I offered to carry her—how, I wasn't sure, but I didn't have to figure it out because she refused everything. A standoff. Mae and I stuck on the side of a slope while the rest of the group was held hostage below.

How do you solve a problem like Mae Mae? This I for sure sang to myself.

I finally convinced her to climb on my back. This girl had been piggybacked around most of Europe. How I was going to do this without falling while carrying two pairs of skis, I didn't know. I just wanted to break the standoff.

Just as Mae was climbing on my back, a guy skied up and asked me something in German. Shaking my head, I asked, "Do you speak English?"

"Would you like me to carry your skis down?" he asked.

Thank God. I pointed to Tim and the group at the bottom and thanked him profusely. He skied them down in seconds.

I slowly sidestepped down the hill in my clunky ski boots, Mae on my back, praying I wouldn't slip and fall and blow out my ACL in the process.

Well, at least you wrecked your knee doing something completely cool, skiing in the Alps, right?

Well, kind of . . .

We agreed at the bottom that I would continue skiing with the boys and the Danners, and Tim and Mae would attempt to salvage the day by going sledding—or "sledging," as they called it there.

I skied that day with a heavy heart. The boys were having fun, but it felt wrong for our family to be separated on Mae's birthday, and I worriedly hoped her day had turned around.

A few runs after lunch, knowing we had at least three lifts and several runs ahead of us before we could even make it to a run that would take us back into Wengen, I suggested that the boys and I split off and head for home; I wanted us reunited with our birthday girl.

Finding our way back to a trail that could take us down to Wengen was a bit harried, with lots of guessing at which lifts to take, which runs to ski down. At one point our trail took us to the tiny train stop of Wengenalp. To the right we could see a trail leading down, the terrain in front of us wide open, blue skies with dusty clouds above us, snow-covered mountains on the horizon, a yellow train cutting across one of them. We crossed over the tracks and followed the trail down to the right, and thirty minutes later we skied up to the ski shop where we'd started our day.

We went to the hotel to find Mae and Tim—who, as it turned out, had had a fabulous day sledging. Mae had turned herself around shortly after they'd rented their sledge, and they had taken a train up to Wengenalp, the station where the boys and I had just crossed the tracks, to use it. Apparently, we had all taken the same run down to Wengen. Tim said he had recorded a video of him and Mae going down next to the train track, racing a train, and then wiping out. He said there had been a few dicey sections with a sheer drop-off on one side, and the sledges weren't easily controllable. But Mae had loved the thrill and her birthday had been salvaged.

That night, we ate dinner just the five of us. The hotel decorated our table with birthday confetti, and they even brought out a piece of cake with a candle for Mae after dinner. We didn't get to choose the cake—lemon with lemon curd next to it, nothing an American child would ever choose as her birthday cake option unless she had suffered a mild head injury in a sledging accident—but Mae was happy to have a piece of cake with a candle, just for her birthday. And I was happy to see her nascent flexibility emerging from her many experiences living abroad. Refusing to budge off the piste that morning notwithstanding.

After the disastrous ski day with Mae, I had texted my sister for advice. She and her family were avid skiers, and her girls were only a few years older than Mae. She said we had to get Mae back on skis again.

Much to Mae's credit, and maybe because she was happily chugging down orange juice she had just pressed for herself at our dream breakfast buffet when we asked the next morning, she said she would try again, especially after we told her we had spied a bunny slope from the gondola that we could check out.

Up the gondola the eleven of us went, mountain goat sighted again, singing restrained, Mae in a fine mood. After making plans to meet up for lunch, Mae and I said goodbye to the circus and made our way to the bunny slope.

Mae quickly rose to the level she'd left off with in Andorra, where she'd done green runs by herself—confident, happy, having a good time. We skied on a broad, wide open, short run high up in the Alps, peaks of mountains right in front of us and at our level, blue sky above and beyond, the sun shining brilliantly. Mae sped down the hill, back up the rope tow, and down again, practicing her turns, never waiting for me, her old self again. This was confirmed when she started going down the hill backwards.

At that point, I suggested we try the blue run we had done the previous day.

"No pressure," I said. "Just you and me, and we'll go as slow as molasses."

She agreed, and it was a totally different experience. We took our time, and she made it the whole way down on her own—no help, no pole across her body trying to hold her back, not even a fall. I was effusive about how proud she should be of herself, taking on this challenge, trying it again, until she cut me off, saying, "Can you please stop saying that? It's going to make me scared to do it again."

We headed to the lunch rendezvous, Mae chattering about how excited she was to tackle the run again, this time with the Danners.

We were meeting at an outdoor picnic area, wooden tables set in the snow in front of a line of grills with a similar view to the bunny slope, mountain peaks as our company. I got myself a beer and Mae a hot chocolate as we waited for everyone. We sat there atop the world, literally and figuratively, looking out at the peaks, friendly German chatter floating by, cold air numbing our throats, and I thought how happy my parents would be to sit there with us. They had lived in Germany for a few years when newly married and had had similar experiences to this. They would be thrilled to enjoy brats right off the grill with us, cold beers in hand, amidst the Alps. I had Mae take a picture of me to send to my parents, raising my stein to them. A special toast to my mom.

After the Breens and Danners had consumed our raclette and giant soft pretzels and brats and beers, we took off as a group for the run Mae and I had just done. Anne and one of her daughters stayed behind Mae and me, probably wanting Mae to feel she wasn't last in the pack. Mae made it down great, so we did the run again, Mae tackling steeper sections of the slope this time. The old Mae was back.

Charles suggested at this point that we zigzag our way to the top, where we could connect with some runs that would take us down the other side into Wengen. He was calculating how long this circus might take to get over to Wengen—and "hours" was the right calculation.

Tim and I were amazed at how well Mae did through all of this, especially since the runs we were having to take were all red now. She snowplowed the steep sections, and snowplowed hard on the really steep sections. And never complained. I think she was thrilled to be part of the gang.

I paused to watch as our group crossed back and forth down a wide-open slope, the sun shining off the peaks all around us but the wind blowing like a storm was wanting to roll in. I felt a pure contentment in that moment, and I thought, *Maybe this is what letting go feels like.* Then I pointed my skis downhill and cut through the powder toward the group.

The next day was our last, but we didn't have to depart until the afternoon for the multiple trains back to Zurich. The night had brought lots of wind but no snow, so our two families opted to go sledging instead of skiing.

As we bought the train passes up to Wengenalp, the ticket lady said, "It's very windy up there, you know."

Sensing this was more of a warning than a remark, I asked, "Should we not sledge?"

"No," she said, "I'm just letting you know."

We got off the train and were met with wind slapping us in the face. When we made our way to the trail the boys and I had skied down two days earlier, Tim gave us the lay of the land. The trail went down and did a hard turn to the left. You couldn't slow down by putting your heels down; they'd just bounce off the icy, hard snow. You had to put your whole foot flat on the ground so the friction slowed you down. And you turned by pressing harder with the foot on the side you want to turn toward.

I was sitting on the sledge with Patrick. I put my foot down, and it just slipped. There was zero friction to be found. The surface was pure ice from a night of whipping wind.

We all tentatively set off down the trail, and I quickly realized that the only way to slow down was to stay on the side of the trail where a little snow was still piled up, with both feet down. After that first turn all the adults realized this was going to be a bit tenuous (Tim's thought), scary (my thought), terrifying (Anne's thought).

On the next section, I said to Patrick, trying to sound in control, "Patrick, I'm going to need your help. When I say, 'Feet down!' you put your feet down too."

Down the next hill we went, rubber soles on ice, no friction, headed toward a curve. When we saw Kieran losing control on his sledge in front of us, I yelled, "*Patrick! Put your feet down!*" to which he yelled back, "*I am!*"

I leaned hard to the right, trying to find some snow to slow us. Feet dug in, legs chattering and bouncing on the icy snow, each contact with the ground reverberating up into my hips, we slowed to a controllable speed and then came to a stop, a bit stunned at our luck.

Kieran, not as lucky, had intentionally bailed, as we'd said he should if he couldn't slow down, and had flipped into the snowbank on our right. He was fine, but this was not turning out to be the fun experience we had envisioned.

We walked a bit of the way, slipping and sliding and falling but more confident doing that than sledging. We came across some young men in uniform ski gear, with rakes and shovels. They were doing sledge-trail maintenance. When we caught up to them, they hopped on their skis and snowboards and headed off to another section to repair. All the kids agreed that was the job they wanted when they grew up.

As we made our way down, the trees became more numerous, the ice lessened, and the snow increased, which meant more drag. The adults felt better about getting back on our sledges, and we enjoyed some nice long runs through the woods, where the scenery was beautiful and the sledging wasn't scary at all, except for the turns. At one turn, Charles and his son accidentally cut me and Mae off, and then Tim and Patrick came barreling down and almost plowed into me and Mae, stuck on the corner; instead of ramming into us, they didn't even attempt the turn and went off the trail straight into the woods, laughing and hooting as they plowed in.

As we came to the end, with the gondola and ski shop just down the hill, the kids decided to keep running back up and sledging down, the eight-second thrill worth the three-minute trudge up. We four adults stood at the top, watching the kids go up and down, cautioning them to avoid the orange snow fence at the bottom.

On Mae's second run down, we could see she wasn't making any attempt to either slow down or turn as she neared the fence.

We watched as she plowed into it, her body thrown backward by the fence and then into the air like a rag doll. She finished with a near belly flop onto the snow.

Tim and I watched, frozen. We knew she had wanted to go into the fence, but none of us, probably Mae included, had expected the stunt-double action that had followed. She was still, then she sat up, and then we could see she was laughing. When Tim and I reached the bottom, the boys were nearly peeing themselves, laughing so hard, reenacting her flight and landing.

Mae's last run was not unlike me on our trip, or any trip: seemingly in control, realizing I wasn't, facing what came due to that lack of control, and finally, when the landing turned out okay, smiling from the realization that I had survived.

And then it was time to pack up. Time to take four trains from Wengen to Zurich, and then a plane back to Barcelona. Time to say farewell and *auf wiedersehen* to Wengen and Switzerland, this time singing it out loud.

Chapter 42

RELEGATION

I had hit my stride living in Spain; curveballs no longer felt like curveballs, but rather, "Huh, that ball almost hit me in the head. Again." But that didn't mean I didn't have to pick myself up and dust off the dirt occasionally; dodging curveballs just felt normal now.

My foray into the Spanish healthcare system was one such curveball. I had had the not-normal-but-apparently-normal dermatology experience, and now the kids would be the guinea pigs: They needed their annual well-child exams. Patrick would be spared; saved by a school trip.

Every year, their school sent the kids off, by grade, to an outing in the country called *Colonias*. The trip involved staying for several days in an old country villa repurposed for this kind of excursion, housing and feeding fifty students, while the kids hiked and did group activities. Kieran's *Colonias*, in fifth grade, was for three nights; Patrick, in third grade, went for two nights; and Mae, being in first, would go for one night. She even had gone on *Colonias* when she was a kindergartner, because it's completely normal for kindergartners to go on an overnight school trip.

So I made appointments for two of my little guinea pigs, Mae and Kieran, to see a pediatrician. Dr. Sala was the only pediatrician in the group who spoke English. Or so the website said. So, he was our man.

On the day of the appointment, Tim was free from work, so I asked him to come along; I could have bumbled my way through, but Tim would pick up much more than I would, and when it came to my kids' health, I preferred to understand more than less. The four of us walked down the hill from our flat, entered the modern hospital, went up three floors to the pediatrics department, gave our insurance card and *NIE*s to the receptionist, and then were directed to the waiting room, filled with light from the room's all-glass front wall. We looked up at the monitor, waiting for our number to pop up, while acoustic music that sounded like the theme from the movie *Dirty Dancing* drifted from unseen speakers.

After about ten minutes, I had to run Mae to the bathroom. On our way back Tim was just entering a room with Kieran, smiling and laughing with an older gentleman in a white coat.

"*¿Podemos hablar en inglés? Mi español es muy básico.*"—Can we talk in English? My Spanish is very basic—I heard Tim ask as Mae and I entered the room.

To which the doctor replied, "*Noooooo, mi inglés es malo*"— Noooooo, my English is bad. He continued, "*Pero tu español es bueno. Podemos hablar en español.*"—But your Spanish is good. We can talk in Spanish.

I understood a good part of the questions Dr. Sala asked Tim, but having Tim field them was so much easier; Tim could turn to me, repeat the question in English, and get the answer from me. Which one would think would clue Dr. Sala in that he should direct the questions to me. But he didn't turn to me as I sat in my chair in the corner. He continued to ask Tim. And when I tried to answer, he mainly kept eye contact with Tim.

When I saw Spanish-speaking patients in the ED, well before I knew any Spanish, I would try to face the non-English speaking patient or family member and make eye contact as they spoke, attempting to understand their body language and nonverbal cues and make them feel heard as they explained their answer to me and whoever was translating. Dr. Sala didn't even attempt that—perhaps because of Spain's culture of machismo, which often translated into *the men are talking*. This had happened to me several times before, even with our Spanish friends. The only time Dr. Sala addressed me was when he wanted to see the kids' vaccination cards. That was obviously a mom's job. And I got reprimanded for not having them. Apparently, one doctor's word to another doctor that her kids' vaccinations were up to date wasn't good enough.

As a physician in the US, I could be in control and call the shots about my family's healthcare. In Spain, because of my inability to speak the language well, my being a physician got me nowhere. Power was reduced to a simple dichotomy: Could you communicate or could you not? Add in a little sexism, and I was relegated to the corner. Recalling the *Dirty Dancing* music from the waiting room, the line "No one puts Baby in the corner" started bouncing around in my skull, trying to get out.

As I was getting sidelined by Dr. Sala, his nurse was having the kids get undressed, weighing them, and getting their vitals. They had to strip down to their underwear. I could sense from them the same discomfort I'd felt in the dermatologist's office. *Right here? In front of everyone? Where's my gown?* As I tried to reassure her with my eyes, poor little Mae sat back on the examining table with her arms folded over her chest, her little legs sticking out; meanwhile, the nurse directed Kieran toward an eye chart with pictures, not letters, and asked him to name the images.

Kieran started rattling off the pictures he saw: "*tortuga, pájaro, casa*"—turtle, bird, house—and then said, pointing to one image, "*Yo sé qué es pero no sé cómo decirlo en español. Es una cosa para un bebé.*"—I know what it is but don't know how to say it in Spanish. It's a thing for a baby.

The object was a pacifier. The nurse smiled at Kieran and, sufficiently impressed with his Spanish, said a slow "*¡Muy bien!*"

When it was Mae's turn, Kieran, again in Spanish, explained to the nurse that his sister's Spanish wasn't good and if it was okay, he would translate for her, but he wouldn't give her the answers, he'd tell the nurse exactly what she said. The nurse winked at Kieran and gave another approving smile.

When it was Kieran's turn to be examined, Dr. Sala chatted Kieran up about his *fútbol*—what club he played for, what position. He told us Kieran was "*muy atlético*" and skinny. As he was pushing on Kieran's abdomen, he said, to Tim, "*Le han quitado el apéndice*"—He's had his appendix removed—pointing to a faint scar in Kieran's lower right abdomen.

He was, understandably, mistaking a scar from a bad scratch Kieran got when he was little for an appendectomy scar.

I said, "*No, tiene su apéndice.*"—No, he has his appendix.

Dr. Sala glanced at me, then turned back to Tim, and said, "*¡Hombre! ¡No!*" and pointed to Kieran's scar again, because obviously I didn't know what I was talking about, and Tim, the only adult in the room with no medical training, was the one whose opinion mattered.

I wasn't concerned; I knew Kieran hadn't had an appendectomy—the diagnosis was irrelevant. I was just fed up with being sidelined. I fully appreciated in that moment how powerless and frustrated and perhaps angry non-English-speaking patients and family must feel in our healthcare system back home and vowed to remember this experience when I returned to work.

When it came time for Mae's exam, the doctor spent a long time listening to her heart. After, he said he had heard a murmur and wanted to get her seen by cardiology, but since I had heard the word "*inocente*" in the sentence, I wasn't that concerned. Once again, where my Spanish failed me I was able to fill in the blanks and make the cognitive leap that he was saying she had what was known as an "innocent murmur," something I knew was not pathological and kids outgrew.

To be sure, he said, we should have cardiology check it out.

Dr. Sala mentioned which test he was going to order with the cardiologist. I was sure it should be an ultrasound, but I hadn't heard the word *ultrasonido*. I also hadn't heard ECG, which was good, because that would be the wrong test to order for working up a murmur. But because I had skipped over the very basics of Spanish like the letters of the alphabet (or numbers, for that matter), I didn't trust what my ears had heard or didn't hear.

Regardless, since I wasn't worried about this possible murmur, I would go along with whatever workup he did order; the test would be noninvasive, and I looked forward to another foray into the Spanish healthcare system.

A week later, Mae and I showed up for the unknown test, which did turn out to be an *ultrasonido*. We got a full checkup of Mae's heart *and* became that much more proficient with the Spanish healthcare system that day. As I sat in a chair in the corner watching Mae being scanned, giving her little reassuring winks, I thought of one small silver lining about our impending return trip home: I would no longer literally or figuratively be relegated to the corner.

Chapter 43

NEW REGRET

hroughout our two years in Spain, I had invariably grappled with one type of regret or another. Regret that I was being too insular, too routinized; regret that I wasn't being adventurous enough, taking advantage of the gift of living abroad. Mostly I tried to ignore these ruminations, willed the regrets away. Sometimes I would think, *Maybe I should change my perspective, not label them as regrets at all.* But one regret that could have no other label, other than perhaps "failure," was my Spanish. It still had not attained the level I had envisioned or hoped for.

Case in point, with our time in Spain drawing to a close, we wanted to make one more visit to our favorite beach town on the Costa Brava, Calella de Palafrugell. And after two years of Spanish, I still could not get my tongue around this town's name.

To be fair, it was a Catalan name, and one of the toughest sounds for me to pronounce was the Catalan double L, of which this name had plenty. No matter how right it sounded to me, Claudia would correct and correct me anytime I tried to say paella. And I couldn't roll my R's, so Calella de Palafrugell was a linguistic landmine for me.

So, with plenty of regret about my Spanish and no regret about how we were living our final weeks in Spain, we headed north toward a town whose name I couldn't pronounce—but our first stop was a town whose name I *could* pronounce.

Girona, a medieval city dating back to the first century BCE, was located close to the Pyrénées and an hour and a half north of Barcelona. Apparently, its preserved old quarter made it a favorite filming spot for shows and movies that needed ancient cityscapes, like *Game of Thrones*. I had been told that Girona was the only town in Spain that had never been captured by a foreign invader, but when I was doing some research for our trip *Wikipedia* had told me Girona had "undergone twenty-five sieges and been captured seven times."

Since Girona was steeped in history, we might have taken some tours while there, or read some plaques to learn that "this cathedral was originally constructed as a mosque in 685 and later turned into a Catholic cathedral in blah, blah, blah . . ." But this being our family, we chose to simply make ourselves proximate to the location of interest and take things in visually. Osmosis.

I felt that what the kids were absorbing through experience was almost more important than what they could have been taught via a guide or reading. I hoped they would be different kids for having played leapfrog on the ancient steps of a cathedral, for having chased one another down pebble-paved alleys cooled from the shade of buildings so close together they could touch both sides with their outstretched arms as they ran, that the experiences were being woven into their fabric, into their being, how they would move through life going forward. No kid was going to remember what year a cathedral was built. But if Kieran watched *Game of Thrones* later in life, he might say, "Hey! I was at that cathedral! I hit my sister in the head with a soccer ball out front of that!"

The next day we set off to bike another section of the Via Verde, like we had down in Andalucía. We drove to the bike rental shop in the morning, which then shuttled us and our bikes to Sant Feliu de Pallerols (the dreaded double L!), a town closer to the Pyrénées. The bike ride back to Girona would be forty kilometers, supposedly all flat or downhill.

The guy from the shop who drove us to Sant Feliu de Pallerols, Ferran, was very nice and chatted with us the whole way. He could not understand how, if we lived in Barcelona, the kids were Real Madrid fans. He kept pausing, looking at one of the kids, and with incredulity saying, "*Pero, ¿por qué?*"—But why?—truly not comprehending.

Ferran dropped us in the small main plaza of Sant Feliu de Pallerols, surrounded by three-story buildings and dotted with trees. A market was being held there, so while Tim and Ferran unloaded bikes, the kids and I loaded up with nuts and fruit and candy (to be used in case of bribery) for the ride.

When we said *adiós* to Ferran, we thought to ask where to pick up the trail—minor detail. "Go down that road," he said, pointing off to the left, "and cross the river and you will see signs for the Via Verde."

These directions proved to lack the detail required to get us there, and we had to ask someone else along the way. Their directions, unfortunately, were equally vague and unhelpful as Ferran's. As opposed to the directions we probably would have received had we been in the US: "Take a right onto X Road, follow the road over the bridge, at the first stop sign take a right onto Y Road, and then look on your left for a yellow sign with green letters for the Via Verde."

Eventually we did find our way to the Via Verde, a sandy gravel path under a sunny sky, and off we went. The kids were so happy to be back on bikes, no cars around. They wove back and forth, crisscrossing each other's path, the angles of their sharp turns defying gravity. Biking, such a staple of life back in Menlo

Park, had been almost entirely absent from our lives in Spain, kind of like attention to detail.

But *I* was paying attention to detail. The sky was blue with giant puffy clouds and the landscape was leafy green as far as the eye could see; rolling green hills beyond pastures and the occasional farmhouse or vineyard; sometimes we followed along a creek, sometimes we passed through a forest.

I had to snap a few pictures on my phone of this idyllic outing. Patrick, being Patrick, was enjoying skidding his bike by slamming the brakes and then continuing on riding—and at one point he skidded right in front of me, which caused me to grab my brake with my left hand, since my right was holding my phone and taking pictures. And since the left brake was the front brake, the front tire locked and twisted, and the bike flipped me over.

I don't remember flying through the air; I do remember the sound I made as I landed, on my stomach, arms beneath me. I was still for about ten seconds as I wondered whether I had broken an arm. Tim had run over and was helping me up, slowly. As I started to push my chest and stomach off the ground, I noticed my phone beneath me, a spider web of shattered glass on its front; the first obvious casualty. The next was my thumb, which was swollen and a bit painful.

As I ran through the differential of possible diagnoses and considered what next steps I would need to take if it were this diagnosis versus that one, I noticed that the kids were silent. A scary realization seemed to have just dawned on them. What happens when the person who usually tends to the hurt person *is* the hurt person?

I looked down to see blood running down my calf from a decent-sized patch of missing skin on my outer lower leg. Luckily just road rash, nothing requiring stitches. ("Just" being an understatement, as anyone who's had the pleasure of any amount of skin being scraped off their body knows.)

After I had shaken off the gravel and other path detritus stuck to my body, decided my thumb was the only potential problem, and reassured the kids all was well, we squeezed water from our water bottles onto my leg, trying to get any bits of dirt and grit out of the wound. As we got back on our bikes to get to our lunch spot, my tender thumb trying to do its opposable job on the handlebar, I tried not to face the question of who wrecks their bike on a flat surface, going five miles per hour, on a pleasure ride. Sure, Patrick had skidded in front of me, but no doubt Kieran, Mae, and Tim all would have deftly and probably easily avoided the spill I had taken. I hoped my bloody leg wasn't going to draw attention when we walked into lunch; I was sure the locals knew the only biking around was a flat scenic path that should be entirely foolproof.

Here's the fool!

No one noticed or cared about my leg when we walked into the restaurant. We took a leisurely hour and a half for our lunch, as we were an hour ahead of schedule anyway. The restaurant was typical for its isolated location—the only gig in town, heavy on meat offerings, with a large space outside to eat and for the kids to run around, a few random cats and dogs wandering around the property, and a waitress who didn't care if you took half an hour or three.

While the bike rental place had overestimated how long it would take us to get to lunch, they'd underestimated the ease of the rest of the trip. The countryside also turned less scenic the closer we got to Girona, and the very last part of the route was in the city. Another thirty minutes was tacked onto our trip trying to find the bike shop after Ferran's exacting description of how to find it—"Just take a left at the train station"—proved woefully inaccurate.

After the bike shop was found and our bikes turned back in, we took a cab back to our hotel in the old quarter. It was time to pack up and drive over to the coast. As Tim checked out, the kids and I sat in the sun in a small plaza, enjoying gelato. Then we piled into the rental car for the one-hour drive to verbal nightmare Calella de Palafrugell.

We arrived at our B&B in time to watch Barça beat Athletic Bilbao 3–1 to win the Copa del Rey finals. It was a very exciting time to live in Barcelona. Barça had already secured the championship title of La Liga, and next weekend they were in the Champions League finals. If they won that, they would accomplish the incredible feat of winning the *treble*, or the trifecta. ¡*Força Barça!*

I'm not sure what I had been thinking, booking a bed-and-breakfast. It was the first time in our two years in Europe that we would be staying in one. And as it turned out, it was run by a British couple. Which made sense, because the Spanish hadn't ever really taken to the concept of paying to stay in someone else's home, according to the British couple.

When I'd made the booking, either I'd been thinking that our kids were such good travelers I wouldn't need to worry about them being rambunctious in someone else's house, even with a few elderly guests, or I hadn't cared that our kids were going to be rambunctious in someone else's house, even with a few elderly guests. But there we were.

We had planned on spending that day and the next on the beach before driving back to Barcelona in the afternoon. The small white-sand coves hugged by brown-black rocks reaching into the sea were beautiful even on an overcast day, but the Mediterranean was cold and the beach was packed. With little room to play and not much motivation to swim, the kids got bored fast. Saint Tim took them exploring on the rocks one cove over for about an hour.

While the kids picked over rocks looking for hidden crustaceans, I anticipated their impending need for food and attempted to understand how to procure a table at the cove's *chiringuito*. I understood that you asked to have your name put on the board and that would get you priority seating when you wanted to eat, so I had our name added to the list.

After Mae found a *gamba*, shrimp, and the kids had scrambled as much territory as they could, they came to me, done and ready for food. There were ten names in front of ours, and though the restaurant had only opened ten minutes prior for service, it was already packed and only two names had been scratched off the list. And they never called out names. We asked for clarification on how the system worked but didn't get a satisfactory answer. Procuring a table at a *chiringuito* was one of the many mysteries of daily Spanish life I was not going to be able to solve.

With the kids peering over the cliff of a food meltdown and no guarantee we'd be getting a table in the next hour, we regretfully went back to where we had eaten the night before for more fast and easy pizza—which at least made three of the five of us happy.

The next day, departure day, our outing to the beach couldn't have been more different from the day before. The sun was brilliant, the beach was much less crowded, and the kids didn't want to leave. We enjoyed talking to a friendly Spanish couple down at the water's edge who eagerly asked about our life in Barcelona as Americans, while the kids had fun on the beach and in the water. It was like the gods were conspiring against us leaving.

In the end, though, we had no choice but to disappoint the gods: We reluctantly left the beach, packed up the car, and started our drive back to Barcelona. As the Costa Brava became smaller in our rearview mirror, Tim and I discussed and marveled at what great experiences were within such easy reach of Barcelona— touring an ancient town, biking near the Pyrénées, sipping a *caña* next to the Mediterranean. Why were we moving back to the States? After so much struggle, I felt like we had finally arrived at a point where our life in Spain felt great, almost easy—or, more likely, I had finally arrived at a point where I was comfortable in my life, not fighting against it, managing it, or overanalyzing it.

As the kids threw pretzels at each other in the back and I stared out the open car window, warm wind whipping my hair, I was surprised to sense that uncomfortable feeling of regret beginning to creep in. It wasn't regret at not having taken advantage of our time in Spain. It actually stemmed from having taken full advantage of the little time we had left. I wanted more of what we'd gotten this weekend—this full, fun, family life that felt so natural, so normal, so right. How could we be leaving Spain?

This was a regret that wasn't going to go away. We were.

Chapter 44

HOW DO YOU SPELL THAT?

*W*e would be moving back to the States in a few short months. Time, especially time with Claudia and Tomás, felt precious. It's not like when friends move to a new town, or even to a new state. We didn't even live on the East Coast, which is a relatively short hop to Europe. This was a move across an ocean and to the far side of another continent. So we had hopes of maybe getting to see each other's families once a year, and even that was ambitious.

Anticipating our impending separation, *la familia* Alemany invited us to spend the weekend with them up in Puigcerdà, a small town Claudia had grown up going to that was located about two hours north of Barcelona and an hour east of Andorra, on the French border. Of course we didn't pass up the chance.

That weekend was as leisurely as they come. No agenda other than exploring Puigcerdà with *la familia* Alemany, as many long, leisurely meals and *cafés* as possible, and one ziplining adventure. The kids loved that part, especially because there were no rules. Our level of alarm was significantly dampened after living in Spain for two years; we weren't shocked that the zipline place didn't have helmets for the kids to wear or that we didn't have to sign any releases of reliability. Or that no one came to oversee the zipline.

When Claudia and Tomás's son David got stuck about two-thirds of the way down the zipline—just petered out of momentum—Tim had to run back and find someone to help us while Tomás stood under David, talking to him. A guy came with a pole to push David to the end. Then he walked away.

Luckily, we kept the pole; it came in handy when the next kid, Patrick, didn't make it to the end either. This time, instead of fretting in needless alarm, we calmly pushed Patrick down the line, soaking in our beautiful surroundings: pine trees, green meadows, a mountain with ski runs cut into the trees, and beyond that snowcapped mountains.

After the zipline and a ropes course, we decided to head back to our hotel for *merienda* (afternoon snack) and *cafés*. It was early afternoon on a beautiful, warm spring day. The hotel had a sizable property, so after having sandwiches and Fantas, the kids took off to do we weren't sure what, but we didn't really care because they were doing what kids should be doing—running around outside with each other.

We four adults remained at the table outside and talked over our *cafés* for another two hours. We talked about our parents, our kids, our kids' teachers, our kids' problems, our kids' friends, our friends, our work, our lack of work, our retirement. Retirement was a big topic for us. We had begun a few months earlier talking about "how great would it be if we traveled together in retirement." But now we started talking about actual destinations and travel preferences—perhaps in desperation, given the ticking of the clock.

We sometimes attempted (or braved, in my situation) conversations in Spanish. Inevitably, not recognizing a certain word someone had said, I would ask them to spell it, my brain needing to "see" the word to process it. *Desesperar.* My brain wouldn't be sure if it was hearing *desesperar,* or *de sesperar,* or *de se sperar.* It would refuse to put that word in its tiny repository until it had seen it written out. *Ah, now I see . . . into your box you go!*

Asking Claudia or Tomás to spell a word invariably stumped them, which always made me and Tim laugh. Here were two highly educated adults, and they always stumbled trying to spell a word. The concept was unnatural to them. Spanish is a phonetic language; you spell words exactly as they sound. My Spanish teacher told me there isn't even an equivalent school subject to "spelling" in Spanish. The closest thing is "writing." So, when I would ask, "How do you spell that word?" Claudia and Tomás would freeze, then look at each other, puzzled, thinking out loud, "How would you spell that word? Why would you even need to know that?" Then they would bumble their way through spelling it, which led to me saying, "Yup, spelled just like it sounds."

The next morning, we eleven took a nice stroll along a country path, passing green pastures with stone barns and stone houses off in the distance, the white tips of the mountains peeking over the roofs. The kids found sticks to play with and kicked a soccer ball as we walked; our adult conversation was sometimes punctuated by the cries of one of Claudia and Tomás's five-year-old twins, which were easily addressed with a hug and a peck.

We worked our way to a river that ran on the outskirts of town and happened to be the border between France and Spain. We stopped on a bridge spanning the river to take pictures of the kids straddling the countries ("Look! I'm in France and Spain at the same time!"), which ended with the boys pushing Mae into France and not letting her back into Spain.

We needed to find a place in town that could take our party of eleven for lunch that day. We found a candidate that had outside seating and looked busy but promising. I followed Claudia up to a maître d' as she asked about seating. I could follow most of the conversation, which went something like this:

Claudia: Excuse me, we are a table of eleven. Can you seat us?

Maître d': We are full right now.

Claudia: I see a few tables that are open.

Maître d': We don't have any that can fit eleven.

Claudia: But you could push those two tables together to make room for eleven.

Maître d': (Turns his back on Claudia)

Claudia: Why aren't you taking my suggestion?

Maître d': (Turning to face her) Why are you telling me how to do my job?

We walked away, and I couldn't help but notice that Claudia was unperturbed by the interaction. Whereas I was anxious and affronted on her behalf, she was not, at all. Annoyed at his attitude, perhaps, but completely unfazed. I couldn't help but envision how the scene would have played out had Tomás been handling the maître d'. Claudia's face, rather than showing any signs of anger or stress, had shown more of an inquisitive look, eyebrows slightly raised, as they'd spoken; she'd been working out logically where we could eat if the maître d' didn't take her suggestion, not focusing on her feelings.

Looking at Claudia's face, I felt something akin to grief. I realized only then in a palpable way that I wouldn't have this friend with me indefinitely. Soon, too soon, I would have her only in the form of memories.

What was the Spanish verb for "to feel loss," and how did you spell it?

Chapter 45

PASO A PASO

I can't believe we made it on the plane.

On our journey home to the US, we had to fly from Barcelona to Frankfurt to Seattle to Spokane. Spokane because we were going to spend three weeks with my mom, who was just starting her chemo, before going back to California.

Our kids, only seven, almost nine, and eleven, were by now veteran travelers. We always waited until the end of boarding to get on the plane, since we rarely packed anything that needed to go in the overhead bin. Over the past two years, Ryanair, with their dollhouse-size overhead baggage compartments, had beaten that out of us.

As we lounged in the Seattle airport waiting for our flight to Spokane, eating our meals and drinking our *cafés*—now just "coffees"—we casually said, with a sigh, "Okay, kids. Time to take the last leg of this trip."

We nonchalantly gathered our backpacks and headed the short distance to the gate, where we found no one but the gate agent. When she saw us, her face registered a look of relief, which quickly rearranged itself into annoyance. "There you are! You're the last ones!" she said, feigning enthusiasm. "We were hoping you'd make it!"

We had been in more than eighteen different airports and taken more than thirty flights in the course of our two-year journey, almost all with signs in a language we were learning or didn't know at all, and we had never missed a flight. But for this last part of our very long trip, we had somehow misjudged our timing, and now we were *those* people—the ones who walk onto the plane ten minutes after everyone is boarded, buckled-in, and wondering why the doors haven't closed.

Tim and I exchanged looks after we had dodged the glares and taken our seats.

"I can't believe we've never missed a flight our whole time in Europe, and we almost missed our very last flight," I whispered. "To *Spokane*."

As the plane leveled off and the gravitational pull seemed to lessen from takeoff, the self-consciousness of being *those* people had diminished; no one was glaring at us. *So here we are, the last leg*, I thought as I closed my eyes, trying to settle. I knew it in my body before my mind processed it: This moment was not only the last part of this latest long journey, it was also a closure. It was final. We had left Spain. We were flying away from friends and a way of life we had come to love, flying toward my mom's battle with cancer and a life back home that I wasn't really looking forward to.

The plane suddenly felt like it was going very fast. Like that time we were on a high-speed train from Córdoba to Barcelona and I was convinced the conductor was blasting past the legal speed limit and we were hurtling toward a possible death.

Now here we were again, hurtling.

When I looked out the window, the clouds under the wing were stationary and bright in their stillness. But my body knew we were traveling at warp speed—away from our life and toward a new one, the electromagnetic pull from Spain straining against the unrelenting pull of an unknown future of chemo and sickness and busyness and work and driving everywhere, a fight to the death for my atoms.

Close your eyes. Deep breaths.

Thoughts and then feelings about our last two years began to shift about behind my eyelids, a jumbled mess. Relief, regret, a sense of accomplishment. Embarrassment, pride, hope. I had struggled, I had lost sight of important things, I had checked boxes instead of living fully. I had flogged and flailed at a language—but persisted. I had questioned myself and been called into question by others. I had broken down in a church and several other places, I had failed as a mother, and I'd had some glorious moments too. I'd made friends and lost friends. I had circled the wagons, questioned why I did that, and then accepted that it was my way of being wholly present with my family while also buffeting myself against change and the uncertainty of a new life. I had learned to put myself out there, to be open to new experiences, and my life was richer for it. I had let myself become comfortable in not knowing, and more open to change, and more able to let go. I didn't ram into windows as often. I was sometimes even able to just sit and *be* now—especially if I had a *gintonic* in hand. I had slowed down, and I was experiencing my days with more contentment and appreciation.

"Watch your feet and elbows!" The flight attendant jolted me out of my thoughts as she pushed her snack cart past my row.

Looking at her cart zoomed me back to a November evening in Sarrià. Mae and I were walking back to our flat from somewhere, Tim and the boys were at *fútbol*. It was dark out, damp and cold, but we were warm in our coats and scarves and buoyed by a festive feeling in the air—Navidad was approaching. We were walking along Plaça d'Artós at the bottom of Carrer de Major de Sarrià, and we saw an older gentleman selling roasted chestnuts, a portable light shining on his cart and pan. No one in our family had ever eaten a roasted chestnut before, so Mae and I bought some for all of us to try. The brown paper bag of *castanyes* was warm in my hands as I handed it to Mae, a prize to carry. That's how we both felt. Any new experience, even one as simple as chestnuts, was glimmering and uplifting.

Sitting in the airplane seat, I felt a sharp need to etch that moment in my memory. I was scared it would be forgotten—bumped by the multiple task lists in my future, pushed behind the mountain of medical information I was going to have to reacquaint myself with, crushed under all the carpool legs I would soon need to keep on top of. I could still feel the contentment of that night as Mae and I walked hand in hand up the hill, both of us upbeat about the warm gift we were bringing home to the boys. Would any experience with my kids in our everyday life in California bring me such joy? Had I grown enough as a person to experience that glow in any moment, or was it only possible for me when experienced through the lens of living in an unknown place where everything was new and therefore shiny and different?

We would have to see. But Spain had slowed me down, given me no choice but to take life *paso a paso*, step by step, and taught me to savor my time. So different from the charge-ahead, eyes-on-the-horizon, speed-walking-through-life working mom I had been on arrival. In going slowly, I had gotten to take in what was happening around me, truly see and be a part of everything. And it turned out I'd been ready to experience everything—to truly live fully. I'd just needed help figuring out how. I wasn't sure that ten years earlier, even if given the opportunity to go *paso a paso*, I would have had the ability to look at anything but forward to the horizon.

Before Barcelona, when I was that charge-ahead mom, I had asked myself a question: *Is this as good as it gets?* Back then, I hadn't been satisfied with the answer. Now, sitting on an airplane, having just left Spain behind, I understood that our adventure there hadn't been "as good as it gets." *How* I experienced that adventure, my life, determined if it was as good as it gets. Small, seemingly insignificant experiences were as precious as big ones.

Lip-synching on the couch, the family dinners on our *terraza*—these were as valuable and meaningful as skiing in the Alps and standing next to the Swiss Guard at the Vatican. Was experiencing a *hammam* with the family in Marrakesh or eating a steak cooked over a volcanic vent on the Canary Islands as good as life gets? No more so than spending hours over *cafés* discussing our joys and failures as parents with Claudia and Tomás while the kids ran around playing tag, or holding my kids' hands every day on the way to and from school.

I took another deep breath. I thought of my mom and what lay ahead for her. I felt my atoms start to vibrate again.

Deep breath.

I understood that a part of me needed to do this, to look ahead—partly as a way to not have to look behind me at the life I was leaving. I would give myself time to let that sorrow heal. But I found solace in where I was. Spain had brought me to this point, where I could and would appreciate every step I would be taking in this next experience with my mom, and in whatever lay beyond. My family would be with me as we went—*paso a paso*, holding hands.

And I would be *tranquila*. I would walk peacefully, purposefully, content in knowing *this* was as good as it gets.

ACKNOWLEDGMENTS

To my team at She Writes Press, thank you for your dedication to the small writers and to female voices. Brooke, Addison, Krissa, and Anne, thank you for bringing the best version of this book into the world.

To my team at Illuminate, thank you for taking on what scared me the most, letting the world know my book was out there.

I want to thank my husband, Tim, for seeing what I wouldn't, that I loved the process of creating this book, and for his unwavering support of me pursuing writing. And thank you for the sacrifices you made so that I could. When it registered that my book was being published, my kids became my biggest cheerleaders, in a teenage kind of way. Thank you to Mae, my social media consultant extraordinaire, to Patrick, who freely provided his valued proofreading skills when made to, and to Kieran, who was mostly "out of office" but delivered Spanish and English editing when he wasn't.

I owe an immense thank you to my early readers, some of whom stayed on for the whole ride without being bribed. Thank you to Jay, whose insights and suggestions never failed to amaze me, and for responding to my many SOS texts, like when you were on a beach, in Colombia, on your honeymoon. Thank you to Meghan, whose opinion on life, literature and clothes is the one I have trusted implicitly since the day we bonded in LAX (and now we can tell your parents all the money they spent on your English major was put to good use). Thank you to Cristina, *mi mejor amiga*, for the many WhatsApp back and forths helping me with all things Spanish, though you should probably be thanking me for greatly expanding your capacity for patience during my editing process. Thank you to Karen for mistakenly leaving me off that email distribution list. I would never have found such a supportive and amazing author sister in the publishing process if you had done your volunteer job correctly. And thank you to my many friends and family members who read, gave advice and opinions, support and encouragement during this process. I am grateful.

ABOUT THE AUTHOR

*A*my Breen is a physician, health advocate, and mother. She lives in Menlo Park, California, with her husband and three children. *Tranquila* is her first novel.

Author photo © Heidi Lancaster

SELECTED TITLES FROM SHE WRITES PRESS

She Writes Press is an independent publishing
company founded to serve women writers everywhere.
Visit us at www.shewritespress.com.

Brave(ish): A Memoir of a Recovering Perfectionist by Margaret
Davis Ghielmetti. $16.95, 978-1-63152-747-0. An intrepid
traveler sets off at forty to live the expatriate dream overseas—
only to discover that she has no idea how to live even her own
life. Part travelogue and part transformation tale, Ghielmetti's
memoir, narrated with humor and warmth, proves that it's never
too late to reconnect with our authentic selves—if we dare to put
our own lives first at last.

Bowing to Elephants: Tales of a Travel Junkie by Mag Dimond.
$16.95, 978-1-63152-596-4. Mag Dimond, an unloved girl from
San Francisco, becomes a travel junkie to avoid the fate of her
narcissistic, alcoholic mother—but everywhere she goes, she's
haunted by memories of her mother's neglect, and by a hunger to
find out who she is, until she finds peace and her authentic self in
the refuge of Buddhist practice.

Heart Radical: A Search for Language, Love, and Belonging
by Anne Liu Kellor. $16.95, 978-1-64742-173-1. As a mixed-
race Chinese American woman, Anne grew up unsure where
she belonged. In her twenties, she travels alone to live and teach
English in China, her mother's birthplace—a long, winding
journey that ultimately teaches her to embrace her many layers of
identity, claim her voice, speak her truth, and live in the present.

Just Be: A Search for Self-Love in India by Meredith Rom. $16.95, 978-1-63152-286-4. After following her intuition to fly across the world and travel alone through the crowded streets of India, twenty-two-year-old Meredith Rom learns that that true spiritual development begins when we take the leap of trusting our intuition and finding a love within.

Rudy's Rules for Travel: Life Lessons from Around the Globe by Mary K. Jensen. $16.95, 978-1-63152-322-9. Circle the twentieth century globe with risk-taking, frugal Rudy and his spouse Mary, a catastrophic thinker seeking comfort. When this marriage of opposites goes traveling, their engaging stories combine laugh-out-loud humor with poignant lessons from the odyssey of a World War II veteran.

Searching for Family and Traditions at the French Table, Book One by Carole Bumpus. $16.95, 978-1-63152-896-5. Part culinary memoir and part travelogue, this compilation of intimate interviews, conversations, stories, and traditional family recipes (*cuisine pauvre*) in the kitchens of French families, gathered by Carole Bumpus as she traveled throughout France's countryside, is about people savoring the life they have been given.